D1499388

LIBRARY OF HEBREW BIBLE/
OLD TESTAMENT STUDIES

486

Formerly Journal for the Study of the Old Testament Supplement Series

Editors
Claudia V. Camp, Texas Christian University
Andrew Mein, Westcott House, Cambridge

Founding Editors
David J. A. Clines, Philip R. Davies and David M. Gunn

PLAYING THE TEXTS

Editor
George Aichele, Adrian College

SUSTAINING FICTIONS

Intertextuality, Midrash, Translation, and the Literary Afterlife of the Bible

Lesleigh Cushing Stahlberg

t&t clark

NEW YORK • LONDON

T & T Clark International, 80 Maiden Lane, New York, NY 10038

T & T Clark International, The Tower Building, 11 York Road, London SE1 7NX

T & T Clark International is a Continuum imprint.

Visit the T & T Clark blog at www.tandtclarkblog.com

The Hebrew font used in this publication, Bwhebb, is used with the kind permission of BibleWorks, LCC. Visit www.bibleworks.com

Library of Congress Cataloging-in-Publication Data
Stahlberg, Lesleigh Cushing.
  Sustaining fictions : intertextuality, Midrash, translation, and the literary afterlife of the Bible / Lesleigh Cushing Stahlberg.
p. cm. -- (The library of Hebrew Bible/Old Testament studies ; #486) (Playing the texts)
Includes bibliographical references and index.
  ISBN-13: 978-0-567-02709-2 (hardcover : alk. paper)
  ISBN-10: 0-567-02709-0 (hardcover : alk. paper) 1. Bible. O.T.--Criticism, interpretation, etc. 2. Bible. O.T.--Translating. 3. Bible as literature. 4. Midrash--History and criticism. I. Title. II. Series.

BS1171.3.S73 2008
  221.6'6--dc22
                    2008012540

06 07 08 09 10   10 9 8 7 6 5 4 3 2 1

This way we write each other's lives—by means of fictions. Sustaining fictions. Uplifting fictions. Lies. This way we lead one another toward survival. This way we point to the darkness—saying: *come with me into the light.*

—Timothy Findley, *Headhunter*

CONTENTS

PREFACE

When *The Preservationist*, David Maine's 2004 novel about the biblical flood, came out, it was met with praise from the critics. One described the novel, which is narrated in turn by Noah (whom Maine calls Noe), his wife, his sons, and their wives, as being replete with "witty, sometimes beautiful touches."[1] Another, who characterized the book as "earthy, funny, oddly moving," declared that it was the way that Maine "twists the tale—familiar, jokey, mildly bawdy and fully immersed in the rugged, relentless activity of building and maintaining the ark—that gives the novel its ruling spirit."[2] Beyond the image of Maine twisting the biblical tale, the reviewers offered little insight into the relationship between telling and re-telling. In his review, Melvin Bukiet depicted the negotiation between ancient text and contemporary literature: "Sometimes the function of fiction is to take the familiar and make it surprising. At other times stories take the surprising and make it familiar."[3] In Bukiet's view, Maine accomplished both, establishing a "pattern of the unexpected and the expected."[4] Reviewer Janet Maslin asked (and answered), "What justifies Maine's appropriation of this biblical story? The author is clearly more interested in imagination than in cannibalization. He envisions the events in Noe's life with a mixture of awe and realism."[5] We could argue that Maslin speaks to the central aspects of retelling: what this book will describe as approach (how a later text gains access to an earlier), stance (the attitude the later text takes to the earlier), and filter (the lens through which the later views the earlier). She accounts for the approach of the retelling (imagination as against cannibalization—the book embellishes rather than devours the biblical text), its stance (appropriation—the novel

1. Ron Charles, "Guess Who Does all the Work on the Ark" (Review), *Christian Science Monitor* (July 20, 2004), Features, Books, 16.
2. Martin Levin, "The Sea, The Sea" (Review), *The Globe and Mail* (July 17, 2004), Book Review, Shelf Life, D13.
3. Melvin Jules Bukiet, "Rain Man" (Review), *The Washington Post* (June 27, 2004). Book World, T06.
4. Ibid.
5. Janet Maslin, "Before there was Global Warming, There was Global Soaking" (Review), *The New York Times* (June 28, 2004), Section E, Books, 6.

takes the biblical story as its own), and, in a way, its filter (the work reads the Bible with a mixture of awe and realism). And yet these are not the terms she uses. In fact, as the survey of the reviews indicates, there is no extant vocabulary for speaking about the relationship of retelling to telling.

The goal of this project is to develop a vocabulary of retelling, one that could be used by a book reviewer or a biblical scholar. Following from Hans Robert Jauss's aesthetics of reception, with its focus on "a dialogical and at once process-like relationship between work, audience, and new work,"[6] this book introduces a language that might allow one to articulate the relationship between work and new work, addressing questions of approach and filter. The idea of stance will allow us to consider audience as well: as Jauss notes, "the new text evokes for the reader…the horizon and rules familiar from earlier texts, which are then varied, corrected, altered, or even just reproduced."[7] Such a vocabulary would also enable more sustained consideration of the generations of a particular text: we could speak not only of Shakespeare's use of the Bible, but of Faulkner's use of Shakespeare's use of the Bible, say.

The hope is that those who teach and study the Bible will avail themselves of the terms put forth here. In the classroom, to identify clearly what is going on in a retelling would allow one to talk about retelling in a way that is not always easily done. Moreover, it would allow one to explore thoroughly the ways in which the Bible is alive in the contemporary situation.

Developing a capacity to speak about retelling would have more than merely pedagogical benefit. As Melanie Wright notes in her introduction to *Moses in America*, "even today, most biblical professionals still view as peripheral activities the study of art, film, literature, or music that retells or depicts biblical stories and themes."[8] While most biblical scholars are versed in Hebrew and Greek, ancient history and philology, in Wright's estimation few are "able to appreciate the distinctive nature of literary texts and artistic forms, so that they can offer an intelligent evaluation of, say, a triptych by Hieronymus Bosch or Bob Marley's 'Exodus.'"[9] Rather, the academy "attend[s] to some readings of the Bible but ignore[s], or treat[s] as trivial diversions, other interpretations and

6. Hans Robert Jauss, *Toward and Aesthetic of Reception* (trans. Timothy Bahti; Minneapolis: University of Minnesota Press, 1982), 19.

7. Ibid., 23.

8. Melanie J. Wright, *Moses in America: The Cultural Uses of Biblical Narrative* (Oxford: Oxford University Press, 2003). 9.

9. Wright, *Moses in America*, 9.

uses that have been of importance to just as many (or maybe more) people."[10] This book fills a lacuna, presenting biblical scholars with a vocabulary for thinking, speaking, and writing about the ways that the Bible has been fleshed out by ancient rabbis and church fathers, smoothed over by poets and short story writers, animated by artists and filmmakers, and popularized by romance novelists and children's book authors. It allows biblical scholars to consider not only the production of the Bible, but its transmission.

This is the project of biblical reception history. David S. Katz has noted, "The English Bible can only be understood against the wide canvas of numerous subjects, such as prophecy, millenarianism, copyright, the occult, Darwin, the novel, American Fundamentalism."[11] Recently, an increasing number of biblical scholars (or scholars interested in the Bible) have turned their attention to the afterlife of scripture—producing reception commentaries and encyclopedias of the Bible in art and literature. Scholars with these interests could avail themselves of the vocabularies presented here when writing about recurrences of biblical phrases, stories, and figures in later culture.

But one hopes that reception history will not always stand at the periphery of biblical studies. Understanding the afterlife of the Bible must become a more established dimension of biblical studies: as Katz argues, "denying the English Bible the scope of its contemporary references is to truncate its influence and to distort its significance in manufacturing the common code of the English-speaking world"[12] (and likewise, the German Bible in the German-speaking world, the French Bible in the French-speaking world, etc.). To understand the creation of code—and to learn to decode—is the project at hand. The focus is literary and artistic, but the undertaking has implications for a multitude of fields, some of which Katz listed above. Knowing how to identify precisely what makes one treatment of a text distinct from another in terms of approach, stance, and filter will allow us to put retellings in dialogue with one another. And to do this will allow biblical scholars to address the nearly imperceptible glide of the literary afterlife of the Bible from scripture to commentary to literature.[13]

10. Ibid., 9.
11. David S. Katz, *God's Last Words: Reading the English Bible from the Reformation to Fundamentalism* (New Haven: Yale University Press, 2004), xi.
12. Ibid., xi.
13. If these can be distinguished: Derrida (in *Of Grammatology*) and Kristeva (in *Desire in Language*) both muddy the line between text (here, scripture) and metatext (commentary).

The many terms offered throughout this work will facilitate thinking and speaking about the interrelationships of approach, stance, and filter, and thereby of scripture, commentary, and literature. For those who elect not to cull for themselves their own lexicons from among the many terms presented in the course of this work, the final chapter presents a vocabulary of retelling that draws from all three fields and provides a baseline for thinking about retelling.

The choice of terms in that lexicon, and the occasional contortion of their original meaning to fit the purposes of this project is entirely my own doing. In addition, the recurring insistence that approach, stance, and filter are the central dimensions of a retelling comes entirely from me: many readers have wondered whether there might be more critical facets than merely these three, and whether these three might have been called something else. I have taken these questions seriously, and yet have returned time and again to this trinity of my own making: any objections should therefore be directed my way.

Lest I appear mulish, I assure you that other queries have caused me to reconsider my ideas and revise my thinking along the way. (That said, any remaining errors are entirely mine.) I am eternally grateful to Peter S. Hawkins and Michael Zank, who have been thorough readers and thoughtful critics from the beginning. Thanks also to Abigail Gillman, Jeffrey Mehlman, and Stephen Prothero for helping me imagine the project as a book. Steven Kepnes pushed me to make the imagining a reality. I am obliged to him and the rest of my colleagues in the religion department at Colgate University for taking a chance on a different kind of biblical scholar, and for their ongoing guidance and support. Barbara Brooks's careful reading and helpful commentary led to a more accessible book. George Aichele agreed to take on this project, and I am indebted for that as well as for his comments on the manuscript. They were invaluable for my thinking about over-arching structure and local concerns alike. When it came to the most minute details, Duncan Burns was an author's dream: an intelligent copy-editor with an incredible eye and unfailing judgment. I am also quite appreciative of Burke Gerstenschlager at T&T Clark/Continuum, who has been both patient and encouraging. The same is true of my beloved husband, Ben Stahlberg, who has been patient, encouraging, and good-humored about keeping the household running on the many nights I worked late. Thank you.

Finally, I dedicate this book to my father, quite certain that the only afterlife he believed in was textual. His faith in literature was profound and his love of books contagious. I know he would have been proud to own this one.

Chapter 1

SPEAKING THE WORLD INTO BEING

From Moses to Moses, There is None Like Moses

When the writer of the biblical book of Joshua set out to describe his title character, he fashioned him as a new Moses, a second leader of Israel who crosses a body of water and climbs a height in the service of the giving of a new law that will bind together the people of Israel. Some seven hundred years later, when the author of the Gospel of Matthew sought to bind the people of Israel to a changing tradition, he too turned to the story of Moses and fashioned a Jesus who crossed the Jordan and climbed a hill in the service of a new law: the Sermon on the Mount. And over the course of the subsequent two millennia, writers have cast and recast the figure of Moses. They have told and retold his story in the service not just of the law, but of art, philosophy, as well as entertainment. In the twentieth century alone, Moses became part of the Harlem Renaissance,[1] the legacy of psychotherapy,[2] the Civil Rights movement,[3] and the Spielberg Empire.[4]

For as soon as canons are fixed (and, arguably, even before: the Bible, as Michael Fishbane and other scholars are quick to point out, is fraught with inner-biblical retelling), new story-(re)telling begins. Unable to edit the original telling from within, later writers alter and revisit it from without. And the phenomenon of retelling is hardly limited to text, of course. There are innumerable examples to be found in film, television, music, and the visual arts.

Thus canon begets counter-canon; scripture begets commentary. Over place and time, both types of response may themselves become

1. In Zora Neale Hurston's 1939 novel, *Moses, Man of the Mountain.*
2. Sigmund Freud, *Moses and Monotheism* (New York: Vintage, 1955).
3. In his last speech, "I See the Promised Land," given the night before he was assassinated, Martin Luther King, Jr. likened himself to Moses, who looks across to the Promised Land but is unable to enter it.
4. *Prince of Egypt*, Dreamworks 1998.

authoritative, may become tellings themselves that will be retold by those without the power, access, or capability to edit them from within. Matthew's new Moses achieved (some would say surpassed) the status of his 'Old Testament' forerunner, and became the telling that begot countless retellings.[5] Why might these transformations have occurred? How do we process, analyze, apprehend this eternal cycle?

The question of why a writer transforms the work of another lies at the heart of this discussion, but the minds of authors—those alive now as much as those in the recesses of history—are difficult to discern. Authorial intention is a thorny issue, and current literary sensibilities avoid trying to determine what a writer sought to convey. To disregard what the author meant is not to disregard meaning, however. Here is where the need for a language to speak about retelling becomes crucial.

There exists no adequate vocabulary—academic or popular, religious or secular, literary or theological—for talking about retellings. The problem is not specific to the English language. French literary theorists, Italian classicists, and Hebrew exegetes all employ loose terms to describe retellings. The Germans have come up with *Nachleben*—afterlife—to describe the phenomenon generally, but this is an umbrella term similar to some of the general words in English, and lacks the precision we seek. English-speaking literary critics, biblical scholars, and book reviewers alike seek recourse in words like adaptation, allusion, echo, imitation, and influence to describe what we might, for lack of better terms, call retellings. Although any of these definitions is possible, none is precise. Allusion, for instance, is premised on the notion that the later text lends greater glory to the earlier.[6] But what if the new text no longer accords the old a place of honor? The question of the later text casting a shadow (of relativism, of doubt, of scandal, even) or even obscuring the earlier is particularly stimulating when the earlier text is the Bible. And yet "allusion" does not help us with this question. Neither do gloss, parallel, nod, rewriting, even the "retelling" I have been using here—all terms that pepper reviews of literature and film that revisit in some way prior works.

5. Abundant examples may be found in Jaroslav Pelikan's *Jesus Through the Centuries* (New Haven: Yale University Press, 1985) and Stephen Prothero's *Jesus in America* (New York: Farrar, Strauss & Giroux, 2003), which both trace later recastings of Jesus.

6. Christopher Ricks, "Beckett's Allusions to Shakespeare" (Boston University Translation Seminar, January 31, 1997). Peter S. Hawkins counters that allusion as glorification is not the case in Dante, whose references to Virgil and Ovid demonstrate the later poet's superiority to his masters.

As popular critics reach to find words that adequately describe the relationship between a text and its *Urtext*, the terms they use seldom touch on the attitude the new text has toward the original: is it an homage? an inversion? a celebration? a subversion? a denial? an amendment? an emendation? an embrace? Words like these might tell us what the author of Matthew is doing with the Moses of Exodus. They could address how the new Moses of Matthew differs from that of Martin Luther King. These, however, are not words that enter the discussion much. Rather, for different reasons, literary theorists and scholars of Jewish hermeneutics have put forth terms to describe intertextual relationships. But even their terminologies are inadequate for speaking with precision and clarity about retelling, for articulating how and why Freud's Moses is different from his contemporary Zora Neale Hurston's, for conveying what the Prince of Egypt has in common with the Man of the Mountain.

We should be able to describe how a retelling relates to a telling. To be able to speak about retelling—and, in particular, to be able to speak about retellings in relation to one another as well as in relation to the texts to which they respond—will bring us closer to being able to speak about what retelling entails. Equipped with the proper language, we might then begin to ask other, bigger questions. What does it mean to retell a biblical story? Is there something substantively different about a revisiting of *Moby Dick*[7] than an analogous return to the Moses story? Is the secular canon more mutable than the sacred one? Is the retelling of secular literature more or less determined than the retelling of sacred literature? We quickly realize we are engaged in a discussion about canon, about the relationship between scripture and interpretation. How do text and tradition relate to one another? In what way does interpretive afterlife have an impact on the life of the canon? Where does text leave off and interpretation begin? When does interpretation become canon? Commentary, literature? The retelling, simply a telling?

The problem becomes especially nuanced when we consider the liminal place of the Bible itself: at this moment, it sits poised between the sacred and the secular. English poet Abraham Cowley (1618–1667) had already begun to see the Bible as literary: hence his claim that "all the books of the Bible are either already most admirable and exalted pieces of poesy, or are the best materials in the world for it."[8] The trend toward viewing it as literature has only blossomed. As David Norton illustrates in *A History of the English Bible as Literature*, the Bible has long since

---

7. This is itself a revisiting of the Bible, most evidently of the book of Jonah.
8. Abraham Cowley, *Poems* (Cambridge: Cambridge University Press, 1905), 14.

entered the literary world, becoming a foundational text in the Western literary canon as well as Holy Writ. And yet, despite this, it not only maintains its own sacredness, but gives rise to literary responses that take on their own sacred status. Most notable are the New Testament and rabbinic midrash, but patristic lore, *responsa* literature, and theological tracts are all part of the corpus.

The case of the Matthew narrative raises the very questions of the interplay between text and interpretation, between scripture, commentary, and literature. The relationship between Matthew's Gospel and the book of Exodus is complicated indeed, but if we were to make a broad comment about it, we could take recourse in the theological vocabulary of supersession. Matthew's goal is to supplant the Exodus story, to offer a new telling of it that is relevant and meaningful to his new audience. Jesus as the new Moses, the giver of a new law, renders the old Moses—and his law—obsolete. In a quite different way, and for different reasons, Freud also seeks to displace the Moses of the Bible.[9]

This project is an attempt to address precisely a lack in the critical language. It has ramifications for the teaching and study of the Bible. In the classroom, being able to offer names for types of retellings will allow us to talk about retelling in a way that we cannot now; furthermore, it will allow us to think more clearly about the ways in which the Bible is alive in the contemporary situation. In our scholarship, knowing how to identify precisely what makes one treatment of a text distinct from another will allow us to put retellings in dialogue with one another, something that is seldom done. As the bibliography indicates, scholarship in this area has tended to focus on one reteller, offering little by way of comparative analysis. Looking at retelling alongside one another will help us to address the ways that the literary afterlife of the Bible glides almost imperceptibly from scripture[10] to commentary to literature.

This work introduces the idea that there are three basic dimensions of a retelling: approach, stance, and filter. These will be introduced shortly. It then surveys the literature that attends, in a variety of ways, to the literary afterlife of the Bible. The body of the book examines three theoretical constructs: intertextuality, midrash, and translation. We will find

9. Freud opens *Moses and Monotheism*, as follows: "To deny a people the man whom it praises as the greatest of its sons is not a deed to be undertaken lightheartedly—especially by one belonging to that people" (p. 3). His project is to show that Moses was an Egyptian nobleman and that the Jewish religion was in fact an Egyptian import to Palestine.

10. The first retellings achieved the level of canon. See the subsection of the bibliography on inner-biblical exegesis.

that the three share much with each other, and that they are not strangers to one another. They collide when Daniel Boyarin brings the theory of intertextuality to his discussion of midrash; when Gerald Bruns wonders about the connection between midrash and translation; when George Steiner extends his exploration of translation to the point that it touches on intertextuality. That said, intertextuality, midrash, and translation have thus far not been engaged in a formal conversation, and certainly not one whose goal is the illumination of yet a fourth area: retelling. Thus one or two chapters will be devoted to each of these overarching constructs from which one might cull a vocabulary for describing literary retellings. These chapters outline the theoretical discourses surrounding each construct, offer some of the terms from the field, and alight on the potential applicability each of these has for our discussion of retellings. In short, these are the tasks at hand: I will introduce relevant extant vocabularies so that, together, author and reader might examine them and develop (from these and from elsewhere) a terminology that applies directly to retelling.

The Three Dimensions: Approach, Stance, and Filter

In an engaging, often funny piece about translation, Gregory Rabassa, best known for his renderings of Gabriel Garcia Marquez in English, talks about Bill Klem, the man who for many years was dean of National League umpires. In Rabassa's account, Klem "eloquently described his position as creator through nomenclature when he said, 'It ain't nothin' till I say what it is. It ain't a ball, it ain't a strike, it ain't nothin'.'"[11]

At this moment, the retelling remains "nothin'." Not an intertext, not a midrash, not a translation, though it could, at some point or another, according to one theorist or another, come to be one or another of these. It is not even a gloss, an allusion, a misreading or a misinterpretation, or any of those words to which critics and reviewers reach in moments of need. The retelling "ain't nothin'" in another respect as well. The double negative betrays that it is *actually something*—not just nothing, as it turns out. The act of retelling, as I will continue to iterate, is pervasive; it is as meaningful as telling itself, despite its apparent subordination. And thus this nothin' deserves to occupy our attention, deserves to be examined, named, and labeled.

---

11. Gregory Rabassa, "No Two Snowflakes are Alike," in *The Craft of Translation* (ed. John Biguenet and Rainer Schulte; Chicago: University of Chicago Press, 1989), 4.

I have pointed to some recastings—or, arguably, retellings, rewritings, transpositions, variations, echoes, etc.—of the Moses narrative. As I have noted, however, if we were to say, "The film *The Ten Commandments*, like the *Decalogue* series, is a rewriting (or transposition, or echo, or recasting) of a canonical text," we wouldn't be saying much. We would be no closer to understanding whether the films of Cecil B. DeMille and Krystof Kieslowski have comparable attitudes to their *Urtexts*, whether they manipulate their respective literary legacies in similar ways, or whether they read the new through a particular ideological and cultural lens than had we not spoken of the two works together. And yet, to understand a retelling properly, we must think in terms of these three concerns and others like them.

Certainly, there are innumerable factors at play in retelling. But the point here is to work toward a way of thinking about the relationship between telling and retelling in a widely applicable (and widely usable) way. I will therefore keep it simple for us. I contend that there are three crucial, inextricably related aspects of a retelling. Let us call these *approach*, *stance* and *filter*.

Approach is the word I use to describe the means by which the retelling gains entry to the telling. Does the author of the later work borrow the plot of the earlier? Does she flesh out an under-developed character? Tell the story from another perspective? Build on a single word? Phrase? Scene? A broad theme? To describe approach is to describe how and how much a writer uses an extant writing.[12] How does *The Prince of Egypt* approach Exodus? It borrows plot and characters, amplifying both.

Stance designates the relationship the retelling has to the telling. Does the retelling supplement the telling or attempt to displace it? Is it an embrace or a conquest of the original? Parody or homage? To consider stance is to consider what one text 'thinks' of its *Urtext*, without entering into the thorny territory of authorial intent. Kieslowski's *Decalogue* is respectful of its biblical roots. The films in this series recognize the complexity of the laws Moses inscribed on the two tablets. They explore the overlapping foci of the Ten Commandments, suggesting that transgression of any one of these laws can have grave moral consequences.

The third dimension, *filter*, is a subset of stance, perhaps, or might be the point of intersection of approach and stance. While every retelling has an approach and a stance toward the telling, not every retelling has a filter. The filter is the lens through which the retelling looks at the telling. Christian exegetes read Hebrew scripture through the filter of the New

---

12. The phenomenon of retelling is hardly limited to text, of course. There are innumerable examples to be found in film, television, and the visual arts.

Testament; the "Old Testament" text cannot be seen except through a Christological lens. Matthew reads Moses through the filter of Christianity (or, more accurately, the beginnings of the Jesus movement). By contrast, Zora Neale Hurston reads Exodus through the filters of the African American experience (particularly of slavery), feminism, and Christianity,

Not every retelling will have a discernible filter, although given their theological underpinnings (or counter-reactions), retellings of biblical tales often do. Chapter two will address some of the issues particular—and peculiar—to the retelling of biblical literature. For the time being, however, it is worth noting that within the realm of biblical retelling, one term exists already that takes into account stance and filter, and to some extent even approach: typology. A uniquely Christian mode of retelling, typology "sets forth a metaphysical point of correspondence between type and antitype, although occasionally...the connection is a point of contrast."[13] Implicit in the very notion of typology are approach, stance, and filter: the approach of the retelling is the recasting of a specific element of the Old Testament[14] in such a way as to suggest that it prefigures a comparable element in the New Testament; inherent in this transformation is stance: "the historical consciousness of typology dictates that its pairings will almost invariably be construed as a relation of 'old' and 'new,' 'then' and 'now.'"[15] Thus the stance of the later to the earlier is supersessionist (and therefore often polemical):[16] the later text is intended to have greater glory than the earlier; the earlier exists only to point to the later. This characteristic is closely related to the notion of filter. "Typology provided the patristic and mediaeval periods with a universally accepted key to reading the [Old Testament] in the light of Jesus":[17] it is Christian (specifically Christological) exegesis.

13. David S. Berkeley, "Typology," in *A Dictionary of Biblical Tradition in English Literature* (ed. David Lyle Jeffrey; Grand Rapids: Eerdmans, 1992), 792.

14. Frequently a figure, as when Paul casts Christ as the new Adam, but also sometimes an object, as when Augustine has the wood Isaac carries up the mountain become the wood of the Cross.

15. Ibid.

16. Barnabas, Justin, Melito and Irenaeus, the church fathers who developed systematic typological exegesis, "always [did] so in a polemical context. The primary concern of all [was] to argue for the unity of the two Testaments: for the first three against the Jews who reject the NT; for Irenaeus against the Gnostics who reject the Old Testament" (Brian McNeil, "Typology," in *A Dictionary of Bible Interpretation* [ed. R. J. Coggins and J. L. Houlden; London: SCM, 1990], 713).

17. Ibid., 713.

Because approach, stance, and filter are woven right into it, typology is on the one hand an exemplar of the potential of descriptive language and a term already too well-defined to be imported into a larger discussion of retelling generally. Thus it joins the vocabularies that touch on the topic at hand, but which do not ultimately allow us to access it. As I have intimated, neither do the languages of literary criticism and theory, nor those of midrashic studies or even translation studies, offer us an entry into the retelling through all three dimensions. However, it is only if we attend to all three aspects, only if we consider the nexus of approach, stance and filter, that we might arrive at a vocabulary that allows us to discuss retellings adequately.

The Three Paradigms: Intertextuality, Midrash, Translation

In their efforts to discuss the literary retelling of canonical texts by later writers, scholars have tended to turn to one of two theoretical frameworks. Those engaged in literary studies frequently label the phenomenon intertextuality. As we will see presently (and discuss in depth in Chapter 3), theories of intertextuality suggest that all texts (either consciously or otherwise) are in dialogue with all other texts, that every utterance of a word echoes and expands upon every prior utterance of it. Retelling, which re-utters prior utterances, would be particularly intertextual. Those scholars treating Jewish sources or Jewish aftertexts often name the phenomenon midrash, which is the rabbinic mode of textual exegesis that frequently fills in gaps in the biblical narrative, smoothing over 'surface irregularities' and fleshing out elliptical verses. We will discuss midrash briefly below; Chapter 4 will be devoted to the topic.

Both intertextuality and midrash are labels that suggest in broad terms that one text is referencing or interpreting another, without communicating fully what actually takes place in that activity. But does either term allow us deep access into a retelling? Will either allow us to talk about the relationship between the telling and retelling? Between two retellings? Here the language of translation study proves itself very useful. Translation is the concern of the penultimate chapter of this work. A quick preview, then, of the chapters that treat our three paradigms of retelling: intertextuality, midrash, and translation.

Chapters 3 and 4 present literary critics and theorists who have developed their own vocabularies to describe the interrelations of later texts to earlier ones. As we will see in Chapter 3, alongside the "allusion" we have just considered, literary critics have put forth an array of possible terms. Aristotle, Horace, and Cicero spoke of "imitation," the adoption of tone, style, and attitude of another writer, a taking of an extant form and giving it a new shape. Spenser, Sidney, and Jonson used "invention," the making of something new out of pre-existent materials or fore-conceits. "Influence" was a concept popular with Pope and Dryden, who understood it as conscious rewriting; it has been revived by Harold Bloom, who sees it as textual inevitability.[18] In more recent criticism, this idea of influence—"the Power of a Superior over an Inferior"—and inter-textuality have gained currency. The latter term, coined by Julia Kristeva, who describes "the 'literary word' as an *intersection of textual surfaces* rather than a point (a fixed meaning), as a dialogue among several writings,"[19] understands all writing to relate to all other writing, intentionally or otherwise. We will consider all of these terms, taking into account their understandings of what takes place in a retelling. We will pay particular attention to how they situate retelling: as conscious act or sub-conscious reflex, as an innovation or as an appropriation, as set in motion by the author of the retelling or by the reader who discerns an earlier work in the later telling. In tying the questions posed back to the retelling of biblical stories, I will apply some of the terms we encounter to poetic retellings centered on the story of the flood.

We will find that intertextuality is the theoretical construct currently championed by literary theorists. As we will explore in greater detail, critic Harold Bloom conceives of literature as fundamentally intertextual, as deriving from and imitating previous texts. This is a notion he intro-duces in *The Anxiety of Influence*, in which he argues that late poets write by misinterpreting and misreading their precursors.[20] As Graham Allen explains, 'strong poets' must both "rewrite the precursor's poems, and in that very act they must defend themselves against the knowledge that they are merely involved in the process of rewriting, or what Bloom calls

18. Bloom asserts that "poetic influence—when it involves two strong, authentic poets—always proceeds by a misreading of the prior poet, an act of creative correc-tion that is actually and necessarily a misrepresentation" (*A Map of Misreading* [New York: Oxford University Press, 1975], 19).

19. Julia Kristeva, *Desire in Language: A Semiotic Approach to Literature and Art* (ed. Leon S. Roudiez; trans. Thomas Gora, Alice Jardine and Leon S. Roudiez; New York: Columbia University Press, 1980), 65. Emphasis in original.

20. Specifically, Bloom claims that all post-Enlightenment English literature returns to Milton. It may be worthwhile at this point to introduce Bloom's notion that all English literature after Milton is "late." In his work on the Romantics, Bloom raises the question of influence. Bloom's poets—Blake, Wordsworth, and Keats—were driven by renaissance and rediscovery, by a rejection of history and a disdain for nostalgia, in short, by a firm belief in the imagination and human creativity. And yet, despite these concerns, as Bloom notes, they consistently returned to Milton. In his view, Milton's poetry was an event and subsequent authors were inevitably late for that event.

misreading."[21] In Bloom's view, "poets employ the central figures of previous poetry, but they transform, redirect, reinterpret the central figures in new ways and hence generate the illusion that their poetry is not influenced by, and therefore not a misreading of, the precursor poem."[22]

Furthermore, for Bloom, the poet "is not so much a man speaking to men as a man rebelling against being spoken to by a dead man (the precursor) outrageously more alive than himself. A poet dare not regard himself as being late, yet cannot accept a substitute for the first vision he reflectively judges to have been his precursor's also."[23] The Freudian struggle between the son (the ephebe) and the father (the precursor) is propelled by two drives: the son wants to imitate the father, from whom he learned the art of poetry, and the son wants to be original, "and defend against the knowledge that all the poet is doing is imitating rather than creating afresh."[24] Bloom's description is premised on the idea that late writers cannot help but grapple with earlier ones: this is the unconscious (Freudian) struggle of the son with the father. Bloom's intertextuality appears almost accidental, as evidenced by his comment that "an ephebe's best misinterpretations may well be of poems he has not even read."[25] But Bloom does not attend to those poets who seek intentionally to refashion the works of earlier poets. How might we speak of intentional rewriting? When the ephebe grapples with a poem he has not only read, but has studied and manipulated, does this constitute another phenomenon entirely? And what do we make of the ephebe who grapples deliberately with not one but many poems he knows well? Is this something else again? Literary theoretical considerations of intentional rewriting will be the topic of Chapter 4.

The process of intentional rewriting is connected with the ancient Jewish enterprise of aggadic midrash—that is, elaborative (sometimes narrative) interpretation. When, in the early second century B.C.E., the authors of the book of *Jubilees* (which, for the most part, adheres closely to the biblical account) rewrote the Noah story, they made small emendations throughout the text.[26] Their (re)writing is usually described

21.   Graham Allen, *Intertextuality* (New York: Routledge, 2000), 135.

22.   Ibid., 135.

23.   Bloom, *A Map of Misreading*, 19.

24.   Allen, *Intertextuality*, 134.

25.   Harold Bloom, *The Anxiety of Influence: A Theory of Poetry* (Oxford: Oxford University Press, 1973), 70.

26.   The authors assert the righteousness of Noah, his unique status among the men of the early generations of Genesis. For instance, the writers of *Jubilees* note that "on account of his righteousness, in which he [Noah] was perfected, his life on

as midrashic. Similarly, when speaking of the ancient translators who, in rendering the Hebrew Bible into Aramaic, incorporated oral traditions or made exegetical expansions of the biblical texts, we label their additions—which range in length from a few words to full paragraphs—midrashic.[27] And certainly, of the rabbis of the second through fifth centuries of the Common Era who wrote aggadic glosses on biblical stories, we must describe their work as midrashic.

Biblical scholar James Kugel explains that the foundational precept of the midrashic hermeneutic is "the dissonance between the religion of the rabbis and the Book from which it is supposed to be derived."[28] Writing in the second century, in exile after the destruction of the Temple that marked the center of their religion, the rabbis felt a loss of connection between their world and the world of their sacred texts. Thus, they wrote midrash, a form of exegesis that simultaneously stressed the ongoing value of the Bible even as the rabbis themselves understood that many of its texts no longer had an immediately evident application for contemporary life. These rabbis composed a series of commentaries[29] on the Bible that filled in perceived gaps and holes in the original text—what Kugel describes as "surface irregularities"[30]—thereby making a compendium

---

earth was more excellent than [any of] the sons of men except Enoch" (*Jub* 10:17). Here they reflect a popular tradition that Enoch, thought to be a sage and astronomer, was lifted to heaven alive by God. Noah is second only to the one man chosen by God not to die as others do, but rather hand-selected to be carried to God. Apart from Noah, nothing else in creation was without blame. By way of justifying the flood, the ancient exegetes, by contrast, explain that the animals too had contributed to the corruption of the earth, asserting that "Lawlessness increased on the earth and all flesh corrupted its way, alike men and cattle and beasts and birds and everything that walks the earth—all of them corrupted their ways and their orders" (*Jub* 5:2).

27. *Targum Neophyti* and *Targum Pseudo-Jonathan* are notable for their inclusion of non-pentateuchal material. For instance, with regard to the post-deluvian Noah story, Gen 9:24 tells us that "When Noah awoke from his wine and knew what his youngest son had done to him," he cursed Canaan. The Bible does not tell us what the youngest son had done, but *Targum Pseudo-Jonathan* offers this gloss: "Noah awoke from his wine, and knew by being told in a dream what Ham his youngest son had done unto him, who was so slight in merit[: he] had contrived that Noah could not beget a fourth son" (John Bowker, *The Targums and Rabbinic Literature* [Cambridge: Cambridge University Press, 1969], 172).

28. James Kugel, "Two Introductions to Midrash," in *Midrash and Literature* (ed. Geoffrey Hartman and Sanford Budick; New Haven: Yale University Press, 1986), 80.

29. This word is slightly misleading; the rabbis' works bore no resemblance to the line by line explication of text we find in modern scholarly commentaries.

30. Kugel, "Two Introductions to Midrash," 93.

that was intended to be accessible to an audience living hundreds of years after the first biblical books were written. David Stern describes midrash in a way that illuminates the rabbis' mode of writing: he states that it "touches upon literature not at the point where literature becomes exegesis, but at what might be called its opposite conjunction, where exegesis turns into literature and comes to possess its own language and voice."[31] Midrash is the ancient mode of bridging the gap between the world of the text and the community that received the text; it is text and commentary, both authority and tradition together.

Chapter 5 explains the rabbinic activity of midrash, particularly as understood by contemporary Jewish Studies scholars, and examines the ways the phenomenon of midrash has been adopted by contemporary literary theorists. In considering traditional midrash as well as the ways in which the vocabulary of midrash has already entered the field of literary studies, we will determine whether the literary theoretical appropriation of midrash, the redefining of the term, is at odds with or complementary to this discussion of retelling.

We will see that the hermeneutic concerns of midrash have come to be understood as literary concerns. Contemporary Jewish poet and literary critic David Curzon speaks of the possibility of modern midrash,[32] such that when a Jewish poet like Yehuda Amichai writes a poem called "Jacob and the Angels" or "King Saul and I," we might label it as midrash. Similarly, David Jacobson uses the term midrash to "refer to the Jewish tradition of the interpretive retelling of biblical stories that began within the Bible itself, developed in the rabbinic periods and...has continued to the present."[33] Occasionally, the term is also put forth to describe retellings of biblical stories by non-Jewish writers.

As Chapter 5 illustrates, Curzon and Jacobson are not the only literary-minded scholars to turn to the area of midrash. Susan Handelman, David Stern, Jacques Derrida, Roland Barthes, and Jorge Luis Borges are among those who have put midrash in dialogue with literary theory. For these thinkers, the draws of midrash are its blending of literature and commentary, its willingness to allow multiple and multiply contradictory interpretations, and its understanding of the text as indeterminate. (Or

31. David Stern, "Midrash and the Language of Exegesis," in Hartman and Budick, eds., *Midrash and Literature*, 105.

32. See two articles by David Curzon in *Tikkun*: "A Hidden Genre: Twentieth-Century Midrashic Poetry," *Tikkun* 9 (March–April 1994): 70–71, 95, and "Tradition Unbound: Poetry from Midrash," *Tikkun* 6 (January–February 1991): 30–31, 95.

33. David C. Jacobson, *Modern Midrash: The Retelling of Traditional Jewish Narratives by Twentieth Century Hebrew Writers* (Albany: SUNY Press, 1987), 1.

their perception of midrash's understanding of the text as indeterminate. The extent to which any contemporary critics shape midrash in the image of their own theory will be addressed at length in Chapter 5.) In weighing the applicability of what may ultimately be a theological construct (midrash) in describing what is generally a secular enterprise (literature), we will consider the ways in which the vocabulary of midrash has already entered the field of literary studies. From there we will determine whether the literary-theoretical appropriation of midrash, the redefining of the term, is at odds with or complementary to this discussion of midrash as a means of describing retelling.

In an effort to determine how broadly we can use the term, we will examine midrash in its traditional manifestation: as the ancient rabbinic exegesis of biblical texts.[34] How did it work? Can we extend the term midrash to encompass contemporary Jewish retellings of the Hebrew canon? Would we describe a work as midrashic because it recalls biblical texts, because it contributes to, builds on, re-imagines, reinvents, or revises the biblical canon? Can we think about midrash as a contemporary activity? As existing outside as Jewish framework? As a viable designator of responses to non-biblical texts? If we could reasonably apply the language of midrash to all these permutations, it would certainly simplify our problems: there exists already a vocabulary to describe the exegetical moves of the rabbis. Chapter 6 defines and describes these hermeneutic principles, putting them to use in an analysis of poetry and literature dealing with the binding of Isaac.

Practitioners and theorists of translation have articulated principles of their own for conveying a text from one language to another. This question of conveyance, of translating (or carrying across) a text from one setting to another, is closely related to the issue of retelling. The reteller imports or transposes something of another work, language, or culture, and renders it in her own work, language, or culture. This is translation: the movement from source to target.

Translation, however, transforms a text. As George Steiner notes, "when we read or hear any language-statement from the past, be it Leviticus or last year's best seller, we translate. Reader, actor, editor are translators of language out of time. The schematic model of translation is one in which a message from a source-language passes into a receptor-language via a transformational process."[35] Here Steiner hits on the most

---

34. Particularly, as read through the lens of contemporary academics Isaac Heinemann, Judah Goldin, David Weiss Halivni, and James Kugel.

35. George Steiner, *After Babel: Aspects of Language and Translation* (Oxford: Oxford University Press, 1992), 29.

compelling reason for thinking about translation in our context: translation is not merely a carrying across of a text from one culture to another, but a carrying across in which the text undergoes a process of transformation. Retellings of canonical texts are intralingual translations, partaking, like interlingual translation, in the afterlife of the parent text.

In the midst of a lengthy consideration of the liberties a literary translator might take in relaying a source into a target language, Steiner offers a cluster of sentences that speak directly to our concerns:

> The relations of a text to its translations, imitations, thematic variants, even parodies, are too diverse to allow of any single theoretic, definitional scheme. They categorize the entire question of the meaning of meaning in time, of the existence and effects of the linguistic fact outside its specific, initial form. But there can be no doubt that echo enriches, that it is more than shadow and inert simulacrum. We are back at the problem of the mirror which not only reflects but also generates light. The original text gains from the orders of diverse relationship and distance established between itself and its translations.[36]

Not only does Steiner point to the necessity for a descriptive vocabulary, he also lays bare the potential pitfalls in developing one.

Steiner's final sentence in particular points to the importance of this study. The echo enriches the text, offers it new meaning. As literary theorists and religious exegetes—or more, as good readers—we must be able to approach the echo as a new life, not merely as a shadow of the old. To apprehend the depth of the retelling, to appreciate the ways that it transforms or transcends or even falls short of the telling, means to develop a vocabulary by which we can talk about the retelling. It seems clear that in Steiner's view, the telling is enriched by the retelling, but the way that this happens cannot adequately be described. Or not, at least, through "any single theoretic, definitional scheme." As Steiner notes, the possible relationships between retelling and telling are indeed too many and too varied for us to rely on general terms like allusion or echo.

Although intertextuality and midrash are most often invoked in thinking about retelling, the terminology of the two subjects is often inadequate for thinking about our three fundamental points in considering retelling: approach, stance, and filter. The varied vocabularies and taxonomies developed by those who concern themselves with the art and act of translation offer some of the precise designations that the languages of intertextuality and midrash do not appear to provide. Thus, in Chapter 7, we will consider writings on translation by Nietzsche, Friedrich, Dryden, Schleiermacher, von Humboldt, Goethe, and Steiner, among others. We

36. Ibid., 317.

will encounter the vocabulary of translation theory—that is, different translators' ideas about the relationships between target and source languages, opinions about bringing a reader to a text versus conveying a text to a reader, conceptions of the respective roles of what I have dubbed approach and stance. Drawing examples from retellings of the David story, Chapter 8 weighs the many terms and phrases used by translators to describe the act of translation, and culls from among them a vocabulary which might be applied to the question of retelling.

We will see over and again that translation theory's concern with the relaying of text from one linguistic (and therefore cultural, historical, aesthetic) locus to another is analogous to the concern here with the relaying of a text from one cultural, historical, or aesthetic locus to another. Unlike theories of intertextuality or midrash, translation theory emphasizes and develops the varying ways a text can be carried forth from one situation to another, and takes into account what is at stake in each. This is not to say, however, that intertextuality and midrash fail us entirely. And indeed, there will be some readers who will be convinced of the applicability of these two fields for their own investigations of retellings. Rather, they present us with rich nomenclature.

This work is replete with terms that have been used and could be used in speaking about retelling. It introduces and defines them, indicating how they have been used and suggesting how they might be applied. They are often presented without editorial comment; the inherent openness to the terms found herein is intentional and allows the reader a less mediated engagement with the terms. This is because words and terms that might not seem viable to one person thinking about retelling may seem quite apt for another. And indeed, there are too many words here to imagine integrating them all into one's thinking or making them all part of general conversation, but the abundance of them will allow the reader to consider and select the ones most appropriate for thinking about the tellings and retellings that occupy her. The reader who wants a working lexicon rather than a history and overview of possibilities will find one in the concluding chapter.

Chapter 2

CREATION IN THE IMAGE

Reception Theory and Literary Afterlives

For nearly two centuries, biblical scholarship was focused almost exclusively on transmission history, on investigating how the Bible came to
be, how it reflects the customs, laws, and cultures of the people who
wrote it, and how archaeological and extra-biblical evidence supports
(or undermines) biblical claims. Beginning with the concentrated scholarly turn to the Bible as literature that took place in the 1980s, there has
been a growing interest in "reception theory"—a consideration of the
ways the Bible has influenced art, literature, culture, and society.

Reception theory—also known as "The Aesthetics of Reception"—
attends to the reading and reception of texts rather than to their production and composition. The two main proponents of reception theory are
Wolfgang Iser and Hans Robert Jauss, who established the Constance
School at University of Constance (then in West Germany) in the late
1960s and early 1970s. While both are concerned with the audience of
the text (what Iser would call the aesthetic pole of a literary work) rather
than its author (the artistic pole),[1] Iser and Jauss focus in somewhat different ways on the role of the reader in the study of texts. Iser examines
the process of reading a literary work, Jauss the role of the audience in
the historical life of a literary work.[2]

Iser sees the reading of a text as a recreation: the reader participates in
a process of creation akin to that undertaken by the author of the work.
The reader, not the author, "establish[es...] interrelationships between
past, present, and future, actually caus[ing] the text to reveal its potential

1. Wolfgang Iser, *The Implied Reader: Patterns of Communication in Prose from
Bunyan to Beckett* (Baltimore: The Johns Hopkins University Press, 1978), 274.
2. Hans Robert Jauss, "Literary History as a Challenge to Literary Theory," in
Toward an Aesthetic of Reception (trans. Timothy Bahti; Minneapolis: University of
Minnesota Press, 1982), 18.

multiplicity of connections" which are produced by the reader as her "mind work[s] on the raw material of the text."[3] These connections are "not the text itself—for this consists just of sentences, statements, information, etc."[4] The reader is the locus of the text's meaning, but this meaning is not static. Each time a reader returns to a text, she is in a different temporal setting and stands in a different relationship to the work (she might know the ending already, for instance, because she has read the book before; she might be older, and bring to the book new experiences of her own—in both cases, her understanding of the book will therefore be changed.). Thus the reader's own anticipation and retrospection alter the text's meaning.[5] Moreover, the reading process is propelled by the reader's instinct to fill in gaps in the text in order to achieve narrative consistency: "we will strive, even if unconsciously, to fit everything together in a consistent pattern."[6] We supply what is not there in the text, making consistency not a function of the author but the reader. As such, consistency arises from the "meeting between the written text and the individual mind of the reader with its own particular history of experience, its own consciousness, its own outlook."[7] The text thus mirrors the reader and the reader, who is changed by the experience of reading, who mirrors the text. For our purposes, Iser's work is relevant because it shifts the focus from author to reader, speaks to the readerly impulse toward gap-filling (which is the starting point for many retellings of biblical narratives), points to the indeterminacy of text, and accounts for the tremendous diversity in readerly interpretation.

Jauss's theory of reception is even more germane. Jauss sought to reposition literary history at the center of literary studies by rethinking how we as contemporary readers in a contemporary culture stand in relation to texts from the past. Whereas literary history was once (in its nineteenth-century incarnation in particular) concerned with establishing the connections between authors and their texts, making literary history a form of biography, Jauss reoriented the discipline. Like Iser, Jauss bracketed the author and foregrounded the reader, centering literary history around the interaction between text and reader (and thereby on the reception of literary works). The reception historian is concerned with the ways that works of literature have had an impact on and been affected by subsequent generations. A literary work "is not an object that

3. Iser, *Implied Reader*, 278.
4. Ibid.
5. Ibid., 281.
6. Ibid., 283.
7. Ibid., 284.

stands by itself and that offers the same view to each reader in each
period. It is not a monument that monologically reveals its timeless
essence"[8]—rather, it is in dialogue with its readers. A work changes as it
passes from reader to reader and from generation to generation. Literature is thus not an object but an event, and its coherence "as an event is
primarily mediated in the horizon of expectations of the literary experience of contemporary and later readers, critics, and authors."[9] Jauss's
theory of the aesthetics of reception insists that we not only look at
works diachronically, that is, considering the varied responses to the text
across time periods, but also synchronically, by investigating the relationships a text has to other texts. In this way, we come to understand
literary history as a "special history" within the general history.[10]

In its attention to how a text has been received, and how it draws from,
connects to, and inspires other texts, Jauss's theory is directly related to
our enterprise. Yet while reception theory has spawned a great deal of
scholarship (including, more recently, work focused on the reception of
the Bible), it has not given rise to a developed vocabulary that allows one
to talk about the relationships between synchronic texts. A few recent
works, all pertaining to the reception of classical figures, can illuminate
our work somewhat.

In *The Figure of Echo*, John Hollander treats "stages of the mytho-
graphy of Echo";[11] he reveals reappearances of Echo in Milton and after.
His very subject matter proffers a descriptive language: he speaks
repeatedly of *echo, reverberation,* and *resonance.*[12] He uses the terms
"figuratively and often synonymously, without regard to their technical
meanings. And yet," he adds, "the acoustic phenomena of echo—caves
and mountains and halls of origin, delays in return, scattering and proliferation, and so forth—will be implicitly and explicitly invoked, as will
certain conceptual problems arising from them."[13] The figurative appropriation of acoustic language allows Hollander to consider aspects of
echo such as fragmentary repetition, the decrescendo, and the presence of
disembodied voice.[14] Hollander contemplates the nature of poetic language, not descriptive vocabularies. He is thus "content…to observe that

8.   Hans Robert Jauss, *Toward an Aesthetic of Reception* (trans. Timothy Bahti;
Minneapolis: University of Minnesota Press, 1982), 21.
9.   Ibid., 22.
10. Ibid., 39.
11. John Hollander, *The Figure of Echo: A Mode of Allusion in Milton and After*
(Berkeley: University of California Press, 1981), 23.
12. Ibid., 3.
13. Ibid., 3.
14. Ibid., 6.

poems seem to echo prior ones for the personal aural benefit of the poet, and of whichever poetic followers can overhear the reverberations"[15] rather than to attempt "anything like a systematic taxonomy of allusive echoic patterns."[16]

He does, however, "exhume" a term that fits neatly into our discussion: "the old rhetoricians' term *metalepsis*."[17] Rarely used even by the ancients, and seldom found in taxonomies of metaphor, since the fifteenth century the derived English form *transumption* has designated a "copy or quotation"; "transfer or translation"; "transmutation or conversion."[18] Quintilian noted that *metalepsis* stands midway between "the term transferred and the thing to which it is transferred"—it merely provides a transition and has no meaning on its own.[19] Hollander takes one of Quintilian's examples and translates it across language and culture: "We might translate the whole sequence [of words in Quintilian's example] into modern English by saying *sing* (for Milton or Pope or Wordsworth) means 'say,' which means 'write,' which means, for us today, 'type.'"[20] It is a transition from one trope to another (one anterior, one posterior) in which "there will be one or more unstated, but associated or understood figures, transumed by the trope, but which are to be reconstructed by interpretation."[21] Transumption is simultaneously allusive and transformative; it is an altered copy or transmuted translation, both of which are intriguing to ponder in our context.

In his introduction to the English translation of Gian Biagio Conte's *The Rhetoric of Imitation: Genre and Poetic Memory in Virgil and Other Latin Poets*, Charles Segal situates Conte's project within modern theory:

> Conte and a small group of disciples and colleagues…have been energetically reexamining the nature of literary allusion in Roman poetry in light of the structuralist and poststructuralist theories of language developed by such critics and theorists as Jakobson, Lotman, Barthes, Genette, Riffaterre, Todorov, and others among the Russian formalists and the 'new' rhetoricians of Paris.[22]

15. Ibid., ix.
16. Ibid.
17. Ibid., 133.
18. Ibid., 134.
19. Ibid., 135.
20. Ibid.
21. Ibid., 140.
22. Charles Segal, "Foreword," to Gian Biagio Conte, *The Rhetoric of Imitation: Genre and Poetic Memory in Virgil and Other Latin Poets* (Ithaca: Cornell University Press, 1986), 8.

As Conte explains:

> A philologist who approaches the text can deconstruct it, dissecting it vertically or at least plumbing the space beneath the tough, compact surface. Seen from below, from the perspective of culture, the text is no longer the neat, checkered chess board of *horizontal* coherence on which words are locked in meter but is now instead a profoundly contextualized network of association, echoes, imitations, allusions—a rich root system reaching down and entwined with the fibers of the culture in its historical dimension. This network of meaning is the used, functionalized culture that, when placed in a poetic context, must be motivated, given coherent meaning within the artistic context of the literary system in which it operates.[23]

Thus his project is not merely source-hunting, the tracing of chains of influence, but an attempt to understand what the later poet's use of earlier poetry *means*.[24] Conte seeks to bring allusion and poetic memory "into a functional rhetorical matrix (defining rhetoric as the ability to motivate the linguistic sign) and thus to make them contribute to the process of poetic signification as constructive elements of poetic discourse."[25] In his reading, "literary echoes are not just the passive repetition of traditional *topoi* but the places where the tradition deliberately intrudes into the text, bringing with it the sign of its own difference from as well as assimilation into the work."[26] What is useful in this—for our thinking at least—is the notion of difference, not in the Derridean sense, but as a counter-response. Unlike with a typology, which will almost always be assimilative, here the later text need not be in concert with the earlier; it need not uphold or trumpet it. Rather, the later text can be a negative departure from it, a reaction against rather than for. The metaphor of intrusion and the designation of difference have tremendous potential for a general discussion of retelling.

Conte is indebted to Giorgio Pasquali, who treats the art of allusion in Italian poetry, and who loops together strings of potential descriptors. In an assertion about the function of allusion, Pasquali touches on ways the later poet may brush up against an earlier text. He explains,

> In reading cultured, learned poetry, I look for what I have for years stopped calling reminiscences, and now call allusions, and would call evocations, and in some cases quotations. The poet may not be aware of

---

23. Conte, *The Rhetoric of Imitation*, 49.
24. It is, in this respect, much like Hollander's undertaking.
25. Conte, *The Rhetoric of Imitation*, 23.
26. Ibid., 11.

reminiscences, and he may hope that his imitations escape his public's notice, but allusions do not produce the desired effect if the reader does not clearly remember the text to which they refer.[27]

To this litany—reminiscences, allusions, evocations, quotations—Pasquali also adds emulations: concerted attempts to mimic the style of another writer.

Pasquali's approach privileges the intentionality of the author, and thus to Conte's mind (as to Bloom and Barthes's, as we will see) is flawed: "the position of the author becomes predominant and the notion of the centrality of the text as a unified, complete, and interlocking system is inevitably weakened."[28] Conte offers his corrective, which is born of philology (in which Conte is trained) and thus does not become embroiled in the psychological readings that beset quests for an author's influences and musings about authorial intent. He contends that

> if one concentrates on the text rather than on the author, on the relation between texts (intertextuality) rather than on imitation, then one will be less likely to fall into the common philological trap of seeing all textual resemblances as produced by the intentionality of a literary subject whose desire is to emulate.[29]

Unlike Pasquali, Conte is not concerned with redeeming the *imitatio*: he asserts that "by assuming that the poet desires to emulate, [Pasquali] attributes authorial intention to the *imitatio*. Whereas he thereby ennobles what is a passive moment, I renounce the nobility and treat the art of allusion as a cog in the general mechanism of textual composition."[30] For him, allusion is "part of the rhetoric that systematically constitutes literary discourse."[31] His concern is with allusion's "simultaneous coexistence of both a denotative and a connotative semiotic,"[32] or, in a plainer argot, with how allusion both points back to an old meaning and creates a new one at once. As such, he is concerned with the "functional character of poetic memory."[33]

The problem with Conte's method, for our discussion, is that the texts about which we speak here make conscious and deliberate use of earlier texts: they *are* intentional. Conte fears that source-hunting reduces poetic

27. Ibid., 25.
28. Ibid., 27.
29. Ibid.
30. Ibid., 28.
31. Ibid.
32. Ibid., 24.
33. Ibid., 36.

memory to the impulse to imitate, and his fears are grounded. There are concordances of biblical allusions in Milton, Shakespeare, Chaucer, and Hardy, for example, that make no effort to describe how the later writer avails himself of the earlier text (let alone explore or explain what transpires when an established text is carried across to a new setting). But here we are concerned with ways of thinking about the deliberate act of carrying texts across time or culture; and so, I would argue, we are not in danger of having "the literary process…center more on the personal will of two opposing authors than on the structural reality of the text,"[34] which is what Conte has witnessed in studies of imitation.

In Conte's view, then, the task of the critic (specifically, the "commit-ted philologist") is to "map the relations of meaning and to show their significance in the context."[35] This mapping privileges the role of (poetic) memory which, with its ability to absorb the past and co-opt it into the present, is dialectic.[36] Allusion, which depends on poetic memory, must then also always operate on two levels of meaning at once, must always be understood twice: once as part of the text whence it comes and once as part of the text which it now inhabits. Herein lies the transformation of culture, the reordering of fragments of history or fact in poetic discourse.

Between those critics concerned with cataloguing influences and allusions, and those theorists concerned with determining what it means to allude and retell, there is little descriptive fodder. Just as critics and reviewers in the popular press sought no specific terminology in their describing later retellings of earlier works, literary critics have been able to speak at length about the return by later writers to earlier texts without using words or terms that have any applicability beyond their own dis-cussions. Thus, with a very few exceptions, the worlds (and words) that we might have plumbed for our own purposes have left us yet at a loss for words. While this is surprising, what is more curious is the fact that even those writers who treat specifically the place of the Bible in later literature have no established vocabulary for talking about retelling.

Talking about the Literary Afterlife of the Bible

As we well know, the biblical canon was not even closed when retellings of it began to appear. After it was closed, however, there was a prolifera-tion of Jewish (and, later, Christian) texts that revisited, reworked, and recast biblical tellings. Standing outside the canon, and therefore denied

---

34. Ibid., 27.
35. Ibid., 49.
36. Ibid.

any authoritative status, these retellings circulated on their own. A small fraction of them achieved authority in their own right—the books of Tobit and Judith, the stories of Bel and the Dragon and Susanna and the elders, among others, were incorporated into the Apocrypha (or Deutero-canon) of the Catholic and Orthodox churches. Those that remained apart, however, have much more recently achieved a secular (or scholarly) canonical status in their being compiled in collections of pseudepigrapha.

James H. Charlesworth published the most well-known edition of pseudepigraphic literature in English. In a 1981 article, he outlines his criteria for including works in his Pseudepigrapha. A work needs to be Jewish or Jewish–Christian and have been written between 200 B.C.E. and 200 C.E. It should claim to be divinely inspired, and be related in form or content to the Old Testament. Ideally, it is ascribed to an Old Testament figure, who purports to be either the speaker or the author of the work.[37] Charlesworth's is a concise list, one which would exclude all of our contemporary literary retellings from consideration, but it is noteworthy in its clear articulation of a set of qualities that link a biblical retelling to the Bible. Some of the characteristics are apparently external to the work itself (date of composition; attribution to another (more known) composer), and thus do not fall within our thinking about a retelling's approach or stance. The concern with the text being "at least partially, and preferably totally, Jewish or Jewish Christian"[38] reflects the significance of filter in any thinking about biblical retellings.

Elsewhere, however, Charlesworth does demarcate the ways that a pseudepigraphic work must stand in relation to the biblical text:

1. *Inspiration.* The Old Testament serves primarily to inspire the author, who then evidences considerable imagination, perhaps sometimes under influences from nonbiblical writings (ranging from the *Books of Enoch* to the *Arda Viraf*).

2. *Framework.* The Old Testament provides the framework for the author's own work. The original setting of the Old Testament work is employed for appreciably other purposes.

3. *Launching.* A passage or story in the Old Testament is used to launch another, considerably different reflection. The original setting is replaced.

4. *Inconsequential.* The author borrows from the Old Testament only the barest facts, names especially, and composes a new story.

---

37. James H. Charlesworth, *LXX: The Pseudepigrapha and Modern Research* (Septuagint and Cognate Studies 7; Ann Arbor: Scholars Press, 1981), 21.
38. Ibid.

5. *Expansions.* Most of these documents, in various ways and
    degrees, start with a passage or story in the Old Testament, and
    rewrite it, often under the imaginative influence of oral traditions
    linked somehow to the biblical narrative.[39]

Here we find a series of words that hold great potential for us, as they
convey a spectrum of approaches to the biblical text. Charlesworth's
adjectives are expressly concerned with how and how much a biblical
trope is used by a later writer.

The categorization of the use of the Old Testament in the pseudepigrapha also occupies Devorah Dimant, who divides the genre into two
distinct categories, which also might prove useful for our thinking about
stance. *Expositional use* is an exegetical strategy in which the pseudepi-
graphist makes explicit reference to the biblical text (designates it with a
clear marker), and explicates it. This interpretative method is seen in rabbinic midrash, Qumranic *pesher*, Philo's commentaries, and at times in
New Testament quotation.[40] *Compositional use* is the literary interweaving of a biblical text into a work without any attribution or marking off
of the text used. Unlike in expositional pseudepigrapha, where the focus
is the biblical text itself, here the biblical text becomes subservient: its
meaning is determined by the new context in which it finds itself. And
while expositional pseudepigrapha are wholly dependent on the Bible,
compositional pseudepigrapha are new and independent texts.[41]

It is intriguing that what could prove to be the most useful terms and
categories for thinking about literary retellings may come not from
literary critics at all, but from biblical scholars. As I will show below,
literary approaches to the Bible (or to the Bible and Literature) offer
much by way of close reading and detailed description, but little by way
of labels or designators (and nothing akin Charlesworth's beginning of a
taxonomy).

We see a broad trend away from source-hunting toward meaning-
making in the scholarly discussion of the use of the Bible by later writers. For those interested in the Bible and literature (as for those interested

---

39. James H. Charlesworth, "In the Crucible: The Pseudepigrapha as Biblical
Interpretation," in *The Aramaic Bible: Targums in their Historical Context* (ed. D. R.
G. Beattie and M. J. McNamara; Sheffield: JSOT Press, 1994), 29.

40. Devorah Dimant, "Use and Interpretation of Mikra in the Apocrypha and
Pseudepigrapha," in *Mikra: Text, Translation, Reading and Interpretation of the
Hebrew Bible in Ancient Judaism and Early Christianity* (ed. Martin Jan Mulder;
Philadelphia: Fortress, 1988), 382–83.

41. Ibid., 383–84.

in the Classics and literature), the 1960s were a period of quantitative assessment, an era of stock-taking that revealed that yes, in fact, the Bible has been a predominant influence on literature. In fact, as Randall Stewart was quick to assert, "The Bible has been the greatest single influence on our literature."[42] Hence the publication of books such as Walter Fulghum's *A Dictionary of Biblical Allusion in English Literature*,[43] James Sims's *The Bible in Milton's Epics*,[44] and *Biblical Allusions in Shakespeare's Comedies*,[45] which merely made note of the allusions.

The Art of Biblical Retelling

At times the surveys provide analyses as well as inventories, as with Carlos Baker's detailed article "The Place of the Bible in American Fiction." Baker determines that "the tradition of secular exploration, fictional dramatization, and lay exegesis…has continued unbroken up to the present moment,"[46] because, as he contends, "great metaphors…have ways of surviving in imaginative literature, especially when they are constantly reinforced by the authors' return to the source-book where they originated."[47] Baker situates biblical retellings in their cultural contexts, noting that "the record shows that times of social *Sturm und Drang* in the United States have often called forth novels in which the teachings of the Bible are reinterpreted—and frequently misrepresented—for popular consumption."[48] The phenomenon is "easy enough to explain. Owing to its infinite variety, and therefore its almost infinite adaptability to a variety of situations, the Bible has been used as the ultimate authority for all sorts of actions, whether for the maintenance of the status quo ante or as a manifesto of revolutionary doctrine."[49] Thus the mode of retelling hangs on the goal of the reteller.

42.   Randall Stewart, *American Literature and Christian Doctrine* (Baton Rouge: Louisiana State University Press, 1958), 3.

43.   Walter Fulghum, *A Dictionary of Biblical Allusion in English Literature* (New York: Holt, Rinehart & Winston, 1965).

44.   James Sims, *The Bible in Milton's Epics* (Gainesville: University of Florida Press, 1962).

45.   James Sims, *Biblical Allusions in Shakespeare's Comedies* (Forsyth, Ga.: Tift College, 1960).

46.   Carlos Baker, "The Place of the Bible in American Fiction," *Theology Today* (April 1960): 71.

47.   Ibid., 55.

48.   Ibid., 62.

49.   Ibid.

Baker is particularly evocative in his outlining of Hawthorne's use of the Bible. He describes Hawthorne's "manipulation of Biblical backgrounds,"[50] his "invok[ing] the memory of the Bible for purposes of plot or characterization,"[51] and his "contriv[ing] to hint at as much of [a biblical] parallel as his story requires."[52] The aim in all this returning to scripture is "to infuse a continuous lurking sense of the remotely antique, the exotically oriental, and the far distant in time to…localized New England novels."[53] Thus, in recalling the Bible, Hawthorne sets his text at a remove from the reader, using the familiar biblical trope to underscore the foreignness of the contemporary work.

The language Baker uses deals with stance, with the relation of the retelling to the biblical telling. This is in part because his concerns are literary rather than historical: he has a grouping of novels containing biblical references, and seeks to explain—or at least explore—what they do with the text that has so influenced them. He is concerned with a sweeping range of literature, yet does little by way of comparison and contrast. This type of singular focus, as we will see, does not change even as the subjects of investigation shift.

If we are tracing general trends, the next move in the study of the Bible in literature is a turn toward the recasting of individual figures. Surprisingly, while this enterprise yields some fascinating reading and some well-developed depictions of the pervasion of biblical events or characters in the culture, it offers little by way of appropriable vocabulary. Jaroslav Pelikan's "history of images of Jesus, as these have appeared from the first century to the twentieth"[54] treats the predilection of each age of history "to depict Jesus in accordance with its own character."[55] He writes of adaptations, blurrings of Jesus' image, reconstruction, tradition, and innovation, but he offers no more precise vocabulary than this. Norman Cohn's book-length study of Noah's flood speaks of Christian typology and Jewish midrash, of reinterpretation and—with specific reference to ancient exegesis—gap-filling.[56] Pamela Norris assesses the interpretations, evaluations, and developments in later depictions of Eve. She marks the proximity or distance of the retelling to the telling, asserting that "Eve's history is as diverse and ingenious as

50. Ibid., 60.
51. Ibid., 59.
52. Ibid., 60.
53. Ibid., 58.
54. Pelikan, *Jesus Through the Centuries*, 2.
55. Ibid.
56. Norman Cohn, *Noah's Flood: The Genesis Story in Western Thought* (New Haven: Yale University Press, 1996).

the imaginations that have so colorfully embellished her story," a story which became "dispersed" and "confused" from the moment it was told.[57] In each of these three books, the descriptions are rich, the descriptors impoverished.

Two works focusing on individual characters offer us a little more by way of nourishing vocabularies. J. Hillis Miller explores the book of Ruth within the context of translation, and this framing allows for a handful of intriguing terms to emerge. Miller reads the book of Ruth as a parable for theory. In his view, it "is a narrative of alienation and assimilation that can exemplify theoretical propositions about the travel of theory."[58] The themes of the story are only part of the connection to theory, however. The text itself has undergone the very changes to which Miller alludes. He contends that "this book of the Hebrew Bible has been alienated from itself, translated from itself. It has been put entirely to new uses, uses by no means intended by the original authors or scribes."[59] The first and most significant of these was the assimilation of the Hebrew book into the Christian canon, which of course gave rise to multiple vernacular translations of the book, and to a widespread understanding of the book as legitimating the claim of Jesus to be the Messiah. This is a significant shift: as Harold Bloom puts it, "the New Testament in its relation to the Hebrew Bible is the most outrageous example of 'misprision' in the history of the West, that is, of 'mistakings' or takings amiss, translations as mistranslation."[60] The New Testament use of Ruth is, however, only the beginning of a series of misprisions of the biblical book, two of which Miller explores in detail. The first is the English folk tradition of *Sortes Sanctorum*, divination by Bible and key. Described in Thomas Hardy's *Far From the Madding Crowd*, the 'reading of the oracles of holy writing' entails a young woman balancing a Bible on a long house key.[61] The Bible is open at the first chapter of Ruth, and the

---

57. Pamela Norris, *Eve: A Biography* (New York: New York University Press, 1999), 6.

58. J. Hillis Miller, "Border Crossings, Translating Theory," in *The Translatability of Cultures: Figurations of the Space Between* (ed. Sanford Budick and Wolfgang Iser; Stanford: Stanford University Press, 1996), 220.

59. Ibid.

60. Ibid., 221.

61. Chapter 13 has Liddy and Bathsheba playing with the Bible on a Sunday, the day before Valentine's Day: "The book was opened—the leaves, drab with age, being quite worn away at much-read verses by the forefingers of unpracticed readers in former days, where they were moved along under the line as an aid to the vision. The special book in the Book of Ruth was sought out by Bathsheba, and the sublime words met her eye. They slightly thrilled and abashed her. It was Wisdom in the

woman repeats the verses following "Whither thou goest I will go" while thinking about the man to whom she is attracted; if the Bible moves, she will marry the man. Miller describes the ritual as "a mistranslation if ever there was one. The verses from the Bible are Ruth's speech expressing her fidelity to Naomi, her mother-in-law. They have nothing to do with her marriage to Boaz, except by unintentional prolepsis, since she has not met or perhaps even heard of him yet." And yet, "the words can be displaced with uncanny appropriateness to a new context in which they fit perfectly. There they can have a new performative function."[62]

Miller's third instance of a mistranslation (or "violent appropriation," which seems to him to be synonymous) of Ruth is Keats's "Ode to a Nightingale." The poem speaks of the nightingale's song, which Keats has heard in a garden in Hampstead, as "something that has sounded the same in many different places and at many different times over the centuries."[63] Among the places the nightingale might have been heard is Boaz's field, where Ruth gleaned: "Perhaps the self-same song that found a path / Through the sad heart of Ruth, when, sick for home / She stood in tears amid the alien corn."[64] The juxtaposition of Boaz's fields with the other settings where Keats's nightingale is heard "associates Ruth with Keats's general presentation of the human situation as forlorn, derelict, haunted by death, even 'half-in love with easeful death' (l. 52)."[65] The atmosphere is all Keats, no Bible. Miller calls it Keats's "invention"; "it is his translation, or mistranslation, of the story of Ruth for his own quite different purposes. Ruth in the Bible is not shown to have suffered one pang of homesickness for the country of Moab, nor to have dropped a single tear."[66] The book of Ruth, which is devoid of both longing for foreign lands and nightingales, "yields without apparent resistance to what Keats does with it."[67] What *does* Keats do with it? He sets it alongside other moments that reflect alienation, thereby making it an expression of alienation as well. Miller calls this mistranslation, or misprision. The use of Ruth by Liddy and Bathsheba he calls unintentional prolepsis. These are fine terms indeed, ripe for the picking.

abstract facing Folly in the concrete. Folly in the concrete blushed, persisted in her intention, and placed the key on the book" (Thomas Hardy, *Far From the Madding Crowd* [London: Pan Books, 1967], 100).

62. Miller, "Border Crossings," 221.
63. Ibid., 222.
64. John Keats, "Ode to a Nightingale," ll. 65–67 (in Miller, "Border Crossings," 222).
65. Ibid.
66. Ibid.
67. Ibid.

Like Miller, Yvonne Sherwood is also concerned to explore what it means to retell as much as to speak of what a retelling entails. In *A Biblical Text and Its Afterlives*, her treatment of the interpretation of the book of Jonah, Sherwood explains that "interpretation comes first, indeed interpretation always overwhelms my text, as if to demonstrate how it also overwhelms, eclipses *and always precedes* the biblical 'original.'"[68] Text and after-text are often simultaneous, frequently indiscernible. Thus the question of the "original," and the problems inherent in it, pervade the book: "biblical texts are literally sustained by interpretation, and the volume, tenacity, and ubiquity of interpretation make it impossible to dream that we can take the text back."[69] The complexity of the original extends to her own self-assessment, too, as Sherwood describes her book as "not 'original,' or at least it foregrounds its reliance on the already-written; like Jonah it works on the basis that knowledge and meaning are *agglutinative*, and that new products can be made by bringing together existing traditions and recombining them."[70] She occupies herself with how the amalgamation and recombination proceed.

Sherwood opens her discussion with a rabbinic perspective on the Bible: "when God gave humankind Torah he gave it in the form of wheat for us to make flour from it, and flax for us to make a garment from it: Torah is the raw material, to be ground, woven, and spun out,"[71] the bread and the cotton of our daily life. Sherwood takes the metaphor and develops it so that it describes the bodies of interpretation with which she is concerned:

> So to the interpretative menu or bill of fare. The book is divided into three sections (starter, entrée, and dessert). The first section ('The Mainstream') takes in the staple diet of Jonah readings: those served up in the Mainstream scholarly and Christian tradition from the first to the twentieth century. The second course ('Backwaters and underbellies') is appropriately and by far the largest, meatiest, most substantial part of the book, and looks at alternative serving suggestions, the way the text is dished up in independent *bijoux* little eating establishments: medieval poetry, Netherlandish art, Jewish interpretation, and other hidden cultural corners and sidestreet cafés. To finish, I stir these new ingredients into the book of Jonah and so cook up a 'new' interpretation, which is also a kind of hash, or jambalaya—a combination of insights from biblical scholarship mixed

---

68. Yvonne Sherwood, *A Biblical Text and Its Afterlives: The Survival of Jonah in Western Culture* (Cambridge: Cambridge University Press, 2000), 2. Emphasis in original.

69. Ibid.

70. Ibid., 5.

71. Ibid., 1.

with older, more piquant, marginal readings. In 'Regurgitating Jonah' I
self-consciously stir up the text, swell it, fatten it, inject it with new
reading idioms: I take this perennial biblical chestnut, turn it into purée,
and serve it up, Terence Conran fashion, with character-grilled peppers
and *pommes de terre*.[72]

She returns to the food metaphor throughout her book, speaking of the
"intellectual chowder"[73] that is the reimagination of the book of Jonah,
and returning toward the end of her work to the menu above.

Food is not, however, her exclusive language of description. She also
seeks recourse in the language of building and construction, which are
concrete ways of thinking about rewriting. She speaks of Augustine's
"recycling exegesis,"[74] the way that he dismantles Noah's ark and from it
builds a crucifix, which he then refashions into the body of Christ cut
through with Roman spears, and ultimately turns into a tomb from which
the resurrected Christ will rise. Likewise, she describes a "midrashic
superstructure erected around the text,"[75] which evinces images of support and protection, but also perhaps of extraneousness.

Sherwood's biblical prooftext itself supplies a string of terms that
enliven her description of the book of Jonah's afterlife: "the ever-
obliging book of Jonah is...a convenient microcosm of the mutations of
'the Bible' in the present. For *these days* it seems that artists and writers
are frequently playing with the tension between *these days* and *those
days* and confusing and domesticating biblical texts."[76] And like Jonah
himself, the book is swallowed (he by the fish, the book by the activity of
interpretation), and is regurgitated (by the fish, by exegetes, scholars,
artists). In fact, it is the regurgitation and thus survival of the book of
Jonah (which parallels the survival of its hero) that intrigues Sherwood.
"What is so fascinating is that this demise, this loss of faith in the biblical, is not so much leading to an exodus of biblical images from Western culture but is *being expressed within the framework and language
of biblical texts*,"[77] she marvels. As she notes, the writers she has presented—Wolf Mankowitz, Norma Rosen, Julian Barnes, Dan Pagis,
Zbigniew Herbert—"are *using the book of Jonah to talk about its own
inadequacy, demise, even uselessness*."[78] Yet, by the very fact of their

---

72. Ibid, 2.
73. Ibid, 5.
74. Ibid, 16.
75. Ibid, 118.
76. Ibid, 206. Emphasis in original.
77. Ibid, 207.
78. Ibid. Emphasis in original.

speaking of the end of the Bible, later writers prolong its demise: by keeping the text in circulation, they resuscitate it. Thus, even the poems that proclaim the death of the book of Jonah ensure its survival. These are sustaining fictions indeed.

Here Sherwood is pointing to a tension in the stance of the poems she treats. And in fact, throughout her readings, Sherwood reflects an awareness of the equal importance of our three areas of concern: approach, stance, and filter. We have discussed stance. She speaks in terms of approach when she considers how later writers are able to bridge the gap between the biblical world and that of the contemporary text. Particularly enjoyable is her discussion of an episode of the television program *Northern Exposure*, in which a Jewish character who has been deliberating about whether his non-Jewish girlfriend can cook a Passover Seder dreams of himself in the belly of a great fish with his rabbi from childhood. Sherwood contends that, for the episode's writers, "the biblical and the contemporary can only be linked by means of the tongue-in-cheek surreal, and for the characters within the whale, who share the scriptwriters' alienation, biblical messages are opaque and notoriously difficult to discern."[79] She considers filter when she begins her work with typological readings: Jonah, in patristic literature, *is* Jesus; equally, somewhat later, he becomes the xenophobic Jew. This latter reading becomes the dominant one through Christian and scholarly readings which hinge on the "othering of the Jew."[80] Throughout her survey, she is quick to note that the Torah becomes the "raw material from which the resourceful interpreter can make endless replicas of the tomb or the Cross"[81]; her goal, in fact, is to counter the tendency of Christian readers and biblical scholars to read the text through the lens of Christian supersessionism.

Sherwood's endeavor is less concerned with the interpretations themselves than with the political and cultural questions and concerns that accompany reading and interpreting. She seeks more to highlight the anti-Judaic strains in biblical studies and to foreground the midrashic tradition and Jewish poetic reading than to trace a history of Jonah in art, more to wonder about the place of the Bible in post-Enlightenment secular culture than about the relationship between individual retellings and their biblical tellings. Thus hers is primarily an investigation of stance—which cannot but touch on approach, and especially (given her treating extensively the perpetuation of Christian theology in biblical studies) on filter.

79. Ibid, 148.
80. Ibid, 288.
81. Ibid, 16.

Her book is reception history, if not a taxonomy of retelling. It offers us a model text for thinking about the ways in which retellings are determined by the worlds from which they come, and the ways in which the reader of the retelling determines his understanding of it. In fact, the relationships between the older text and the new, as well as the significance of the act of retelling, drive Sherwood's enterprise.

This is also the case with two relatively recent volumes that examine the role of the scripture in literature. Robert Alter's *Canon and Creativity* and Piero Boitani's *The Bible and Its Rewritings* both consider the place of the Bible in a range of literature and thus both held the promise of offering descriptive vocabularies. Alter works with specific authors, treating Bialik, Kafka, and Joyce's "engagement"[82] of canon; Boitani, by contrast, works with specific texts, treating the "re-Scripting"[83] of Joseph and Susanna.[84] The two projects are closely related. Alter seeks "to explore the dynamic of canonicity, attending to the ways in which the exemplary canonical corpus of the Western tradition, the Bible, is assimilated and imaginatively reused by poets and writers of fiction."[85] Boitani has "taken a limited number of direct or oblique re-Scriptures, separated across time and space"[86] and considers what it means to "re-Script." Based on the understanding that "re-Scripting is necessarily preordained by Scripture is itself,"[87] Boitani's contention is that "every Author or author sees his task as that of rewriting God and humanity."[88]

Both Alter and Boitani proclaim the uniqueness—and the necessity—contained within the rewriting of the Bible. Alter attributes the prominence of the Bible in later literature to scripture's universal message. The writers he treats "provide in their work potent antidotes to the

---

82. Robert Alter, *Canon and Creativity: Modern Writing and the Authority of Scripture* (New Haven: Yale University Press, 2000), 8.

83. Piero Boitani, *The Bible and Its Retellings* (trans. Anita Weston; New York: Oxford University Press, 1999), vi.

84. He also examines the genre of animal fables in considering "the problems of interpretation, particularly those arising from the conflict between the literal sense on the one hand and the moral, allegorical and analogical on the other" (ibid., 78) and brings these questions to bear on William Faulkner's short story "Go Down, Moses." His final chapter treats the theme of recognition in Euripides' *Helen*, John 20–21, Shakespeare's *Pericles*, T. S. Eliot's "Marina," and Joseph Roth's *Job*. What connects these re-scriptures is the recognition of God: to recognize God is to rewrite; to "re-script" one's own existence in light of that recognition (ibid.).

85. Alter, *Canon and Creativity*, 6.

86. Boitani, *The Bible and Its Retellings*, vi.

87. Ibid.

88. Ibid.

disappearance of the inherited canon from effective cultural memory precisely because they recognize in it eloquent images of their own urgent concerns."[89] This is the case not only of the Faulkners, Melvilles, and Joyces, but of Hebrew modernists as well. Alter contends that "the nearly ubiquitous presence of allusions to the Bible in postbiblical Hebrew literature is a major index of this binocular vision of the Bible." On the one hand, "the allusions occur because the Bible provides later Hebrew writers a thick concordance of phrases, motifs, and symbols that encode a set of theological, historical, and national values (a canon in the strict sense of the *O.E.D.*)"; on the other, there is a proliferation of allusions "because the Bible in Hebrew speaks resonantly, even to the most pious readers, as a collection of great works of literature."[90] The biblical literature is great in and of itself, and great also because of its source, subject, and content (which are, for the traditional reader, one and the same).

Canon and Creativity examines the ways that three modern writers—Kafka, Joyce and Hebrew poet Nahum Bialik—have "interwoven biblical material into the fabric of a new work." Thus these three belong to a litany that includes Milton, Dante, Blake, Melville, and Faulkner.[91] Faulkner is, in fact, Alter's starting point. His project being the role of Hebrew scripture for the modernists, Alter contends that the modern writer is gripped by the Bible "because of his acute consciousness of it as a body of founding texts, marking out one of the primary possibilities of representing the human condition and the nature of historical experience for all the eras of Western culture that have followed antiquity."[92] The modernist's return to foundational texts did not necessarily lead him to "revealed truth or theological principle,"[93] although the Bible's canonicity evinced the traditional conviction in its divinity. Nonetheless, "Faulkner [and other modernists] saw something true and deep in the Bible that spoke to [their] own sense of the world... [Faulkner's] relation to Scripture, like that of his literary contemporaries, illustrates how a canon is a dynamic transhistorical textual community and not a timeless inscription of fixed meanings."[94] Alter's assessment of Faulkner's use of

89. Alter, *Canon and Creativity*, 19.

90. Ibid., 32.

91. Other scholars have, to varying degrees, tackled questions of the relationships these writers had to the Bible. None to my knowledge has developed a descriptive vocabulary that can be applied beyond the parameters of their own study of their own author or figure of choice.

92. Alter, *Canon and Creativity*, 17.

93. Ibid.

94. Ibid., 18.

scripture in *Absalom! Absalom!* is representative: he asserts that "it is clear that the imaginative texture of the Bible pervaded his decidedly unbiblical prose."[95] He notes that the "intricate correspondence (as well as ironic divergence) between Faulkner's plot and the biblical one are fascinating to contemplate, but what [he] want[s] to stress is how an underlying relation between story and historical reality in Faulkner's novel is enabled by the Bible."[96]

The case, he maintains, is the same for Joyce as it is for Faulkner. Behind Joyce's *Ulysses* lie two fundamental intertexts: the Bible and the Odyssey. Joyce works the two together, such that the Odyssey provides *Ulysses* with the theme of setting one's house in order while the Bible structures its world, giving it a place in the recurring cycle of human experience. Leopold Bloom looks back on his romancing of Molly on Ben Howth: "All quiet on Howth now. The distant hills seen. Where we. The rhododendrons. I am a fool perhaps. He gets the plums and I the plumstones.[97] Where I come in. All that old hill has seen. Names change: that's all. Lovers: yum yum." Alter notes that Bloom's concession, "Names change: that's all" is "a reflection on the endless generations of lovers that succeed one another. Behind this stands Joyce's notion that human life is, after all, an eternal cycle of recurrences: the names change, but one Leopold Bloom may also be Abraham and Moses and Elijah, while his own name hints at two biblical ones—the Lion of Judah (Leopold) and the messianic restorer whom Zechariah calls Zemach, 'shoot' or 'bloom.'"[98] That the names change and all else remains the same is Joyce's nod to Qohelet's refrain that there is "Nothing new under the sun." The absence of the new, the reuse of the old is what fuels the writing of the modernists: "by conjoining the Bible with the Odyssey, Joyce's novel is able to take stock of the literary origins of the Western tradition and suggest how they might be relevant to a cultural future. The notion of a single authoritative canon that sets the limits for the culture is tacitly and firmly rejected, while the perennial liveliness of the old canonical texts as a resource for imagination and moral reflection is reaffirmed."[99] The extraction of the Bible from its religious context, its re-articulation in a secular one, does not detract from the power of scripture. Rather, the Bible itself inspires: the "imaginative power of the

95. Ibid., 8.
96. Ibid., 10.
97. The "he" here is Blazes Boylan who has had a tryst with Molly.
98. Alter, *Canon and Creativity*, 178.
99. Ibid., 182.

Bible energize[s] a writer,"[100] and the newly energized text breathes a new life back into the Bible. This is the "supple interweave"[101] of the biblical and the non-biblical in modern literature.

Alter's strength is his ability to describe what happens in a retelling—he walks his reader through Kafka, Bialik, and Joyce's playing with, subverting of, and returning to the Bible. He develops no distinctive vocabulary, no means of speaking about the texts in relation to one another, but he offers descriptions and analyses that make evident what the work at hand is doing to the scripture. Samuel HaNagid's poetry is "an extraordinary condensation of meaning through allusion to the Bible"[102] in which the poet makes "audacious and frankly erotic use of the devotional text from the Bible";[103] Mapu's *Ahavat Zion* is a "florid pastiche of biblical phrases that reflects an analogous aspiration to build on the aesthetic resonances of the Bible and make out of them a new edifice of secular culture in Hebrew";[104] the purpose of a Tchernikovsky poem is " to tease out of the shadowy margins of the biblical world the sunlight of poetic attention what biblical doctrine opposed and suppressed."[105] Kafka, in revisiting Babel in *Amerika*, "reads the biblical text against the grain, teasing out of it an idea that contradicts the explicit condemnation"[106] in Genesis of the builders of the Tower of Babel. The beginning of the work "shares with the midrash an impulse to flesh out the spare biblical tale and to make it intelligible in more or less contemporary terms."[107] And Alter goes so far as to assert why the biblical tale should be made intelligible in more or less contemporary terms: it has something significant to say to contemporary readers. What he does not articulate, however, is precisely how this significant message can be transmitted and retransmitted, apprehended and appropriated, told and retold.

Boitani focuses on the greatness, on the divine in the text: he sees its rewriting as simultaneously an emulation of the divine act of creation and the human act of recognizing the divine. He notes these two activities form a line of tradition that "stretches, continual but not continuous, from the Yahwistic document of Genesis (known as J) to Mann's *Joseph*

---

100. Ibid., 52.
101. Ibid., 38.
102. Ibid., 40.
103. Ibid., 47.
104. Ibid., 52.
105. Ibid., 58.
106. Ibid., 68.
107. Ibid., 70.

and His Brothers (henceforth M), across thousands of years of rewriting, commentaries, *midrash*, and exegesis, M simply 'fulfilling' or 'filling in' J."[108] The fulfilling or filling in must be consonant with the prior text: it cannot abandon or undermine the central problem of the biblical text, the problem of recognizing God. Boitani assures us that, "far from 'ruining the sacred truths', however, M re-enacts all their mystery, humanizing it, discussing it, and creating a metaphysics, a theology, and a mystique of narrative right in the middle of the twentieth century."[109] Mann recognizes what J knew: "God cannot be known, cannot be the product of cognition but only, if at all, of re-cognition, and all Scripture is therefore a re-scripting, a re-Writing."[110]

Boitani proposes to discuss the recognitions, the rewritings themselves "without offering a theory or even analysis of rewriting as such, if only because it would be next to impossible."[111] What hinders the endeavor is the sheer volume of rewriting, the fact that it is concomitant with writing itself. As Boitani notes,

> Rewriting takes place within the Bible itself: Genesis rewrites Genesis, John rewrites Genesis, and the whole of the New Testament rewrites the Old, with the intention of 'fulfilling' it. Hundreds of Apocrypha exist of both, and interminable rewritings in all languages and all mediums in Western culture, from painting and sculpture to music, theatre, and cinema.[112]

The Bible is not the only thing to be rewritten either, particularly in literature—in Boitani's view, after the *Iliad* there is nothing other than rewriting.[113]

While both scholars treat an assortment of writers and writings in relation to the Bible, neither Alter nor Boitani develops comparative vocabularies for talking about a variety of texts and their relations to their *Urtext*. What they offer instead is description—thick description even—that treats each text on its own terms and in its own relation to scripture. Consequently, they employ descriptive phrases, but do not develop descriptive vocabularies.

We risk coming away from this chapter with a sense of defeat. Although reviewers and critics alike speak often and at length of later works retelling earlier ones, the vocabularies they offer for describing the

108.   Boitani, *The Bible and Its Retellings*, viii.
109.   Ibid.
110.   Ibid.
111.   Ibid., vii.
112.   Ibid., vii.
113.   Ibid., vii.

literary afterlife of texts is undefined indeed. The reviewers gave us the coy "nudge wrapped in a wink" and "intellectual tennis match." Our survey of criticism was somewhat more productive: from it we reaped Hollander's *transumption*; Conte's *intrusion*; Pasquali's *reminiscences, allusions, evocations,* and *quotations*; Charlesworth's relations of *inspiration, framework, launching, inconsequential,* and *expansion*; Dimant's *expositional* and *compositional use*; Miller's *mistranslation, misprision,* and *unintentional prolepsis*; Boitani's *rescripting*.

The list, however, is short, if we consider how many works went into its compilation, and the words on it touch on aspects of approach, stance, and filter, but never offer the potential of treating all three elements. Thus, over the ensuing three chapters, we will turn to three developed theoretical frameworks: literary theory, midrashic studies, and translation theory. The first two have been toward discussions of retelling; the third has not. As we consider each in detail, we will determine their viability for the present enterprise.

Chapter 3

ACCORDING TO THE LIKENESS

Literary Criticism and the Interrelationships of Texts

The impulse to retell is hardly limited to the Bible. Certainly, Adam, Noah, Moses, David, and Jesus—to name only the most revisited figures in Scripture—have all had long and varied literary afterlives. Beyond the Bible, it seems that just about everyone of note—Penelope and Percival, King Lear and Captain Ahab, Conrad's Marlowe and Carroll's Alice—has been recast by later writers. As tellings beget retellings, so closed canons (of sacred writ and great books alike) beg to be reopened. This, to an extent, is how literature is sustained.

Neither the phenomenon of turning to previous texts nor the impulse to name this activity is new to the field of literary study. While, as we have seen, many have managed to discuss retelling without ascribing to it specific names, literary theorists have developed various vocabularies to describe the interrelations of later and earlier texts. Historically, imitation and invention were used to indicate one text's echoing another; in recent literary criticism, influence and intertextuality have gained currency. We begin this chapter with an overview of these terms, as well as of the shifts over the centuries in the understanding of texts' referring to other texts. We will then move to a consideration of the usefulness of the terms for a discussion of the literary afterlife of the Bible.

Imitation

From the beginning of criticism we find the term *imitation* to describe not only the representation of the world in images or words, a copying of an original form (as Plato uses the word), but also the adoption of the tone, style, and attitude of another writer. Aristotle views the poet's taking of a form from nature and giving it its own shape as an emulation of the divine process; the poet is both imitator and creator. Even in taking from someone else's poetry, the poet imitates *and* creates. Aristotle thus advocates rather than discourages a later poet's reworking of an earlier poet's work, construing the literary activity of reworking as a manifestation of change, which he saw as a creative force with direction. What results—when the poet draws on nature or on poetry—is an improvement upon the original.[1]

Similarly, Horace and Cicero also assert that a poet should learn as much as possible from his precursors, echoing and adopting from them freely. For Horace, the crucial element in art is the exercise of good taste. In his "Art of Poetry," he adjures poets, "either follow tradition, or, if you invent, see that your invention be in harmony with itself."[2] Horace offers the following guidance to the poet who follows tradition:

> It is a hard task to treat what is common in a way of your own; and you are doing more rightly in breaking the tale of Troy into acts than in giving the world a new story of your own telling. You may acquire private rights in common ground, provided you will neither linger in the one hackneyed and easy round; nor trouble to render word for word with the faithfulness of a translator; nor by your mode of imitating take the 'leap into the pit' out of which very shame, if not the law of your work, will forbid you to stir hand or foot to escape.[3]

The use of tradition is an act of appropriation, of taking what is written and giving it a new voice. It is, in Horace's view, a more noble achievement than giving the world a new tale.

The perception that a writer not only can, but *should*, borrow from those writers who came before him was championed in the literary criticism of the Renaissance. Thomas Greene's *The Light in Troy* examines the literary uses of *imitatio* in Italy, France, and England during the Renaissance. Greene contends that "the imitation of models was a precept and an activity which during that era embraced not only literature but pedagogy, grammar, rhetoric, esthetics, the visual arts, music, historiography, politics and philosophy."[4] The idea of imitation, however, was not fixed: "the concept and praxis were understood to be repeatedly shifting, repeatedly redefined by the writers and artists who believed themselves to be 'imitating'"[5] during the Renaissance era. There were, in Greene's telling, three key characteristics of *imitatio*: it was an attempt to

1. Aristotle, *Poetics* XV.8.
2. Horace, "Art of Poetry," in *Critical Theory Since Plato* (ed. Hazard Adams; New York: Harcourt Brace Jovanovich, 1971), 70.
3. Ibid.
4. Thomas M. Greene, *The Light in Troy: Imitation and Discovery in Renaissance Poetry* (New Haven: Yale University Press, 1982), 1.
5. Ibid.

deal with the "newly perceived problem of anachronism";[6] it "assigned the Renaissance creator a convenient and flexible stance toward a past that threatened to overwhelm him";[7] and it came to determine the character of poetic intertextuality for the next three centuries. A distinctly European phenomenon, imitation shaped the literary relationship between texts generations.[8]

Renaissance imitative theory did, as I have noted, evolve and change, and concepts of imitation varied across the continent.[9] Greene foregrounds Petrarch's "rich and crucial" role in determining imitative practice. In a letter to Boccaccio, Petrarch determined what imitation entails:

> A proper imitator should take care that what he writes resembles the original without reproducing it. The resemblance should not be that of a portrait to the sitter—in that case, the closer the likeness the better—but it should be the resemblance of a son to his father. Therein is often the great divergence in particular features, but there is a certain suggestion, what our painters call an 'air,' most notably around the face and eyes, which makes the resemblance. As soon as we see the son, he recalls the father to us although if we should measure every feature we should find them all different. But there is a mysterious something there that has this power.[10]

Petrarch goes on to argue that the similarity must only be a beginning point: a writer should tailor his imitation so that a plenitude of dissimilarities clouds the underlying similarity. Only through a literary excavation of sorts might the original be revealed.[11]

In England, the metaphor was not filial but faunal. The imitative poet, according to Ben Jonson, was "to draw forth out of the best, and choicest, flowers, with the Bee, and turne all into Honey, worke it into one relish and savour."[12] The sense here is that the poet is to sample broadly from other writers, select judiciously from the best of them, and produce a perfect poem of his own. The process of imitation was not mechanical but entirely natural.

Jonson's contemporary Sidney, however, had a different understanding of nature in light of artifice. In his discussion of the interrelationships

6.   Ibid., 2.

7.   Ibid., 2.

8.   There are a great number of critical works about the use of earlier sources in Latin and Greek poetry.

9.   Greene himself identifies four categories of imitation: reproductive, eclectic, heuristic, and dialectic.

10.   Greene, *The Light in Troy*, 105.

11.   Petrarch, Letter 190, in ibid.

12.   Donna B. Hamilton, *Virgil and the Tempest: The Politics of Imitation* (Columbus: Ohio State University Press, 1990), 110.

of Sidney's, Spenser's, and Shakespeare's re/tellings of King Lear,[13] Andrew D. Weiner looks to Sidney's *Defense of Poetry*.[14] Here, Sidney outlines a poetics in which intentionality does not fall on "the 'literary work' but on the author of the work."[15] The activity of the author—specifically, the poet—is the creation of a new world. The basis for this new world is not the one in which the poet lives, but that of poetic fore-conceit. More worthy of emulation than nature itself is poetry, which "bringeth forth, or, quite anew, forms such as never were in nature, as the Heroes, Cyclopes, Chimeras, Furies, and such like."[16] This world of forms lies outside the "narrow warrant" of nature. In Sidney's view, which is based in an Aristotelian notion of the poet as completing that which nature cannot, "nature never set forth the earth in so rich tapestry as diverse poets have done.... Her world is brazen, the poets only deliver a golden."[17] In the poet, the heavenly Maker creates an earthly maker who, in striving to represent the beauty of nature through his creation, surpasses it,[18] thus rendering the brazen golden.

The poet's creation is, to use Aristotle's term, mimesis—an imitation of reality. Or, as Sidney has it, "a representing, counterfeiting or figuring forth—to speak metaphorically, a speaking picture."[19] For Sidney, there are three kinds of mimetic poets. The "chief, both in antiquity and excellency, were they that did imitate the inconceivable excellencies of God";[20] Sidney counts among these David, Solomon, Moses, and Deborah, who were moved by the Holy Spirit to create the Holy Writ. And though the ancient pagans wrote "in a full wrong divinity,"[21] he also places Orpheus, Amphion, and Homer within this category. The second type of poets consists of "them that deal with matters philosophical,"[22] either moral or historical. These, Sidney likens to "the meaner sort of painters, who

13. Leyr, Leir, Lear, respectively.
14. An essay written by Sir Philip Sidney between 1580 and 1583, published as two different posthumous editions—*An Apologie for Poetrie* and *The Defense of Poesie*—in 1595. The essay was a response to Puritan Stephen Gosson's attack on poetry, *School of Abuse*.
15. Andrew D. Weiner, "Sidney/Spenser/Shakespeare: Influence/Intertextuality/Intention," in *Influence and Intertextuality in Literary History* (ed. Jay Clayton and Eric Rothstein; Madison: University of Wisconsin Press, 1991), 246–47.
16. Sir Philip Sidney, *An Apology for Poetry*, in *Critical Theory Since Plato* (ed. Hazard Adams; New York: Harcourt Brace Jovanovich, 1971), 157.
17. Ibid., 158.
18. Ibid.
19. Ibid.
20. Ibid.
21. Ibid.
22. Ibid.

counterfeit only such faces as are set before them, and the more excellent, who, having no law but wit, bestow that in colors upon you which is fittest for the eye to see."[23] In Sidney's description, these latter paint the lamenting Lucretia who punished herself for another's fault, while the third category of artists will not paint Lucretia at all, but the "outward beauty of such a virtue."[24] This third group is comprised of "they which most properly do imitate to teach and delight, and to imitate borrow nothing of what is, hath been, or shall be; but range, only reined with learned discretion, into the divine consideration of what may be, and should be."[25] These too are the poets held up by Aristotle.[26] They are the poets who begin not with the created world but with a creative work, and fashion from that earlier work the sublime, the idealized version of both nature and the prior depiction of it.

These poets' understanding of what may and should be is a product of their own construction; "the skill of the artificer standeth in that idea or fore-conceit of the work, and not in the work itself."[27] The poet delivers forth the beauty and virtue that nature cannot concoct. His "'sources,' then, are whatever has enabled him to glimpse that 'golden' world—other texts, broadly accepted commonplaces, ideology."[28] The poet is more indebted to those poets who came before him than to the world around him, for it is their invention that he imitates. Sidney focuses on the author of the new telling echoing not the work itself, but the idea behind the work: "the world being imitated is not a text—the 'brazen' world of nature that we experience directly—but the nontextual intention, what Sidney called the artificer's 'idea or fore-conceit' behind the text."[29] The fore-conceit, the predecessor, was crucial to Sidney's understanding of "making," which was inextricable from the contemporary notion of "invention."

Invention

For Sidney, "invention" was the "source from which the poet's golden world originates, and 'imitation' the deliberate and deliberative process by which the poet reworks both the 'facts' of the visible world and

23. Ibid.
24. Ibid.
25. Ibid.
26. Sidney's *Defense* is strongly influenced by Aristotle's *Poetics*; here he draws on IX.2.
27. Sidney, *An Apology for Poetry*, 157.
28. Weiner, "Sidney/Spenser/Shakespeare," 247.
29. Ibid.

materials inherited from his predecessors,"[30] but this understanding of invention was only one of the complex notions current among Renaissance writers. Historically, invention has had a complex interrelation of meanings, "linking the senses of discovering (accidentally or deliberately) with contriving or devising, including the possibilities of creating something new out of something preexistent, as well as the possibility of devising something first."[31] This cultural perception is Shakespeare's as well as Sidney's; his writing is based in "the assumption that a writer creates by taking the raw materials left him by his predecessors and transforming them into images that represent the *idea* or fore-conceit he wishes to present through his work"[32] as well. For English writers of the Renaissance, then, poetic invention involves not merely the making of something new, but the making of it from pre-existent materials or fore-conceits. Theologically, we might see this as an imitation of God, whose creation is not *ex nihilo* but is a refashioning of pre-existent matter.

More descriptive than Sidney's naming this double act of creation and re-creation 'making' is Ben Jonson's "purposeful remaking." As we have seen, Jonson—like Sidney—adhered to Renaissance understandings of rewriting, making "creative use of the thoughts and words of the ancients in a spirit of emulous rivalry."[33] The reteller did not subordinate himself or give himself over to the teller; rather, he retold in the spirit and fashion of the telling. His goal was not to conquer the text but to challenge it. He did so through "that process of judicious gathering in, assimilation, and transformation or turning whereby a good writer, and by extension a good man, shapes an original and coherent work of art of a virtuous life."[34] This transformation or turning of the old into the new was the "purposeful remaking." It was a moral as well as aesthetic activity.

Jonson's 'purposeful remaking' or 'invention' holds great potential for our thinking here. It allows us to consider what one text is doing to another, without needing to account for what one writer thought she was doing with the work of another. For English writers of the Renaissance, the writing process always involved invention. That was an aesthetic given. Furthermore, the term 'purposeful remaking' is nuanced in a way that literary critical terms adopted later are not. Unlike influence, which suggests one writer asserting himself on another, invention accounts for

30. Ibid., 248.
31. Ibid.
32. Ibid., 266.
33. Richard Peterson, *Imitation and Praise in the Poems of Ben Jonson* (New Haven: Yale University Press, 1981), xiii.
34. Ibid.

the direction of flow, with the focus on the later writer turning back to the earlier text. Unlike intertextuality, Jonson's term attributes agency to the author of a work, seeing the act of (re)writing as intentional and not something inherent in the nature of language or born of the public quality of writing.

When Weiner sets out to treat the interrelationship of Spenser, Sidney, and Shakespeare's histories, he does so feeling "some discomfort in trying to fit the interrelations of Renaissance texts into late-twentieth-century boxes."[35] Far more comfortable is the language of invention and imitation. Where some contemporary theorists might discuss the connections across the works in terms of influence or intertextuality, Weiner contends that the anachronism of this usage is problematic. He argues that "the burden of proof is on 'influence' and 'intertextuality' to prove that they can do something that a theory contemporary with the writers cannot *and* that they can do it from without, so to speak, without writing over contemporary history."[36] In his view, the activity of his writers is best described using terms with which these writers would themselves have been familiar. Rather than make his Renaissance writers post-modernists, he defines them in their own terms.

Weiner's reticence serves as a caution: he is arguing that we must be mindful of the contexts of a text's creation, taking into account if not the intention of a writer then at least the literary world in which he lived. If this is the case, can terms like invention, which served him so well, be used to talk about retelling in contemporary film, for instance? Or, reaching back in time, could one reasonably speak of Matthew's using Moses in his portrayal of Jesus as imitation?

Influence

Whereas the Renaissance ideal was a text infused with the transformed writings of a literary predecessor, attitudes toward retelling shifted over the century between Jonson's death (1637) and Pope's (1744). In his neoclassical "Essay on Criticism," reminiscent of Horace's address to poets, Alexander Pope advises critics first and poets second about poetry. Pope urges the poet to imitate nature—"First follow nature, and your judgment frame by her standard, which is still the same: Unerring nature! still divinely bright, one clear, unchanged and universal light!"[37] —and

35. Weiner, "Sidney/Spenser/Shakespeare," 246.
36. Ibid., 245–46.
37. Alexander Pope, "An Essay on Criticism," in Adams, ed., *Critical Theory Since Plato*, ll. 68–71.

to the critic to assess the poet based on such imitation. And yet, he allows that the poet may learn of nature not merely by observing it himself, but through knowledge of it supplied by the ancients. Pope conceives of the Greeks and Romans as providing a key to thinking about nature. In their writings were "those rules of old discovered, not devised...nature still, but nature methodized."[38] Hence Pope encourages the writer to immerse himself in nature's "useful rules" as distilled by the Greeks, declaring: "Be Homer's works your study and delight, / read them by day, and meditate by night; / thence form your judgment, thence your maxims bring, / and trace the Muses upward to their spring."[39] Ultimately, for Pope, as for the critic to whom he addresses himself, "Nature and Homer were [to be]...the same";[40] of ancient rules, Pope contends "to copy nature is to copy them."[41] These expressions, directed as they are to the critic and reflecting critical views of transformation and reworking, evince the close of a particular attitude toward retelling. On this point, we can see Pope as bridging two key perceptions: the Renaissance view of the imitation of fore-conceit as surpassing the imitation of nature, and the early Enlightenment view of nature as surpassing imitation. A generation after Pope, a good poet was measured not by his dependence on the ancients, who were themselves synonymous with nature, but by his exclusive dependence on nature for inspiration.

The shift in attitude is marked by a new critical pursuit, one quite distinct from that advocated by Pope. The mid-eighteenth century brings us the term *influence*, a word Shakespeare had used to mean "inspiration."[42] The contemporary understanding reflects the word is a concept that had been unknown to Dryden and Pope but, two generations later, was quite familiar to Coleridge and his contemporaries as a means of describing an author's use of prior texts.[43] Nathan Bailey's *Universal Etymological English Dictionary*, published in 1721, offers a first glimpse of the significance the term was to take on; Bailey defines influence as "a flowing into, a sending forth of Power or Virtue; the Power of a Superior over an Inferior."[44] From the outset, the influence was thought to exceed the influenced.

38. Ibid., ll. 88–89.
39. Ibid., ll. 124–27.
40. Ibid., l. 135.
41. Ibid., l. 140.
42. Bloom, *The Anxiety of Influence*, xii.
43. Ibid., 27.
44. Jay Clayton and Eric Rothstein, "Figures in the Corpus," in *Influence and Intertextuality in Literary History* (ed. Jay Clayton and Eric Rothstein; Madison: University of Wisconsin Press, 1991), 5.

By 1774, when Thomas Warton wrote the first literary history of English poetry, influence was considered to be an important tool for understanding hierarchies in literature. The more an artist imitated nature—rather than art—the greater his claim to genius. Thus, because dependence on other writers was understood to be a marker of lesser writing, the major critical enterprise in the eighteenth and nineteenth centuries was the cataloguing of the writer's borrowings from others. The quest for a writer's influences was therefore evaluative; it was a means of establishing a writer's merit. Shakespeare and Sidney were deemed to exhibit creative genius as their work, in the view of those who measured influence, drew primarily from the world and not from prior works. A fixation with the mapping of literary reworkings continued through the nineteenth century into the first half of the last century. So much so, in fact, that in his long-running debate with literary critic F. R. Leavis, literary historian F. W. Bateson described the predominant activity in Leavis's field as a reliance on establishing relations of influence.[45]

There were disparities in understandings of what influence suggests. In his 1919 essay, "Tradition and the Individual Talent," T. S. Eliot notes that "tradition" has come to be seen as a negative, so that in assessing the strength of a writer "we dwell with satisfaction on the poet's difference from his predecessors."[46] Eliot counters that "if we approach a poet without this prejudice we shall often find that not only the best, but the most individual parts of his work may be those in which the dead poets, his ancestors, assert their immortality most vigorously."[47] Note that Eliot speaks of the dead poets who enter into the new work: he is careful to distinguish between the influence of the ancestors and that of the "immediate generation."[48] In the distinction we hear a valorization of tradition. It is, according to Eliot, more than mere "handing down, [which] consisted in following the ways of the immediate generation before us in a blind or timid adherence to its successes" (this should "positively be discouraged").[49] Rather,

> tradition is a matter of much wider significance... It involves, in the first place, the historical sense...and the historical sense involves a perception, not only of the pastness of the past, but of its presence. This historical

45. Ibid.
46. T. S. Eliot, "Tradition and the Individual Talent," in *Selected Prose of T. S. Eliot* (New York: Harcourt Brace, 1975), 38.
47. Ibid.
48. Ibid.
49. Ibid.

sense, which is a sense of the timeless as well as of the temporal and of the timeless and of the temporal together, is what makes a writer traditional.[50]

The interplay of past and present is central to Eliot's understanding of the role of the poet: the past is altered by the present just as the present is altered by the past, and "the poet who is aware of this will be aware of great difficulties and responsibilities."[51] The poet who grasps the significance of the past will by necessity "surrender" to the earlier: "the progress of the artist is a continual self-sacrifice, a continual extinction of personality."[52] This extinction, or depersonalization, is related to tradition in that the poet does not parlay his own experiences and emotions, but becomes a "receptacle for seizing and storing up numberless feelings, phrases, images."[53] The poet is a medium rather than a maker.

Eliot, as he was well aware, stood apart in his understanding of the role of tradition in poetic writing. Other critics, as I have intimated, were concerned to detail the poetic appropriation of earlier works, rather than to champion the surrender of one poet to his predecessors. Up until the early 1960s, then, the question of influence generally turned on identifying one author's concerted allusions to or borrowings from another, as opposed to an author's use of commonplace phraseology or imagery. Critics were concerned to "distinguish between resemblances that inhere in the common subject matter of two poems and resemblances that may really be due to direct imitation."[54]

The idea of imitation, which suggests a conscious act, was for centuries central to discussions of influence. The critical perception was that a poet sought in some way to follow or echo a literary precursor. This makes for a curious twist on the very idea of influence. As Clayton and Rothstein note, "an author becomes a 'precursor' only when someone else uses his or her work, so that at best the line of intentionality runs from the later to the earlier author, or does not run at all, since one usually does not intend to be influenced by another."[55] Where, in other settings, influence is exerted—an agent intends to have an influence on a subject—influence is here assumed by the subject and not intentionally deployed by the agent. Art critic Michael Baxandall points to the

50. Ibid.
51. Ibid., 39.
52. Ibid., 40.
53. Ibid., 41.
54. R. E. Neil Dodge, "A Sermon on Source Hunting," *Modern Philology* 9 (1911): 215–16.
55. Clayton and Rothstein, "Figures in the Corpus," 7.

problems inherent in this flow of agency, offering up alternative descriptions of the phenomenon. His challenge is long but evocative:

> 'Influence' is a curse of art criticism primarily because of its wrong-headed grammatical prejudice about who is the agent and who the patient: it seems to reverse the active/passive relation which the historical actor experiences and the inferential beholder will wish to take into account. If one says that X influenced Y it does seem that one is saying that X did something to Y rather than that Y did something to X... If we think of Y rather than X as the agent, the vocabulary is much richer and more attractively diversified: draw on, resort to, avail oneself of, appropriate from, have recourse to, adapt, misunderstand, refer to, pick up, take on, engage with, react to, quote, differentiate oneself from, assimilate oneself to, assimilate, align oneself with, copy, address, paraphrase, absorb, make a variation on, revive, continue, remodel, ape, emulate, travesty, parody, extract from, distort, attend to, resist, simplify, reconstitute, elaborate on, develop, face up to, master, subvert, perpetuate, reduce, promote, respond to, transform, tackle...—everyone will be able to think of others. Most of these relations just cannot be stated the other way round—in terms of X acting on Y rather than Y acting on X. To think in terms of influence blunts thought by impoverishing the means of differentiation.[56]

Here Baxandall hits on the two semantic issues central to our discussion: grammar and vocabulary. The problem of grammar is seen in his concern with the direction of flow of influence, as well as in our concern with stance;[57] the problem of vocabulary is seen in his litany of possible words that might be used to describe what I have been calling the approach.

This former question, of grammar or stance, takes on a new tenor with Harold Bloom's appropriation of the term influence. The central principle of his seminal *Anxiety of Influence* is that "poetic influence—when it involves two strong, authentic poets—always proceeds by a misreading of the prior poet, an act of creative correction that is actually and necessarily a misinterpretation."[58] Bloom allows for the possibility of failed, or at least not fruitful, poetic influence. Even in the best of situations, influence is a fraught enterprise. In Bloom's account, the grand notion of imitation is replaced with "self-saving caricature." To Baxandall's generally constructive catalogue of approaches, Bloom adds "distortion"

---

56. Michael Baxandall, *Patterns of Intention: On the Historical Explanation of Pictures* (New Haven: Yale University Press, 1985), 58–59.

57. The question of conscious versus unconscious rewriting is also a question of grammar: to what extent is retelling a transitive verb, as opposed to an intransitive one.

58. Bloom, *A Map of Misreading*, 19.

and "perverse, willful revisionism."[59] To the vocabulary of what we might call stance, he inserts the idea that retelling might better be understood as "misreading."

Misreading, counter intuitively, does not imply reading. As noted in the introduction, Bloom contends that all post-seventeenth-century English literature returns to Milton, that all English literature after Milton is "late." In Bloom's view, Milton's poetry was an event: subsequent authors were late for that event. Thus Milton is a "poetic father," an Oedipal figure to whom all later poets return, making the poet

> not so much a man speaking to men as a man rebelling against being spoken to by a dead man (the precursor) outrageously more alive than himself. A poet dare not regard himself as being late, yet cannot accept a substitute for the first vision he reflectively judges to have been his precursor's also.[60]

The Freudian struggle between the son (the ephebe) and the father (the precursor) is propelled by two drives: the son's desire to imitate the father, from whom he learned the art of poetry, and the son's quest for originality, his effort to "defend against the knowledge that all the poet is doing is imitating rather than creating afresh."[61] What is most interesting about Bloom's struggle between father and son is the fact that the son need not necessarily know the father. Bloom asserts that, in considering the flow of influence from an earlier writer to a later one, "source study is wholly irrelevant here; we are dealing with primal words but antithetical meanings, and an ephebe's best misinterpretations may well be of poems he has never read."[62] Thus Bloom is not concerned to trace lineages, to determine whether one poet had knowledge of another's poem, to engage in the "wearisome industry of source-hunting, of allusion-counting."[63] Rather, influence, in his view, seems to take place on the level of the subconscious. In this respect, his idea of influence marks a sharp departure from that of previous literary critics.

As Bloom pushes past the texts, occupying himself instead with primal words, he may seem to be effacing the precursor. Even his focus on the ephebe as being predestined to struggle with his (known or latent) literary father(s)—a concept in keeping with Bloom's psychologizing of the act of writing—suggests that he is not concerned with the author's intention or conscious action. Poems "are necessarily about *other poems*;

59. Ibid.
60. Ibid.
61. Graham Allen, *Intertextuality* (New York: Routledge, 2000), 134.
62. Bloom, *The Anxiety of Influence*, 70.
63. Ibid., 31.

a poem is a response to a poem, as a poet is a response to a poet, or a person to his parent."[64] Further, Bloom's assertion that "the meaning of a poem can only be another poem"[65] would seem to underscore a dismissal of the author. And yet Bloom insists that "those like Derrida and Foucault who imply...that language by itself writes the poems and thinks"[66] encourage a "humanistic loss." For while Bloom conceives of influence as meaning "that there are no texts, only relationships *between* texts,"[67] he also understands influence to be personal: "influence remains subject-centered, a person-to-person relationship, not to be reduced to the problem of language."[68] Ultimately, it *is* the struggle of one author with all others before, not the response of one text to another.

Thus we see in the centuries from Pope to Bloom a shift not only in the ways that influence is understood, but in the very reasons for attending to the topic. Where influence was once the conscious decision of a writer, it becomes over time both subconscious and inevitable. And where borrowing was once the marker of genius, once dubbed influence it becomes a marker of poetic weakness. With Bloom, influence ultimately becomes the means the late poet has for accessing the early, the weak for drawing near the strong. In those cases when poetic influence involves two strong, authentic poets, it involves a misreading that results in a creative correction. It is this correction that makes art: coming around, in some respects, to the Renaissance view of influence, Bloom construes influence as assuring the survival of poetry.

Intertextuality

Bloom was the last of the literary theorists to concern himself with influence, in part because he was one of the last literary theorists to be at all concerned with the author:[69] many of the critical concerns connected

---

64. Bloom, *A Map of Misreading*, 18.
65. Bloom, *The Anxiety of Influence*, 94.
66. Bloom, *A Map of Misreading*, 60.
67. Ibid., 3.
68. Ibid., 77.
69. Barthes urged critics to do without the [author] and study the work itself; mere months later Foucault asserted that Barthes's declaring the author dead was much less radical than it appeared to be (Michel Foucault, "What is an Author?," in *Modern Criticism and Theory* [ed. David Lodge; London: Longman, 1988], 198). Similarly, Foucault contended that "a certain number of notions that are intended to replace the privileged position of the author actually seem to preserve that privilege and suppress the real meaning of his disappearance" (ibid.). Stated otherwise, his rival Derrida's focusing on the text was simply a shifting of attention away from the

to the author were not picked up by postmodern literary theorists. Those deemed passé included analysis of biographical data (which might be relevant to influence); the ascription of authority to the author (such as transpires when the stress is placed on his being influenced or his influencing); the making of normative judgments about originality (which often accompany discussions of influence).[70] Bloom's contemporaries— Roland Barthes, Mikhail Bakhtin, and Julia Kristeva—ushered in a new understanding of the relationships between texts, one that all but effaces the author. These theorists conceive of the allusions to a first author made by a second, and the phenomenon of phrases and ideas echoing across texts, as intertextuality.[71]

Northrop Frye, in *Anatomy of Criticism* (1957) had focused on systems of verbal relationships which position major authors and minor figures according to likeness and difference. He was not, however, the one to introduce the world of criticism to intertextuality. The term is Julia Kristeva's and refers, perhaps surprisingly, not to connections between texts but to the coming into being of any text. She describes "the 'literary word' as an *intersection of textual surfaces* rather than a point (a fixed meaning), as a dialogue among several writings: that of the writer, the addressee (or the character), and the contemporary or earlier cultural context."[72] Her rather specific and somewhat counter-intuitive definition is not the only one to adhere to the term. Intertextuality comes to be so widely adopted as to lose any stable meaning.

It is easy enough to see "intertextuality" as merely another designator for the phenomena of appropriation or retelling. Clayton and Rothstein

---

author's power and a resituating of the same concerns on "writing" or "language itself." In Foucault's view, neither Barthes nor Derrida resolve the author question. Hence he proposes his own resolution: "the author function." The author is not significant in terms of his being the flesh and blood writer of a work, but in terms of his being a function of the sociohistorical discourse that limits and restricts meaning (ibid., 196–210).

70. Clayton and Rothstein, "Figures in the Corpus," 12.

71. Strongly influenced by Lacan, Kristeva develops the idea of the semiotic and thetic phases. The semiotic phase, which derives from Lacan's *infans* (the preverbal child who has not separated his identity from his mother's), is a state of drives, impulses, and bodily movements that have no symbolic value. These are mostly cast off in the thetic phase, the period during which humans enter into the social framework. At this point, self-identification borne out of distinction from the mother allows for a subject, an "I," thought to be able to present singular meaning. Of course, Kristeva ultimately concludes that there are only split subjects, no singular ones.

72. Kristeva, *Desire in Language*, 65.

note that "the new and voguish 'intertextuality' has served as a genera-
tional marker for younger critics who end up doing very much what their
elders do with influence and its partners, like 'context,' 'allusion,' and
'tradition.'"[73] However, as Clayton and Rothstein break down the
concept, they point to the way in which intertextuality departs radically
from influence, and takes retelling in the very direction that Bloom
refused to go: "Strictly, influence should refer to relations built on dyads
of transmission from one unity (author, work, tradition) to another."[74] In
this respect, intertextuality and influence are closely linked—"the shape
of intertextuality in turn depends on the shape of influence."[75] There are
two possible explanations of the relationship between the two terms.
Either intertextuality is "the enlargement of a familiar idea or…an
entirely new concept to replace the outmoded notion of influence."[76] The
extension of influence would come to include unwitting textual depend-
ency, as it does for Bloom. Here,

> intertextuality might be taken as a general term, working out from the
> broad definition of influence to encompass unconscious, socially prompted
> types of text formation (for example, by archetypes or popular culture);
> modes of conception (such as ideas 'in the air'); styles (such as genres);
> and other prior constraints and opportunities for the writer.[77]

The alternative, however, is to have intertextuality be something that is
wholly conscious. It "might be used to oust and replace the kinds of
issues that influence addresses, and in particular its central concern with
the author and more or less conscious authorial intentions and skills."[78]
Which of the divergent theories of intertextuality one upholds has
everything to do with how one understands the role of the author. The
intellectual climate if the late twentieth century was disposed to efface
the author.

The virtual disappearance of the author comes to a head in the 1970s
and 1980s, when theoretical concerns shifted and the author's intentionality became irrelevant to both the text and the text's relation to other
texts. The new perception was that texts cannot help but refer to one
another, that "all language responds to previous utterances and to pre-
existent patterns of meaning and evaluation, but also promotes and seeks

---

73. Clayton and Rothstein, "Figures in the Corpus," 3.
74. Ibid.
75. Ibid.
76. Ibid.
77. Ibid.
78. Ibid

to promote further language."[79] Every use of a word holds within it every prior use of that word, and signals every possible future use of it. Barthes contends that "a text is made of multiple writings, drawn from many cultures and entering into mutual relations of dialogue, parody, contestation, but there is one place where this multiplicity is focused, and that place is the reader, not, as was hitherto said, the author."[80] I cannot emphasize enough the stark shift from Bloom to Barthes here, with the locus of relational activity moving from author to reader. Thus the reader is left to "hold together in a single field all the traces by which the text is constituted";[81] to connect across the texts; to chart the intertextual map. These three dimensions constitute a readerly activity in which Barthes himself partakes; in *The Pleasure of the Text*, he follows the rippling of texts across texts:

> Reading a text cited by Stendahl (but not written by him) I find Proust in one minute detail. The Bishop of Lescars refers to the niece of his vicar-general in a series of affected apostrophes (*My little niece, my little friend, my lovely brunette, ah, delicious little morsel!*) which remind me of the way the two post girls at the Grand Hotel at Balbec, Marie Geneste and Celeste Albaret, address the narrator (*Oh, the little black-haired devil, oh tricky little devil! Ah, youth! Ah, lovely skin!*). Elsewhere, but in the same way, in Flaubert, it is the blossoming apple trees of Normandy which I read *according* to Proust. I savor the sway of formulas, the reversals of origins, the ease which brings the anterior text out of the subsequent one. I recognize that Proust's work, for myself at least, is *the* reference work, the general *mathesis*, the *mandala* of the entire literary cosmogony—as Mme. de Sevigne's letters were for the narrator's grand-mother, tales of chivalry for Don Quixote, etc.; this does not mean that I am in any way a Proust "specialist": Proust is what comes to me, not what I summon up; not an "authority," simply a *circular memory*. Which is what the inter-text is: the impossibility of living outside the infinite text—whether this text be Proust or the daily newspaper or the television screen: the book creates the meaning, the meaning creates life.[82]

There are a number of distinct agents in this description. Barthes, as a reader, finds Proust in a line quoted by Stendahl; he reads Flaubert *according* to Proust. These acts of reading seem merely to happen: through "sways" and "reversals" the subsequent text "brings out" the

79. Allen, *Intertextuality*, 19.

80. Roland Barthes, "The Death of the Author," in *Image–Music–Text* (trans. Stephen Heath; New York: Hill & Wang, 1977), 148.

81. Ibid.

82. Roland Barthes, *The Pleasure of the Text* (trans. Richard Miller; New York: Hill & Wang, 1975), 35–36. Emphasis in original.

anterior. The latter evokes, not invokes, the former. Proust is not asserting himself in the other works, and neither is Barthes inserting Proust there. Barthes does not "summon" him up. In this respect, the author is not authority, but rather part of a wide-reaching web of textual connection.

Text exists only within the network of texts. It is the text—the book itself—that creates meaning, not the author. In Barthes's view, "an institution, the author is dead: his civil status, his biographical person have disappeared; dispossessed, they no longer exercise over his work the formidable paternity whose account literary history, teaching, and public opinion had the responsibility of renewing."[83] Yet while the author is dead, no longer relevant to the text at all, the text continues to give meaning, a meaning that "creates life." This life is constructed by the reader, the person who replaces the author as the orderer of texts. As Barthes has it, "the reader is the space on which all the quotations that make up a writing are inscribed without any of them being lost; a text's unity lies not in its origin but in its destination"[84] (that is, the reader). This reader may not actively seek to read in a particular way or in conversation with a particular other text (as Barthes's own description of reading indicates): his intertextual reading may simply be something that happens.

It is important to distinguish Barthes's centering of the reader from reader response criticism. In this latter vision, the reader brings her biography to her reading. She reads the text through the lenses of her education, experience, emotion: her *self*. For Barthes, however, this is not the case. The destination—the reader—"cannot any longer be personal: the reader is without history, biography, psychology; he is [as we have noted] simply that *someone* who holds together all the traces by which the written text is constituted."[85] The reader is merely a vessel. She is responsible for containing the text, for "holding it together in a single field" when the propensity of text is intertextual. A text's life extends beyond the covers of the book, reaches outside to other books, other utterances, other texts.

Mikhail Bakhtin has a similar understanding of texts as being in conversation with one another, although he does not do away with the author. In his view, the author "still stands behind his or her novel, but s/he does not enter into it as a guiding authoritative voice. Bakhtin's author cannot be said to spin his or her characters out of an original imagination."[86] Dostoevsky, according to Bakhtin's description, does not express himself:

83. Ibid., 27.
84. Barthes, "The Death of the Author," 148.
85. Ibid., 148. Emphasis in original.
86. Allen, *Intertextuality*, 24.

his speech already "exists as reiterations, parodies, transformations and other kinds of appropriations of existing speech genres, utterances and words associated with particular ideological, class and other distinct social and cultural positions."[87] Bakhtin's Dostoevsky must draw on the language of the world in which he lives and of which he reads; like Bloom's author, he cannot avoid rewriting what writing precedes him.

This is because, in Bakhtin's view, language is communal. "Language, for the individual consciousness, lies on the borderline between oneself and the other. The word in language is half someone else's";[88] language is always shared. Because others have spoken and written a word before, their use of that word is bound up in any subsequent speakings and writings of that word. This is the crux of Bakhtin's understanding of language as dialogic, the assertion that "the most important feature of the utterance, or at least the most neglected, is its *dialogism*, that is, its inter-textual dimension. After Adam, there are no nameless objects, nor any unused words."[89] Bakhtin contends that:

> The speaker is not the biblical Adam, dealing only with virgin and still unnamed objects, giving them names for the first time… In reality…any utterance, in addition to its own theme, always responds (in the broad sense of the word) in one form or another to others' utterances that precede it. The speaker is not Adam, and therefore the subject of his speech itself inevitably becomes the arena where his opinions meet those of his partners (in a conversation or dispute about some everyday event) or other view-points, world views, trends, theories, and so forth (in the sphere of cultural communication). World views, trends, viewpoints, and opinions always have verbal expression. All this is others' speech (in personal or imper-sonal form), and cannot but be reflected in the utterance. The utterance is addressed not only to its object, but also to others' speech about it.[90]

Although Bakhtin will argue that all utterances reflect all other similar utterances, he does place some parameters around his understanding of trans- and inter-textual relations. He tends to read poetic forms—the epic and the lyric—as essentially monologic, presenting and enforcing a singular authoritative voice. In sharp distinction, and unique in its dialo-gism, stands the novel. While each genre may be more or less monologic or dialogic, for Bakhtin language in and of itself is multiple:

87. Ibid.

88. Mikhail Bakhtin, *The Dialogic Imagination: Four Essays* (trans. Caryl Emerson and Michael Holquist; Chicago: University of Chicago Press, 1981), 293.

89. Tzvetan Todorov, *Mikhail Bakhtin: The Dialogical Principle* (trans. Wlad Godzich; Manchester: Manchester University Press, 1984), x. Emphasis in original.

90. Mikhail Bakhtin, *Speech Genres and Other Late Essays* (trans. V. W. McGee; Austin: University of Texas Press, 1986), 93–94.

> At any given moment of its historical existence, [the novel] is heteroglot
> from top to bottom: it represents the co-existence of socio-ideological
> contradictions between the present and the past, between differing epochs
> of the past, between tendencies, schools, circles and so forth, all given a
> bodily form. These 'languages' of heteroglossia intersect each other in a
> variety of ways, forming new typifying 'languages.'[91]

Language, then, is both dynamic and public, determined as much by
points in history as by personal use.

Like Bakhtin, Julia Kristeva views language as inseparable from the
cultural framework: every text is part of a larger fabric of social relations.[92] Paraphrasing Bakhtin, she describes intertextuality as the point
where the "horizontal axis (subject–addressee) and vertical axis (text–
context) coincide, bringing to light an important fact: each word (text) is
an intersection[93] of words (texts) where at least one other word (text) can

91. Bakhtin, *Dialogic Imagination*, 291.

92. As Clayton and Rothstein note, Kristeva's intertextuality is itself intertextual.
The concept comes out of her knowledge of the structuralist theory of Swiss linguist
Ferdinand de Saussure. Saussure contends that language is a social phenomenon, a
structured system that is both synchronic (existing at any given time) and diachronic
(changing over time), and that comprises both a private tongue ("parole," the speech
of the individual) and a public one ("langue," the systematic, structured language of
a given society at a given time). Saussure's approach highlighted the relativity of
language, showing that the meaning of a sign is determined by the network of relations that make up the synchronic system of language. What was true of the linguistic
sign must be, for Kristeva at least, even more true of the literary sign (word, plot,
genre, character, imagery, narration), which is always drawn from previous literature.
Kristeva marries her background in structuralist linguistics to her understanding of
Freud. She thus distinguishes between the symbolic and the semiotic in language
(recognizing that the semiotic cannot exist apart from the symbolic (Allen, *Intertextuality*, 50). The first is thetic, the second prethetic. She adds to displacement and
consideration (Freud's designations for the two processes of the unconscious) a third
process, "the passage from one sign system to another" (Julia Kristeva, *Revolution in
Poetic Language* [trans. Margaret Waller; New York: Columbia University Press,
1984], 60). To show the split nature of language as text, she introduces two new
terms. The "phenotext" is the part of the text that communicates, the "thetic thesis"
that reflects structured information presented by a unified voice. The "genotext"
emanates from the subconscious; it makes up not the information but the arrange-
ment and rhythm thereof (ibid., 60). Intertextuality allows "Kristeva to move from
the thetic of the subject to the thetic of the text" (Janet Rex, "Heterogeneous Contradiction: Toward a Kristevan Practice," *Poetics Today* 7, no. 4 [1986]: 767). As we
will see, Kristeva then set this structuralist thinking on intertextuality in dialogue
with the theoretical writings of Derrida, Bakhtin, and Lacan.

93. Bakhtin's understanding of a horizontal axis of subject–addressee and a
vertical one of text–context, and Kristeva's pinpointing of the intersection of the

be read."[94] The slight edit—the insertion of the word 'text' in parentheses—allows Kristeva's concept of intertextuality to emerge fully. Where Bakhtin is concerned with the historicity of the word—the unique historical context of its every utterance—Kristeva is not interested in the meaning of a given word (text) at a given moment. Rather, influenced by Derrida, whom she cites on the very first page of *Desire in Language*, she is drawn to the indeterminacy and ahistoricity of meaning.

Furthermore, Kristeva does not want to analyze the way that the intertext transforms, and in fact seeks actively "to avoid the reduction of intertextuality to the traditional notions of influence, source-study and simple 'context.'"[95] Whereas Bakhtin "considers writing as a reading of the anterior literary corpus and the text as an absorption of and a reply to another text,"[96] Kristeva (as John Frow notes) does not discuss what happens to a fragment of the social text when it is "absorbed and transformed" by literature, nor does she account for how specific social texts are chosen for "absorption." In her view, "any text is constructed as a mosaic of quotations; any text is the absorption and transformation of another."[97] This is symptomatic of the profound ahistoricity of her approach.

One further way Kristeva departs from Bakhtin is her attempt to identify when writers became *self-consciously* intertextual. She turns her focus to late nineteenth- and early twentieth-century avant-garde writing. She conceives of this literature as explicitly inter-textual, the product not of great originals but of split subjects.[98] In her view, "the subject is split between the conscious and unconscious, reason and desire, the rational and irrational, the social and presocial, the communicable and incommunicable."[99] She is not, however, concerned with sifting through these dichotomies. Rather, she attends to the "altering of the thetic position—the destruction of the old position and the formation of a new one."[100]

two, provides a useful paradigm if one sees approach and stance as the two axes of a retelling.

94. Julia Kristeva, *Séméiôtiké: recherches pour une sémanalyse* (Paris: Edition du Seuil, 1969), here citing the English translation: *Desire in Language: A Semiotic Approach to Literature and Art* (Oxford: Blackwell, 1980), 66.

95. Allen, *Intertextuality*, 53.

96. Kristeva, *Desire in Language*, 69.

97. Clayton and Rothstein, "Figures in the Corpus," 20.

98. Closely linked to this is Kristeva's summation of Bakhtin: "The notion of *intertextuality* replaces that of intersubjectivity, and poetic language is read as at least *double*" (Kristeva, *Desire in Language*, 66).

99. Allen, *Intertextuality*, 47.

100. Kristeva, *Revolution in Poetic Language*, 59.

Because of her concern with position, Kristeva ultimately discards the term intertextuality, adopting instead transposition, which better reflects the transformation of the text and its consequent thetic position. As she puts it,

> the term *intertextuality* denotes this transposition of one (or several) sign system(s) into another; but since this term has often been understood in the banal sense of 'study of sources,' we prefer the term *transposition* because it specifies that the passage from one signifying system to another demands a new articulation…of enunciative and denotative positionality.[101]

Kristeva's move from intertextuality to transposition also reflects her lack of interest in the reader. On this front, she stands at a remove from Barthes, who (as we have seen) views the reader as the organizing principle behind the disparate intertexts that make up a text. While we might have expected Kristeva to come closer to offering a vocabulary that depicts the phenomenon of conscious and intentional retelling than do Bloom, Barthes, or Bakhtin, her interest in the author's activity is only slightly more pronounced than her interest in the reader. And even then, Kristeva's interest in the writer is, fundamentally, an interest in the writer as reader. That is, "the only reader in Kristeva is the writer reading another text, a figure that becomes 'no more than a text rereading itself as it rewrites itself.'"[102] Ultimately, while her theory is concerned with the subject—in this case, the one who partakes in the transpositional practice—Kristeva's dismissal of the possible unity of a subject means that the subject melds back into the text. Not only does the writer not intentionally rewrite, the writer scarcely exists.

In the two-thousand years from Aristotle to Kristeva, literary critics (and, later, theorists) have held a wide variety of views about the use of earlier writing by later writers. Retelling has been upheld as a reflection of artistic genius and a sign of artistic weakness. It has been considered supremely original and distressingly derivative. And just as there has been no consistent attitude toward retelling, so there has been no single term to describe it. Imitation, invention, influence, and intertextuality have all been in fashion. Each, as we have seen, denotes something distinct about the relationship of text to *Urtext*. Each requires amplification and explanation if it is to be used to describe how a later text uses an earlier (rather than the artistic merit of a later text using an earlier). The next chapter introduces literary theories that attend not simply to texts that recall other texts, but to texts that make deliberate appeal to other texts.

101.   Ibid., 59–60.
102.   Clayton and Rothstein, "Figures in the Corpus," 21.

Chapter 4

NAMING THE ANIMALS

Intentiveness in Retelling

Implicit in the idea of influence is directionality: to speak of an earlier text influencing a later writer suggests that the agency lies with the earlier written work rather than the later reader cum writer. Because of this grammatical flaw, it might make more sense to speak in terms of imitation, as was historically popular. (Invention, by contrast, is a word that makes little sense in this context, despite its having been widely used to describe the phenomenon that interests us.) But the terms imitation and influence seem to have had their day, and these antique ideas have yielded to the modern notion of intertextuality. Intertextuality suggests interrelationships between texts, but might not be as useful a concept as we might have hoped. Recent trends in literary theory have tended either to situate the reader as the locus of intertextual relationships, or to understand language as inherently communal and texts therefore as unavoidably intertextual. Neither allows for the possibility that a later writer might be making intentional use of or reference to an earlier text.

As we saw, art critic Michael Baxandall sought to reorder the understanding of influence, so that agency belongs to the *re*-teller not the teller. He is interested in the very question of purposefulness, of intentional reuse. These are not concerns of Kristeva, Barthes, or Bakhtin. Instead, Baxandall returns to the question of purposefulness raised by Sidney. His book, *Patterns of Intention: On the Historical Explanation of Pictures*,[1] is an attempt to "address pictures partly by making inferences about their causes":[2] in the book, he outlines the critic's limitations in assessing intention. His hermeneutics is similar to those outlined here, which offer the language of textual approach and stance as alternatives to

1. Michael Baxandall, *Patterns of Intention: On the Historical Explanation of Pictures* (New Haven: Yale University Press, 1985).
   2. Ibid., 41.

the far more sticky authorial intent, but Baxandall has a different way around the problem of intent. He pursues the idea of intention not in terms of what the author or artist was thinking or meaning, but as "a general condition of rational human action."[3] He notes, "The intention to which I am committed is not an actual, particular psychological state or even a historical set of mental events inside the heads of [the artist], in the light of which—if I knew them—I would interpret the [work of art]."[4] Rather, his intention is pragmatic rather than psychological. He sketches a "triangle of reenactment," which looks like this:

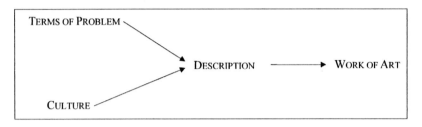

The work of art is conditioned by the problem the artist faces—in the case of an architect, a bridge to be built, or in that of a painter, a model to be sketched, say—and the culture in which she lives. She negotiates between the two, and our analysis of her work—our description—provides the connector between the finished project and her incorporation of the problem and the culture. What Baxandall calls 'inferential criticism" "brings all three corners of the triangle, in an active relation to each other, to description of the object. Description and explanation interpenetrate one another."[5] Our moving about on the triangle of re-enactment

> assumes purposefulness—or intent or, as it were, "intentiveness"—in the historical actor but even more in the historical objects themselves. Intentionality in this sense is taken to be characteristic of both. Intention is the forward-leaning look of things. It is not a reconstituted historical state of mind, then, but a relation between the object and its circumstances.[6]

Thus Baxandall can speak of purposefulness, or intentionality, in reference to paintings rather than painters—just as "approach" and "stance" allow us to focus writings rather than writers. Baxandall answers the

3. Ibid.
4. Ibid.
5. Ibid., 34.
6. Ibid., 40–41.

question of intention without having to ask 'What did this artist think she was doing when she…?" Instead, the product rather than the producer's insight accounts for intent.

Intentional Interrelationships

It is only with French theorist and narratologist Gérard Genette that we find a detailed vocabulary for describing the interrelationships of texts, and specifically, a writer's intentional engagement with previous text. His 1982 *Palimpsestes: La littérature au second degré* is a consideration of the many possible relationships between *hypotext* (telling) and *hypertext* (retelling). He good-humouredly describes the project as "nothing other than the faithful transcription of a no less faithful nightmare, stemming from a hasty and, I fear, sketchy reading, in the dubious light of a few pages by Borges, of I know not what Dictionary of Works from All Times and All Countries";[7] a flip through the index reveals that he is exaggerating only slightly. His specimens span time and place, from ancient Greece to modern France; his prooftexts are as diverse as *Roman de la Rose* and *Robinson Crusoe*; his theory is equally in conversation with Aristotle as with Derrida.

The book is an effort to examine and catalogue the many ways that later texts not only reveal the presence of earlier ones (as the image of a palimpsest suggests), but also of the ways that they rework them. He celebrates the interweaving of the earlier text (the hypotext) into the later (the hypertext):

> That duplicity of the object, in the sphere of textual relations, can be represented by the old analogy of the *palimpsest*: on the same parchment, one text can become superimposed upon another, which it does not quite conceal but allows to show through. It has been aptly said that pastiche and parody "designate literature as a palimpsest." This must be understood to apply more generally to every hypertext, as Borges made clear concerning the relation between the text and its foretexts. The hypertext invites us to engage in a relational reading, the flavor of which, however perverse, may well be condensed in an adjective recently coined by Philippe LeJeune: a *palimpsestuous* reading. To put it differently, just for the fun of switching perversities, one who really loves texts must wish from time to time to love (at least) two together.[8]

7. Gérard Genette, *Palimpsestes: La littérature au second degré* (Paris: Seuil, 1982), here (and unless otherwise indicated) citing from the English translation: *Palimpsests: Literature in the Second Degree* (trans. Channa Newman and Claude Doubinsky; Lincoln: University of Nebraska Press, 1997), 394.
8. Ibid., 399.

Genette's exploration of the links between hypotext and hypertext is not a matter of "source hunting" but of love. To read the retelling in light of the telling is to derive the greatest joy from it.

According to Genette, the reading of two texts in relation to one another is an *open structuralism*.[9] The reference to structuralism reveals some of Genette's own influences (foretexts). Drawing on Claude Lévi-Strauss' idea of a "bricoleur," the primitive myth-maker, and on Kristeva's intertextuality, which "provides [him] with [his] terminological paradigm,"[10] Genette in his earlier works had put forth the argument that "the subject of poetics[11]...is not the text considered in its singularity (that is more appropriately the task of criticism), but rather the *architext* or, if one prefers, the architextuality of the text."[12] By architextuality, he meant "the entire set of general or transcendent categories—types of discourse, modes of enunciation, literary genres—from which emerges each singular text."[13] In *Palimpsests*, however, he revisits this opinion, emending it to "the subject of poetics is *transtextuality*, or the textual transcendence of the text...defined roughly as 'all that sets the text in a relationship, whether obvious or concealed, with other texts.'"[14] Transtextuality, then, both goes beyond and subsumes the earlier designator, architextuality.

Genette recognizes five types of transtextual relationship. These are not "separate and absolute categories without any reciprocal contact or overlapping"; rather, "their relationships to one another are numerous and often crucial."[15] The five, however, can be distinguished from one another, and they represent a range of abstractions and relationships to the text.

The first type is intertextuality, which Genette defines more tightly than does Kristeva.[16] Her definition is broad: intertextuality is not a classification of texts but "an aspect of textuality."[17] This is itself a notion that, to Genette's mind, "makes no sense, since there are no texts without textual transcendence."[18] Genette claims he "can also trace in just about

---

9. Ibid.

10. Ibid., 1.

11. Here we are back at Aristotle.

12. Genette, *Palimpsests*, 1.

13. Gérard Genette, *Architext: An Introduction* (trans. Jane E. Levin; Berkeley: University of California Press, 1992), 87.

14. Genette, *Palimpsests*, 1.

15. Ibid., 7.

16. He credits her with initially exploring the term that "obviously provides [him] with [his] terminological paradigm" (ibid., 1).

17. Ibid., 8.

18. Ibid.

any work the local, fugitive, and partial echoes of any other work, be it anterior or exterior."[19] Thus, in its broadest definition, the whole of literature could by rights rest under the blanket of intertextuality. Genette therefore limits his understanding and application of the term to works "in which the shift from hypotext to hypertext is both massive (an entire work B deriving from an entire work A) and more or less officially stated."[20] What is attractive about his narrowing the term is the attention to deliberate act: all texts may resonate with all other texts, but there are certain texts that make intentional recall to others. To speak in these terms is not necessarily to get into questions of what the author intended in revisiting a text—something, as I have noted, that we usually cannot know[21]—but it does allow us to acknowledge a purposefulness in a revisiting even if we cannot speak to its motivation.

Here intertextuality refers to the actual presence of one text within another. Genette's usage includes one text's explicit and literal quoting of another; the less explicit plagiarism, which he describes as "an undeclared but still literal borrowing";[22] and the still less literal practice of allusion, which is "an enunciation whose full meaning presupposes the perception of a relationship between it and another text, to which it necessarily refers by some inflections that would otherwise remain unintelligible."[23] The three—quotation, plagiarism, and allusion—are comparable at the level of approach:[24] all three make direct use of specific

19. Ibid., 9.

20. Ibid.

21. Not because we distrust a writer's assertion of his intentions or assessment of his own work (although this might sometimes be the case) but because so many writers have left their drives unarticulated and their influences undocumented.

22. Genette, *Palimpsests*, 2.

23. Ibid.

24. The question of whether the distinctions between the three are entirely semantic is interesting to contemplate. A few years ago, The *New Yorker* printed a letter from Henry Louis Gates, Jr., shortly after it ran his piece on "The Bondswoman's Narrative by Hannah Crafts, A Fugitive Slave, Recently Escaped from North Carolina," a handwritten manuscript that "may indeed have been the work of a fugitive slave." Gates had read echoes of Harriet Beecher Stowe and Frederick Douglass in the manuscript, but once he published it, *New Yorker* readers "pointed out borrowings—occasionally verbatim—from another source: Charles Dickens's Bleak House." Gates's response to these "verbatim borrowings" is fascinating and speaks to that point at which quotation, allusion, and plagiarism can become curiously commingled. He writes: "The use of 'Bleak House' suggests that Crafts was not merely seeking to 'testify' about a slave's experience: she was seeking a relation to a canonical tradition, finding in Dickens a language and rhetoric that she sometimes assimilated and sometimes appropriated. No doubt, further study will uncover

phrases or paragraphs found in the original. In terms of stance, however, the three depart significantly. Quotation, whether it turns to the original for support or in order to detract from it, engages the original in some sort of dialogue. Plagiarism takes directly from the original as a means of furthering its own purpose; in not acknowledging the original, in its sur- reptitious drawing from it, the plagiarized text seeks to bar the original from dialogue. Allusion draws openly (though perhaps subtly) from the original; it nods at the original, and in so doing points away from itself toward the earlier text.

The second of Genette's five categories of textual transcendence is the "less explicit and more distant relationship that binds the text properly speaking, taken within the totality of the literary work, to what can be called its *paratext*."[25] The paratext, or the text's paratextuality, is that which lies on the threshold of a text. It consists of the *peritext* (the titles, chapter headings, prefaces, and notes)[26] and the *epitext* (interviews, pub- licity announcements, reviews by and addresses to critics, private letters, and other authorial and editorial discussions). The paratext is both inside and outside the text; it is that which Derrida describes as "paradoxically fram[ing] and at the same time constitut[ing] the text for its readers."[27] Genette recognizes the role of the paratext for the reader, acknowledging that peritext and epitext "provide the text with a (variable) setting and sometimes a commentary, official or not, which even the purists among readers, those least inclined to external erudition, cannot always disregard as easily as they would like and as they claim to do."[28] Like Barthes's Proust, paratext and epitext inform a reading often without the reader intending them to.

The third type of transcendence, *metatextuality*, is that which is gen- erally labeled commentary; it "unites a given text to another, of which it speaks without necessarily citing it (without summoning it), in fact

other instances of influence and borrowing. But the image of a fugitive slave turn- ing to the greatest English novelist of her day—a novelist known for his vivid descriptions of poverty and powerlessness—to help fashion her story carries with it at least one lesson: that the republic of letters has always transcended the bounds of identity" (*The New Yorker* [March 4, 2002]: 5). Quotation and plagiarism become enmeshed with assimilation and appropriation; the use of the canonical text is in the service not merely of fashioning a story, but of transcending the bounds of identity.

25. Genette, *Palimpsests*, 3.

26. Presumably also the physical object of the text—typeface, paper binding, jacket, cover illustrations, etc.—although Genette does not specify these.

27. Jacques Derrida, *The Truth in Painting* (trans. Geoff Bennington and Ian McLeod; Chicago: University of Chicago Press, 1987), 13.

28. Genette, *Palimpsests*, 3.

sometimes even without naming it."[29] This relationship Genette calls the "*critical* relationship par excellence."[30] In biblical studies, metatextuality is the prevalent mode of discourse about text, but this hardly suggests that commentary is monolithic. In its presentation of the philological, archaeological, and historical aspects of scripture, the Anchor Bible Commentary, for instance, offers a scholarly means of engaging the text; with its suggestions for sermons and devotions, the *New Interpreter's Bible*, by contrast, offers a devotional tack in addition. Their disparate "motives" aside, however, the format and style of the two are similar: both offer a line by line elucidation of the biblical text.

Fourth, and most important to his investigation in *Palimpsests* is *hypertextuality*, the relationship that unites text B (the hypertext) to an earlier text A (the hypotext). Hypertextuality is "too obviously to some degree a universal feature of literariness: there is no literary work that does not evoke (to some extent and according to how it is read) some other literary work, and in that sense all works are hypertextual."[31] Thus Genette is compelled to narrow his terms: he describes hypertext as "a text derived from another preexistent text"[32] in a more "properly literary" way than that in which the metatext derives from the text. This derivation may occur in one of two ways: through simple transformation, which Genette labels merely *transformation*, or through indirect transformation, which he labels *imitation*.[33]

Fifth[34] is "the most abstract and implicit"[35] of these relationships: *architextuality*. Defined above, it

> involves a relationship that is completely silent, articulated at most only by a paratextual mention, which can be titular (as in *Poems*, *Essays*, *The Romance of the Rose*, etc.) or most often sub-titular (as when the indication *A Novel*, or *A Story*, or *Poems* is appended to the title on the cover) but which remains in any case of a purely taxonomic nature.[36]

Not only does Genette offer a framework for discussing interrelationships of texts, he concerns himself directly with the problem of intertextual allusions, or what he calls hypertextuality. The supposition

29. Ibid., 4.
30. Ibid.
31. Ibid., 9.
32. Ibid., 5.
33. Ibid., 7.
34. Genette actually describes this fifth relationship before the fourth, so as to give proper emphasis to hypertextuality.
35. Genette, *Palimpsests*, 4.
36. Ibid.

underlying all of Genette's discussion here is that hypertextuality "adds a dimension to a text":[37] a text that uses another is somehow enriched.

Within his broad rubric of hypertextuality, Genette offers a number of subcategories we will do well to keep in mind. These are not genres: as Genette himself notes, "above all, hypertextuality, as a category of works, is in itself a generic, or more precisely *transgeneric* architext: … a category of texts which wholly encompasses certain canonical (though minor) genres such as pastiche, parody, travesty, and which also touches upon other genres—probably all genres."[38] To speak in terms of genre, however, does not get us to a vocabulary describing either the relationship of a text to its precursor or how the later text accesses the earlier. Genre, as a framework, offers a hint of what a text's stance might be, though, in Genette's hand, the question of approach is brought somewhat to bear on genre.

Genette takes terms generally associated with genre and infuses them with an undercurrent of what we are calling approach. In describing and analyzing parody, travesty, caricatures, and pastiches, which he works through in some detail, he enacts transformations of his own. He "(re)baptize[s] as *parody* the distortion of a text by means of a minimal transformation";[39] he has *travesty* "designat[e] the stylistic transformation whose function is to debase."[40] *Caricature* comes to be "the satirical pastiche," while *pastiche* itself refers to "the imitation of a style without any satirical intent."[41] The first two genres comprise *transformation*, and differ primarily in the degrees of distortion inflicted upon the hypotext. The latter two genres are *imitation*, and differ only in their function and the degree of their "stylistic aggravation."[42] The criterion for this new distribution is "the type of relationship (transformation or imitation) that they create between the hypertext and its hypotext."[43]

In his discussion of parody, for instance, Genette turns to the Abbé Sallier's identification of five approaches in parody: the changing of a single word in a line; a changing of a single letter in a word; the subversion, without textual modification, of a quotation's intended meaning; the composition of an entire work that deflects a complete work or significant portion of one; and the composition of verses in the taste and style

37. Ibid., 200.
38. Ibid., 8.
39. Ibid., 25.
40. Ibid., 25.
41. Ibid., 25.
42. Ibid., 25.
43. Ibid., 25.

of a lesser writer.[44] Moreover, he describes how approach links to the stance of genres: "parody can be characterized as a limited, even minimal, modification, or one reducible to a mechanical principle... Travesty is defined almost completely by a single type of stylistic transformation (trivialization). Pastiche, caricature and forgery are only functional inflexions bearing on a single practice: imitation."[45] Thus approach and genre become inextricable. Furthermore, in Genette's account, "all these practices can produce only brief texts, for fear of losing the reader's interest";[46] the success of these hypertextual genres is contingent on the original.

Mere imitation (understood here in its most common sense, as meaning attempts to be like something else) does not get the writer far. The new work has to go beyond the old. According to Genette, "Contrary to what is true of painting, the 'literary fake'... is assuredly not the principal mode of expression of serious imitation. That mode... is much rather to be sought in the practice that the Middle Ages (which did not invent it) called *continuation*."[47] Here he introduces a new idea: the continuation, which, as the name itself suggests, is the completion of a work that is somehow incomplete. It is distinct from the sequel—*la suite*—in that the completion is picked up by another teller; the sequel is written by the original author.[48] In its taking up a piece already begun, continuation is "not like other imitations, since it must abide by a certain number of additional constraints: first, naturally—given that any satirical caricature is prohibited—imitation here must be absolutely faithful and serious... But above all, the hypertext must constantly remain continuous with its hypotext, which it must merely bring to its prescribed or appropriate conclusion while observing the congruity of places, chronological sequence, character consistency, etc."[49] To ensure "the unity of the whole and the invisibility of the seams,"[50] the writer of the continuation must internalize the writing and writer of the work continued.[51]

44. Ibid., 19.
45. Ibid., 212–13.
46. Ibid., 213.
47. Ibid., 161.
48. Or, as Genette has it, the one is autographic, the other allographic (ibid., 161).
49. Ibid., 162.
50. Ibid., 163.
51. The *Romance of the Rose* is, according to Genette, a "rare example...of an official continuation that is emancipated from any stylistic mimeticism, indeed from any ideological faithfulness" (ibid., 192); Jean de Meun continues in his own style (reflecting his own philosophy) the allegorical narrative Guillaume de Lorris left incomplete at his death.

In typical fashion, Genette does not let this category stand unqualified. Under the general umbrella of continuations are *conclusions*, which may be either *garrulous* or *concise*. The latter "add to their hypotext only the prolongation and the conclusion that the continuator thinks it fit (or profitable) to adduce."[52] The former, on the other hand, view the telling as "flawed by an inadequate beginning, or even—as Aristotle would put it—an inadequate middle or inadequate sides, and decide to correct those flaws."[53] How the hypertext deals with the inadequacies of the hypotext is a question of approach: the *corrective continuation*[54] may be *proleptic* (continuing the story forward), *analeptic* (moving backward, illustrating what came before), *elliptic* (filling in a "median gap" or ellipsis), or *paraleptic*[55] (bridging paralepses, or lateral ellipses[56]).[57] All four categories are explanations of approach; they identify how (and at what point) the later text gains access to the earlier.

The category of continuation, however, can to a degree illuminate the question of stance as well. Continuation demands stylistic and thematic faithfulness.[58] When these qualities are not apparent, the continuation is "unfaithful." Genette provides a vocabulary for this permutation too. There is the *complement*, an unfaithful continuation that is "careful not to exhibit a betrayal that is perhaps not conscious and intentional";[59] complements are "modest and respectful"[60] in their treatment of the original work.

In sharp contrast is the *supplement*, which "bears a more ambitious significance"[61] than does the complement. "The postscript here is wholly prepared to substitute for—that is, to displace and therefore to erase—that which it completes";[62] it eclipses the earlier. Genette puts forth as a more specific designator the *murderous continuation*, the one that

52. Ibid., 177.
53. Ibid.
54. Ibid., 175.
55. As in, "Meanwhile, back at the ranch..."
56. Genette, *Palimpsests*, 177.
57. All four varieties, Genette asserts, are found in "the post- or para-Homeric epic cycle called the Trojan Cycle, written after or around Homer's time by poets intent on completing and extending the narrative of which the *Iliad* and the *Odyssey* were seen as merely two erratic episodes or fragments" (ibid., 177). This brings him, of course, to a discussion of cyclical continuations as a genre.
58. Ibid., 198.
59. Ibid., 202.
60. Ibid.
61. Ibid.
62. Ibid.

"almost entirely erases the continued work."[63] The murderous continuation supplants the original;[64] "the hypotext [rises] to the surface and abolishes its own hypertext."[65] On this point, Genette sounds like Bloom: just as Bloom spoke of the Oedipal struggle of the ephebe with his precursors, Genette refers to the unfaithful continuation as parricide.[66] The murderous continuation raises a problem of method and principle, rather than merely of taxonomy. What, Genette asks, "is a hypertext whose hypotext has been forgotten and which everyone reads as an autonomous text?"[67] Does this alter status, transforming the hypertext into mere text? Not quite, answers Genette, punning: "the hypotext is no longer anything but a pretext, the point of departure for an extrapolation disguised as an interpolation."[68] (In Genette's lexicon, an interpolation is "substitutive by its content";[69] it is complementary. The extrapolation, however, "brings about a transmutation of meaning of value in [its] hypotext";[70] it is supplementary.)

These distinctions do not close out Genette's consideration of hypertexts that pick up where their hypotexts left off. As against the continuation, which is, as I have said, thematically and stylistically consistent with the text to be continued, and is therefore within the bounds of imitation, stands the unfaithful continuation that "extends beyond the category of serious imitation to that of transposition, actually a very marked, at times very aggressive, variant of transposition—i.e., *thematic correction*, or even *refutation*."[71] Here, the significance of the original text is reversed; the refutation modifies an essential aspect of the hypotext, such as its setting, tone, or plot. Genette offers two examples of the refutation: Fabre d'Eglantine's *Philinte de Molière, ou La Suite du Misanthrope*, a 1790 version of *Misanthrope* that does not "side with" Philinte, and D. H. Lawrence's 1930 short story, "The Man Who Died." Genette describes the latter as "less impertinent but at bottom much more subversive" than the former,

63. Ibid., 196.

64. This type of continuation, as seen in *Pantagruel* or *Orlando furioso* "entails oblivion for its hypotext, unfairly or not and with the exception of scholars" (ibid., 200).

65. Ibid., 196.

66. Ibid., 198.

67. Ibid., 200.

68. Ibid., 203.

69. Ibid., 205.

70. Ibid.

71. Ibid., 198.

since the man in question is none other than Jesus Christ who, having
risen from the dead, wanders about the world and discovers physical
love—and through it Lawrence's own gospel. This very beautiful tale is
thus both a continuation and a refutation of the Christian Gospel—unless
we are expected, as is my inclination, to take in a Lawrentian sense the
precept "Ye shall love one another."[72]

Such reversals, in Genette's view, "are as a matter of course the most
interesting and the most successful, for it stands to reason that a gifted
artist, however piously disposed to a great forebear, cannot be content
with a task as menial as a simple continuation."[73] It is not because
Genette has invoked piety that we find ourselves now in the realm of
much of the literature that sparked our discussion. We are concerned
with those retellings that, like Lawrence's "The Man Who Died," carry
the scriptural telling into a new realm.

This carrying across, which Genette labels "serious transformation, or
transposition, is without any doubt the most important of all hypertextual
practices."[74] The weight he ascribes it is based on the aesthetic merit and
historical significance of many of the works that fall within this designation; Genette lists *Faust* and *Ulysses* as exemplars of the transposition.
Their "textual amplitude and aesthetic and/or ideological ambition may
mask or even completely obfuscate their hypertextual character":[75] their
greatness comes by virtue of their using many transpositional practices at
once. Genette turns to Michel Tournier's 1967 novel *Vendredi*, a retelling of *Robinson Crusoe*, to illustrate transpositional practices. These
include "*thematic transformation* (ideological reversal), *transvocalization* (the switch from first to third person[76]), and *spatial transfer* (a shift
from the Atlantic to the Pacific)."[77]

Transposition can take a number of other forms. Most obvious, of
course, is translation, the transposition of a text to another language.
There are also transpositions of form: *versification*, where prose is rendered as poetry, and *prosification*, in which poetry is rendered as prose.[78]

72. Ibid., 199.
73. Ibid., 199–200.
74. Ibid., 212.
75. Ibid., 213.
76. This move from autodiegetic to heterodiegetic is characteristic of summary.
77. Genette, *Palimpsests*, 213.
78. There are gradations within this last subgenre. *Unrhyming* is rendering a
rhymed text unrhymed, while otherwise maintaining its verse form. *Transfiguration*
is shifting a poetic system that is metaphoric to one that is comparative and/or
metonymic. *Transmetrification* is changing a poem from one meter to another (ibid.,
222–26).

Less obvious as a category is *transstylization,* "a stylistic rewriting,"[79] as in journalistic or editorial corrections that substitute a "good" style for one "less good."[80]

When transformation is quantitative, as against stylistic or qualitative, Genette introduces another series of terms. The two basic categories of this are *reduction*[81] and *augmentation,*[82] but, as "there are certainly many ways to reduce or extend a text,"[83] Genette will not let such broad characterizations stand. He begins with the most radical case, out and out *suppression,* which "is the [activity] most brutal and the most destructive to [a text's] structure and meaning."[84] More constrained than this is *excision,* the removal of "some useless and therefore noxious part,"[85] which, unlike suppression, may serve to improve a work. *Amputation—* "a single massive excision"[86]—is routine for editors, but as Genette notes, readers do it frequently too, skipping over chunks of text when interest wanes or time runs short. Less drastic still is *trimming* (or *pruning*), the process the classics undergo when they find their way into *Reader's Digest* editions. When reducing takes on a moral or censorial function, it becomes *expurgation*—Thomas Bowdler's infamous versions of Shakespeare are perhaps the best known English example of this phenomenon.

All of the above are variations on a theme of cutting. Genette also speaks of *concision,* wherein "a text is abridged without the suppression of any of its significant thematic parts."[87] Unlike excision, however, where parts of the text are cut out, here the whole text is made more concise. Genette knows of only one exemplar of this: Cocteau and his reworkings of *Antigone* (1922), *Romeo and Juliet* (1924), and *Oedipus Rex* (1925).[88] Cocteau's contraction of *Antigone* "emphasizes, exaggerates and at bottom updates Sophocles' own concision...[he] pushes Sophocles

---

79. Ibid., 226.

80. The *Good News Bible* is a perfect example.

81. He notes, "I have a vague notion that augmentations have been favored by literary expression much more often than reductions—although there is a sizable number of those—and I have an even vaguer hunch of their thematic repercussions. I shall therefore first gropingly explore the process of reduction" (ibid., 229).

82. He also calls this breed of quantitative transformation "translongation" (ibid.).

83. Ibid., 228.

84. Ibid., 229.

85. Ibid.

86. Ibid.

87. Ibid., 235.

88. Ibid., 236.

to the limit, but in Sophocles' own direction,"[89] argues Genette. In fact, Genette goes so far as to contend that "Sophocles rewritten by Cocteau is more Sophocles than the original."[90] Genette here introduces a dimension we have not yet considered: the ephebe might not merely improve upon, but could in fact surpass, the precursor aesthetically.

Whereas the result of both excision and concision is a new version of the original telling, a third category of reduction, *condensation*,[91] favors relaying the general meaning over the retention of some sentences or scenes at the expense of others. There are, in Genette's taxonomy, various means of condensing. *Summary*[92] can be either *extraliterary* (outlines[93] or "administrative condensation or other synthetic reports"[94]) or *metaliterary* (e.g. précis of works in encyclopedias, summaries of plays, critical discourse about literature, descriptive summary). The metaliterary summary "never lets [the hypotext] out of its sight, or so to speak, its discourse."[95] It is always contingent on the text it summarizes; it expects that the reader knows the text, perhaps even in its full form.

The *digest*, on the other hand, is a condensation in which there is no expectation that the reader will turn to the hypotext. Whereas summary is bound up in commentary, here we have pure narration. The digest "presents itself as a perfectly autonomous narrative"[96] and thus takes direct charge of the action of the other. While itself a hypertext, the digest is much less metatextual than other types of summary; title aside, it never mentions the hypotext. Further, it not only abbreviates the hypotext, but emends it, telling it in its own way. For readers of English,[97] the prime

89. Ibid., 237.

90. Ibid. One wonders whether a much less refined art might also fall under this heading of concision: is this how we might also describe the cutting/culling of lines when scripts are made closed captioned for the hearing impaired?

91. Also known as digest, *abridgment*, *résumé*, *summary*, or *text contraction*.

92. French *résumé*.

93. Which, as Genette points out, can enter the realm of the literary: he points to examples from Henry James and Emile Zola, whose outlines of research in progress are deeply creative and original (Genette, *Palimpsests*, 274–76). But in these cases, the outline precedes the work itself. The outline that comes after seems inherently extraliterary.

94. Ibid., 238.

95. Ibid., 241.

96. Ibid.

97. Indeed, for Genette as well, who, following Harald Weinrich, even in the French calls this type of summary without commentary *reader's digest*: "Résumer le contenu d'un roman n'est past faire un *reader's digest*. Il s'agit bien plûtot de commenter une oeuvre ou de donner à d'autres la possibilité de le faire sans defaillance de mémoire" (Genette, *Palimpsestes* [original French edition], 283).

example of this is *Reader's Digest* itself, which takes articles, essays, and stories from the popular press and rewrites them in a more accessible condensed version.

Again, the concern with condensation has to this point been with the *approach* of the hypertext to the hypotext, but there is also stance to consider. A condensation can have the effect of trivializing the original, of aggrandizing it, of highlighting its moral points at the expense of its aesthetic ones. The mode of condensation does not imply stance: a metaliterary summary does not by definition hold the hypotext in higher regard than a digest, for instance.

For each of the modes of reduction, there is a corresponding mode of expansion. By virtue of its altering the text, adding to—like subtracting from—"involves significant distortions."[98] *Extension*, Genette's first brand of augmentation, involves massive addition. Seventeenth- and eighteenth-century French neoclassical drama, though it adapted Greek tragedy for the contemporary stage, deemed the classics insufficient for the current day and subjected them to "all kinds of extensions that might more appropriately be called 'padding.'"[99] The padding included adding characters,[100] heightening passions,[101] and extending the action.[102]

The second subset of augmentation, "the antithesis of concision, proceeds not through massive additions but through a kind of stylistic dilation."[103] Taking place at the level of the sentence, in which each one is elongated, Genette labels this type of amplification[104] *expansion*. As Genette illustrates using the fable of the wolf and the lamb, expansion can take place through *hypotyposis* (the vivid description of a scene) or *sermocination*[105] (a recounting using only dialogue without introductory statements). He then points to Raymond Queneau's *Exercises in Style*[106]

98. Genette, *Palimpsestes*, 254.
99. Ibid.
100. As in Corneille's giving Jocasta and Laius a daughter, and therefore Oedipus a sister, in his *Oedipus Rex* of 1659.
101. See Voltaire's "annexing" Philoctetes, a hero from outside Thebes and an old love of Jocasta, as a means of making Jocasta less "insipid" (Genette, *Palimpsestes*, 256).
102. As with Houdar La Motte's 1726 prose version of *Oedipus Rex*.
103. Genette, *Palimpsestes*, 260.
104. A term he reserves for later use.
105. Also *dialogism* (Genette, *Palimpsestes*, 261).
106. The plot of Queneau's book is simple. It takes up five lines on the back jacket of the book: "On a crowded bus at midday, Raymond Queneau observes one man accusing another of jostling him deliberately. When a seat is vacated, the first man appropriates it. Later, in another part of town, Queneau sees the man being

for further examples of expansion, most pertinent of which are *hesitation*, the infusion of doubt or delay into the authorial voice;[107] *specificity*, the transmission of the most minute details;[108] *definitional transformation*, the narrowing of terms;[109] and *preciosity*, the affectation of a fastidious literary style.[110]

Whereas extension and expansion both correlate with types of reduction, Genette's third subcategory of augmentation, *amplification*, has no equal and opposite form.[111] Prevalent in classical drama, amplification is an author's contribution of his "own variations upon the themes of [his] predecessor."[112] Continuing the cycles of intertextual (or, in Genette's terms, transtextual) relationships, it is interesting to think that the hypotext of the amplified hypertext may easily stand as its summary.[113]

Genette describes Thomas Mann's *Joseph and His Brothers* as a "vast amplification (from 26 to 1,600 pages) of the biblical narrative, or as a transformation of a very spare mythical narrative into a kind of vast historical *Bildungsroman*."[114] It amplifies not only Genesis, but the Qur'an, Firdusi and Djani's versions of "Yussuf and Suleika," and the medieval Spanish "Yussuf's Poem" as well.[115] Mann's *Joseph*, which spans four volumes, stretches the biblical figure's life far outside the scope of the Bible. Mann begins with Joseph's childhood, and continues through his maturity (which is coincident with his father's death). In his use of literary flashbacks to Jacob's own childhood, Mann extends Joseph's biography well beyond the years of Joseph's own life, into the

---

advised by a friend to sew another button on his overcoat" (Raymond Queneau, *Exercises in Style* [trans. Barbara Wright; New York: New Directions, 1981]). The premise, however, is more complex: Queneau retells the "story" ninety-nine times, each time in a different style.

107.   "A zebra, at least I think it was a zebra—it might, I suppose, have been a white horse with black stripes…"

108.   "A zebra, 7 ½ feet high, 8 feet long, weighing 978 pounds…"

109.   "An equus boehmi, of the class mammalia, order perissodactyla, family equidae…"

110.   "A cascade of black mane rippling across the strong sinewy neck, an expanse of white hide interrupted with ebon strokes, brushed stripes, a zebra…"

111.   Although it could at "least be inaccurately described as the obverse of a condensation," concedes Genette (*Palimpsestes*, 262).

112.   Ibid.

113.   Genette uses as his example here Thomas Mann's *Joseph and His Brothers*. When cited throughout *this* work, the edition used will be H. T. Lowe-Porter's translation (New York: Knopf, 1948).

114.   Genette, *Palimpsestes*, 265.

115.   Ibid.

lives of earlier and later patriarchs.[116] These Jacob stories, which take up the last two-thirds of the first book of Mann's opus, Genette describes as *metadiegetic analepsis*, addition that takes place afield of the (temporal) confines of the original but supports the initial theme. This, in Genette's taxonomy, is one of a number of ways narrative amplification can proceed; it may also transpire through "*diegetic development* (...*expansion*: distension of details, descriptions, multiplication of episodes and secondary characters, maximum dramatization of an adventure hardly dramatic in itself)," as well as through "*metadiegetic insertions* (...*extension*: episodes that are extraneous to the initial theme but whose incorporation makes it possible to extend and invest it with its full historical and religious significance[117])...and through the narrator's *extradiegetic interventions*."[118]

Here, the extradiegetic interventions (or intrusions, as Genette also calls them), are the verbose insertions of Mann's omniscient narrator, who "misses no opportunity to claim his right to amplify his predecessors' versions."[119] This narrator "demands his right to restore in its entirety the story that tradition had omitted to pass on but that had nevertheless been told once upon a time" but that had succumbed to "the inexorable laws of abridgement."[120] He offers the "'how,' the dramatic amplification of the 'what' handed down by tradition,"[121] and supplies the 'why'[122]—the desires and motives[123] to all the characters[124] of the Genesis story.

---

116.   Genette offers an analysis of Mann's broadened periphery: "It seems as if Jacob's narrative were for Thomas Mann a simple pretext to look back into the past, as if his tetralogy began in *media res* with Joseph's childhood and thereafter moved back to its true starting point: Jacob's birth. But such a description would not account for the essential fact that the hero, the principal object and the quasi-unique *focus* (subject) of this narrative, is not Jacob but indeed Joseph himself: despite its pseudodiegetic reduction, Jacob's narrative remains one that is *addressed to Joseph* and is heard by him. It is included in the novel only as an element in Joseph's education..." (ibid., 265–66.)

117.   Genette came to the category of amplification when he considered Saint-Amant's *Moyse sauvé* (1653), which "amplifies into 6,000 lines the few lines devoted in Genesis (sic) to the exposure of the child Moses" (ibid., 264).

118.   Ibid., 264–65.

119.   Ibid., 266.

120.   Mann, *Joseph and His Brothers*, 983.

121.   Genette, *Palimpsestes*, 267.

122.   Mann states that in the volume *Joseph in Egypt*, he attempts to answer the question *Why?* Most notably, Why does Mrs. Potiphar attempt to seduce Joseph, and Why does he rebuff her? (ibid., 325).

In this case at least, the approach—amplification—becomes bound up in genre. *Joseph and His Brothers* is ostensibly a comic work;[125] the "outward characteristics of humor here are an affectation of official pompousness and the constant pastiche of biblical turns of phrase and the formulaic style,"[126] all of which demand and make for the growth of the text. The amplification allows the comic reversals to take place; the shift in form allows for a shift in meaning.[127] Once again, approach and stance are interrelated.

Genette's last type of "purely formal transposition" is *transmodalization*, alteration of the mode of presentation of the hypotext,[128] which he distinguishes from change of genre. Fiction's two modes are narrative and dramatic. Modal shifts may be intermodal ("involving a shift from one mode to another"[129]) or intramodal ("involving changes within the internal function of the mode"[130]). The potential transformations of the dramatic mode are relatively limited: a writer can excise vestigial remnants of narrativity (i.e. cut out the chorus); redistribute dramatic discourse (give or take lines from pre-existing characters); shift the spotlight (relegate certain scenes to the wings); or reset the scene (introduce flapper costumes in a Shakespeare production).[131] The narrative

---

123.   The working with the motivations of an extant character can include *overmotivation* (extending personal motives to a broader political or historical framework), *demotivation* (as in Wilde's *Salomé*, which in its shifting form from novel to play removes the inner lives given to the characters by Flaubert in his *Herodias*), or *transmotivation* (where the motive known in the hypotext is replaced by another. Jacob, in Anita Diamant's *The Red Tent*, does not toil all those years for his beloved wife, as the Bible tells us he does, but with the specifically goal of becoming rich and powerful).

124.   Even to God.

125.   Exhibiting, Genette contends, "Thomas Mann's well-known—and misunderstood—humor, which spares no one: neither his hero, who never loses his seductive charm or self-satisfaction; nor the hero's father, Jacob the Patriarch, shown as wily, sectarian, and always standing upon formality; nor even...the Supreme Power; nor, of course, his own source, who otherwise would be nothing but a vulgar ironist" (Genette, *Palimpsestes*, 268).

126.   Ibid., 268.

127.   As he later notes, "no great merit has been involved in stating, and no great effort in verifying, the plain fact that there is no such thing as an *innocent* transposition: i.e., one that does not in one way or another alter the meaning of its hypotext" (ibid., 294).

128.   Ibid., 277.

129.   Ibid.

130.   Ibid.

131.   Ibid., 285.

mode has greater potential for alterations: Genette lists among them transformation of temporal order;[132] of duration and frequency;[133] of mood/distance;[134] and of mood/perspective.

This last is the most significant for Genette. Here the hypertext modifies the hypotext's point of view, or what the French call its *"focalisation."* A *transfocalization*, then, would be the shifting from one character's point of view to another's—a *Dr. Bovary* told through Charles's, rather than Emma's, eyes, for instance.[135] A *defocalization* would be the removal of overt perspective—a *Moby Dick* that begins "Call him Ishmael." Most significant for our consideration of retellings of biblical stories would be simple *focalization*, the giving of an evident perspective to a non-focalized work.[136] While the Bible is relayed by an omniscient narrator, many retellings offer the account or perspective of a specific character.[137]

Genette takes his reader through a tremendous number of potential permutations of the text. His task, however, is not yet finished. To see the formal ways a hypotext may be transposed is to address only in part the question of the hypertext. He admits:

> True enough, the semantic alterations entailed by translation, versification, and most of the "formal" transpositions we have just been discussing generally result from unintended distortions inherent in those procedures, rather than any deliberate purpose. The sole aim of a translator, a versifier, or the author of a summary is to say "the same thing" as the hypotext in another language, in verse, or in more compact form; such transpositions

---

132. A shift in narrative agent can allow for "the introduction of anachronies into an initially chronological narrative" (ibid., 286) or the opening of a work in *media res*.

133. Specifically, "the pace of a narrative can be modified at will; summaries can be turned into scenes and vice versa; ellipses or paralipses can be filled in or segments of the narrative deleted; descriptions can be deleted or introduced; singulative segments can be converted into iterative ones and vice versa" (ibid., 286).

134. Wherein the proportion of direct to indirect discourse, or of " 'showing' to 'telling'" is inverted (ibid., 287).

135. Such tellings would also involve, to some extent at least, transmotivation.

136. Genette puns with the term, noting there might also be *vocalizations* in which a speaking 'I' is introduced to an otherwise impersonal account (ibid., 288). The term itself brings forth possibilities of revocalizations, transvocalizations, devocalizations—the emphasis in all being not whose perspective, but whose voice.

137. Such retellings often end up being, in part, paraleptic sequels: the shift in focalizaton "[affords] opportunities of responding to questions left unanswered by gaps in the hypotext, such as, 'While this is happening to X, what is becoming of Y?'" (ibid., 287)—or, "Meanwhile, back on the ark…"

are thus *in principle* purely formal. In the various types of augmentation, however, or in transfocalization, the intent itself appears to be more complex, or more ambitious, since no one can boast of lengthening a text without adding text, and therefore meaning, to it; nor can "the same story" be told from a different viewpoint without altering its psychological resonance at the very least.[138]

And thus, in the latter portions of *Palimpsests*, Genette shifts his attention from the alterations of meaning that come mostly as byproducts of the alteration of form to those transpositions that in their very design alter the meaning of the hypotext.

At this next stage of inquiry, Genette concerns himself with "thematic transposition in its own right, as it operates in those procedures of which it constitutes the chief intent and dominant effect."[139] In this constituting of effect, the transposition becomes semantic. Most often, semantic transpositions involve a *diegetic* transposition[140] or a *pragmatic*[141] transposition. By the former, Genette intends alteration of "the spatiotemporal world designated by the narrative"; by the latter, "a modification of the events and actions in the plot."[142] The one turns on the story, the other on the world in which the story takes place. Genette cautions that pragmatic transformations "will be constantly subsumed within semantic transformations from which they cannot be dissociated or even distinguished";[143] he nonetheless parses modes and means of both diegetic and pragmatic transformations in turn.

Genette identifies as *homodiegetic transpositions* "all classical tragedies that take up mythological or historical themes, even if they significantly modify those themes";[144] he notes that most maintain signs of diegetic faithfulness—they keep the character's name, nationality, gender,[145] family background, and so on.[146] Conversely, a *heterodiegetic*

138. Ibid., 294.
139. Ibid., 294.
140. Keeping with the grammar of Genette's categories, a *transdiegetic transformation*, then, could be a moving of an ancient work to modern times: the transposed text cannot behave in every way as its predecessor did, and thus its meaning is changed. Herein lies the semantic shift.
141. Which he takes from the Greek *pragma*, "which, in Aristotle and elsewhere, designates any kind of event or action" (Genette, *Palimpsestes*, 461).
142. Ibid., 294.
143. Ibid., 317.
144. Ibid., 297. He counts among these Anouilh's *Antigone* and Mann's *Joseph and His Brothers*.
145. Transsexuation, a mark of heterodiegetic transformation, is most interesting when "a change of sex suffices to upset and sometimes to cast ridicule upon the

transposition involves a change of setting and thereby also of the identity of the characters.[147] A change in nationality, for instance, is always a matter of proximization: "the hypertext transposes the diegesis of its hypotext to bring it up to date and closer to its own audience (in temporal, geographic, or social terms)."[148] In drawing teller and told closer together, the retelling alters the meaning of the telling. Genette notes that heterodiegetic and homodiegetic approaches might seem to be incompatible, as the first "emphasizes the thematic analogy between its plot and that of its hypotext ('my hero is not Robinson [Crusoe], but you will see that he goes through a very similar adventure')" while the second "emphasizes its own freedom of thematic interpretation ('I am rewriting the story of Robinson after so many others, but let there be no mistake: I am giving it an entirely new meaning')."[149] Despite their different attitudes toward the text, however, both heterodiegetic and homodiegetic transpositions enact semantic shifts. Likewise, pragmatic transformations[150] (changes in the course of the action and "its material support"[151]) may also constitute semantic transformations.[152] Broadly speaking, however, "diegetic transformation...might be said to bear on the questions *Where?* and *When?* and pragmatic transformation on the questions *What?* and *How?*"[153]

Central also to the question of meaning is what Genette terms *valuation*—"the operation of an axiological nature bearing on the value that is implicitly or explicitly assigned to an action or group of actions: namely, the sequence of actions, attitudes, and feelings that constitutes a 'character.'"[154] As one might by now expect, valuation takes any number of forms. The *revaluation* of a character involves "investing him or her—by way of pragmatic or psychological transformation—with a more significant and/or more 'attractive' role in the value system of the hypertext

whole thematic intent of the hypotext," says Genette (ibid., 298). This is the case with the masculinization of Pamela in *Joseph Andrews*.

146.   Ibid., 297.

147.   In Dublin, Ulysses becomes Leopold Bloom.

148.   Genette, *Palimpsestes*, 304.

149.   Ibid., 310.

150.   Which include de-, trans- and remotivation and other activities introduced as thematic transformations.

151.   Genette, *Palimpsestes*, 311.

152.   The interesting question of Pierre Menard's *Don Quixote*—which I will discuss in some detail in the fourth chapter—creeps in here as well: can a hypertext enact a semantic transposition without altering the hypotext at all?

153.   Ibid., 464.

154.   Ibid., 343.

than was the case in the hypotext."[155] This can transpire in varying degrees. *Secondary revaluation* is adding benefit (in the value scale of the hypotext) to a less prominent figure in a work; it usually involves foregrounding a lesser character.[156] *Primary revaluation* is the revaluation of the hero and his deeds, but—as the hero already has prominence in the hypotext—here the increased valuation is of his merit or symbolic value rather than of his presence in the story.[157] The inverse, of course, is *devaluation*, the "demystification"[158] or even debasing of a character.[159] *Transvaluation*, finally, is the "double movement of devaluation and (counter)valuation bearing on the same characters":[160] in reworkings of classics this can entail stripping the hero of his heroic stature, but instilling him with a new value (as generally measured in a more common, human context.)

As is evident, in *Palimpsests*, Genette introduces and explains a litany of terms that allow us to think and speak about the relationships between telling and retelling. This summary offers a glimpse at the full spectrum of Genette's undertaking. What becomes clear, when the terms are referenced in rapid succession, is that he is writing a whole new language. Consequently, his work has the potential either to illuminate or to overwhelm. On the one hand, one has the sense that there is no aspect of retelling that Genette has not named. On the other, one finds daunting the idea of committing this formidable lexicon to memory. Moreover, if the aim of our investigation is not merely to be able to think in a sophisticated manner about retelling, but to be able speak with others about it also, the broad sweep of Genette's vocabulary seems (paradoxically) to be restrictive. Are his terms ones that might realistically be picked up (and passed on) by those who have not immersed themselves in his thorough, thoughtful tome? Might we be best served by culling some of his terms as part of a cluster of words that speak to the questions of retelling? We might better be able to answer these questions after we have seen how Genette's taxonomy might work for us. The final section of this chapter will apply the language we have encountered so far to literature that falls under our purview.

155. Ibid.
156. Ibid., 344–50.
157. Ibid., 350.
158. Ibid., 354.
159. Genette cites Fielding's *Shamela*, which sought to refute Richardson's *Pamela* (ibid.).
160. Ibid., 367.

Naming the Animals

Bakhtin rejects the idea that we can be like Adam, and name the world afresh. Words come to us already used; they have all been written and spoken previously. They have attached to them the meanings and connotations others have appended to them. All the same, the idea of naming —specifically, of being the primeval namer—has a certain appeal. It is a notion that has captured the imagination of numerous writers. What follows is a collection of six recent poems,[161] all hypertexts of a common hypotext. The text is Genesis, of course—a text about the impulse to name things. We will test out the new words and terms we have just encountered as we consider poems that return to the biblical account of Adam's naming of the animals:

> The LORD God said, "It is not good for man to be alone; I will make a fitting helper for him." And the LORD God formed out of the earth all the wild beasts and all the birds of the sky, and brought them to the man to see what he would call them; and whatever the man called each living creature, that would be its name. (Gen. 2:18–20)

We will use Genette's taxonomy to label and describe each poem, thus offering a glimpse of how his terminology might be put to use in the naming of beasts. I will be selective in using Genette's vocabulary: once I note that the initial poem evidences a paratext (the title), I will not make the same observation about the others. I will use his taxonomy only insofar as it allows us to talk more specifically and intelligently about a poem, or allows us to speak about two poems together. The latter is particularly important for, as I stated at the outset, there is a dearth of literature that puts hypertexts in dialogue with one another, that allows us to think broadly about the afterlife of a hypotext.

Three transtextual relationships are immediately evident in our first poem, John Hollander's "Adam's Task" (1971). Like most poems, it opens with paratext: the title, which stands in relation to the text of the poem in its announcing the subject. The introduction of a partial verse from Genesis (which is ascribed) is intertext (in Genette's narrowly defined sense)—one text's explicit use of another. With the citation, and the quotation marks designating the beginning and end of the intertext, this is clearly a quotation. Like the title, it indicates subject, but more it makes evident what kind of hypertext will ensue. The quoted text is merely 21 words long; the poem itself is 110. The hypertext, the third of the transtexts, is an augmentation, then:

---

161. They were written between 1971 and 2002, and appear in chronological order.

Adam's Task

"And Adam gave names to all cattle, and to the fowl
of the air, and to every beast of the field..." (Gen. 2:20)

> Thou, paw-paw-paw; thou, glurd; thou, spotted
> Glurd; thou, whitestap, lurching through
> The high-grown brush; thou, pliant-footed,
> Implex; thou, awagabu.
>
> Every burrower, each flier
> Came for the name he had to give:
> Gay, first work, ever to be prior,
> Not yet sunk to primitive.
>
> Thou, verdle; thou, McFleery's pomma;
> Thou, thou; thou—three types of grawl;
> Thou, flisket; thou, kabasch; thou, comma-
> Eared mashawk; thou, all; thou, all.
>
> Were, in a fire of becoming,
> Laboring to be burned away
> Then work, half-measuring, half-humming,
> Would be as serious as play.
>
> Thou, pambler; thou, rivarn; thou, greater
> Wherret, and thou, lesser one;
> Thou, sproal; thou, zant; thou, lily-eater.
> Naming's over. Day is done.

The poem consists of dialogue, without introductory material (beyond the intertext) which makes it a sermocination. The shift to a telling by Adam also makes it a transfocalization. Additionally, it is a transvocalization: the omnipresent, omniscient narrator has disappeared and is replaced by an implied *I*. Given its attention to detail—the Bible has Adam giving names to "all cattle, and to the fowl of the air, and to every beast of the field," but Hollander has him naming the paw-paw-paw and the glurd (spotted and otherwise), the sproal, the zant, the lily-eater each—the mode of expansion could conceivably be described as a definitional transformation.

All of which brings us closer to an understanding of the poem, of the ways that it works. What the vocabulary of transformation does not allow us to do is discuss what this poem thinks of the biblical text.[162] The value of Hollander's Adam is slightly different from that of the Bible's;

---

162.   No, texts do not think; the authors of texts do. But I have already addressed the difficulty of the author, and so take recourse to the text for the case of simplicity.

this is, to an extent, a secondary revaluation, in which the lesser character of Adam—who is supporting actor to Genesis's God—becomes not only the subject and full focus of the story, but a very echo of God. He speaks a new creation into being; he punctuates the days with his declarations. Does the poem replace the biblical account? Hardly. It coexists with the verses in Genesis, making them more immediate, less remote. And in expanding upon them, it lightens them, without becoming parody or caricature. Here Genette's moods are useful: the once serious naming of the animals has become playful. But Genette's moods are linked to generic transformations. Is the poem a pastiche, then, Genette's "imitation without satiric intent"? Not precisely, because this hypertext is less imitation than expansion, a category that seems to stand separate from generic qualifiers.

By contrast, Anthony Hecht's "Naming the Animals"[163] (1989) more than lightens the Genesis story: it renders it comic. This is not the same as satirizing it, however, which points again to the limits of Genette's extensive taxonomy. First, how do we communicate that something serious has been made funny, and second, how do we communicate that a switch in mood to humorous does not necessarily signal a dismissal of the serious original?

> *Naming the Animals*
> Having commanded Adam to bestow
> Names upon all the creatures, God withdrew
> To empyrean palaces of blue
> That warm and windless morning long ago,
> And seemed to take no notice of the vexed
> Look on the young man's face as he took thought
> Of all the miracles the Lord had wrought,
> Now to be labeled, dubbed, yclept, indexed.
>
> Before an addled mind and puddled brow,
> The feathered nation and the finny prey
> Passed by; there went biped and quadruped.
> Adam looked forth with bottomless dismay
> Into the tragic eyes of his first cow,
> And shyly ventured, "Thou shalt be called 'Fred.'"

Using Genette's vocabulary, we can communicate a fair amount about the poem. To begin, it is a transmodalization: the narrative becomes poetic. The already defocalized account becomes even more defocalized

---

163. Anthony Hecht, "Naming the Animals," in *Chapters into Verse*, Vol. 1 (ed. Robert Atwan and Laurance Weider; New York: Oxford University Press, 1997), 25.

here the omniscient narrator becomes more omniscient, this is a hypotyposis[164] that provides details about the whereabouts and perceptions of
God that are far more informed (and intimate) than those we find in
Genesis. In this respect "Naming the Animals" is an amplification, both
in terms of its adding to the text and by virtue of its adding the author's
own themes to the original. It is the insertion of the new themes —the
wrenching twist of the punch line at the end—that is difficult to communicate. What makes the poem work is its shift in style: the simplicity
of the biblical account is replaced by a specificity and preciosity that
make fun of themselves, not the biblical account. The conclusion of the
poem, the ridiculousness of Adam's declaration—"Thou shalt be called,
'Fred'"—undermines the weight of the new poem, not the weight of its
hypotext. The poem is a joke, but the joke is on the poem and its reader,
somewhat on its new Adam, not on the Bible. Which thus removes it
from the generic categories Genette puts forth—this is not satire, or
caricature, or pastiche—and leaves us asking what precisely it *is*. How
do we describe its stance?

It is somewhat easier to label the stance of Susan Donnelly's take on
Gen 2:20. Her "Eve Names the Animals" (1985)[165] is a secondary
figuration and transvocalization as well, with Eve gaining prominence
and voice. This Eve's naming of the animals is a response to Adam's, a
corrective to a naming by a man who, Eve swears, "never knew
animals." His designations do not fit their objects: "Words he lined up
according to size," oblivious, it seems, to their reality. He names her a
name that sticks her to him, an effort to "comfort [her], for not being
him." To herself, however, she is not that name but "palomino / raven /
fox." Her words capture her world: "*dove*, / a burrowing, blind creature";
"pickerel / hopped on branches above [her/]… / running up to lick [her]
hand." Her words she strings together "by their stems and [wears] them /
as garlands…" In the morning, the garland stems are wilted, but this not
troubling: this Eve is quick to assert "I liked change."

In its expansion of the biblical story, its adding of detail (expansion
and amplification) the poem puts distance between the reader and the
Bible: it inserts a voice that detracts from the biblical one. The authority
of Adam is undermined: "I swear that man never knew animals," asserts
Eve, who knows animals intimately. They hop on the branches above
her, accompany her everywhere, go looking for her. And in her undermining Adam's authority, Eve (with Donnelly) undermines the authority

164. "Vivid description of a scene."
165. Susan Donnelly, "Eve Names the Animals," in *Modern Poems on the Bible*
(ed. David Curzon; Philadelphia: Jewish Publication Society, 1994), 62–63.

of language itself: the names given to the animals are misnames. The alternative to names that do not apply, to names that stick one being to another, is names that may be strung together into garlands that wither and need to be changed. The fixed language—the canon—is replaced with a transient one; the voice of authority is replaced with the voice of authorial arbitrariness. The poem is a continuation, certainly, but it is one of Genette's unfaithful continuations: a refutation.

The inscription of this story in a woman's voice does not always undermine or override the biblical version. We presume it is a woman, a mother of a young boy, who speaks "The Gift," Louise Glück's 1996 poem about the naming of the animals.[166] She presents herself to the Lord, tells him, "I have a son." This child "likes to stand at the screen door, calling / oggie, oggie." She wonders, when a dog does stop or come up the walk, whether the boy might believe he caused the dog to act:

> *The Gift*
> Lord, You may not recognize me
> speaking for someone else,
> I have a son. He is
> so little, so ignorant,
> He likes to stand
> at the serene door, calling
> *oggie, oggie*, entering
> language, and sometimes
> a dog will stop and come up
> the walk, perhaps
> accidentally. May he believe
> this is not an accident?
> At the screen
> welcoming each beast
> in love's name, Your emissary.

As in Genesis, the namer of the animals is the male, but unlike in Genesis, the version given is the female's. The speaker recognizes the foreignness of her own (female) voice; she entreats, "Lord, You may not recognize me speaking for someone else." How do we understand this? Has she otherwise spoken only for herself, or is she usually the other for whom someone else speaks? Here, she is the one who classifies the other. She names the Lord; she identifies the child as her son; she translates "oggie" as dog. If she is Eve, she is the possessor of knowledge—which, given her instigating the eating of the fruit of the forbidden tree,

---

166. Louise Glück, "The Gift," in *First Four Books of Poems—Louise Glück* (San Francisco: HarperCollins, 1996), 144.

ought not to surprise us. The child, by contrast, is "so little, so ignorant." His ignorance, however, is celebrated: he is the innocent entering into language like a new Adam; he welcomes each beast in the spirit of the Lord who shaped him.

The relationship between the poem and the biblical text is primarily allusive (not one of Genette's terms.) The invocation of the Lord draws us toward the Bible; the naming of the beasts points us to Genesis. In Genette's terminology, however, this is a diegetic transposition—and, by extension, a semantic transposition. The poem takes us out of the spatio-temporal world of the Bible; it transforms the biblical characters. What else might we say of Donnelly's poem? That it is a secondary revalua-tion, a transfocalization, and a transvocalization. All these transforma-tions and transpositions raise the question of stance, which is quite dis-tinct in this poem. Donnelly's poem takes issue with the biblical account. In its grappling with Gen 2:20, "Eve Names the Animals" demands to be read alongside the biblical account (and demands too that the biblical text not be read independent of it). By contrast, "The Gift" gently points the careful reader back to Genesis. Glück's allusions are veiled, and her poem can be read independently of Genesis—in fact, it can be under-stood to be complete apart from Genesis. Moreover, Genesis remains viable without the modern work.

In "Linnaeus,"[167] a poem, like Glück's, set in a post-biblical world populated by non-biblical characters, Czeslaw Milosz makes direct reference to Adam's naming of the animals:

Linnaeus

He was born in 1707 at 1:00 A.M. on May 23rd, when spring was in beautiful bloom, and cuckoo had just announced the coming of summer.
                                                    from Linnaeus's biography

Green young leaves. A cuckoo. Echo.
To get up at four in the morning, to run to the river
Which streams, smooth under the rising sun.
A gate is open, horses are running,
Swallows dart, fish splash. And did we not begin with an overabundance
Of glitterings and calls, pursuits and trills?
We lived every day in hymn, in rapture,
Not finding words, just feeling it is too much.

167. Czeslaw Milosz, "Linnaeus," in *Provinces: Poems 1987–1991* (trans. Robert Hass; Manchester: Carcanet Press, 1993), 6.

He was one of us, happy in our childhood.
He would set out with his botanic box
To gather and to name, like Adam in the garden
Who did not finish his task, expelled too early.
Nature has been waiting for names ever since:
On the meadows near Uppsala, white, at dusk
Platantbera is fragrant, he called it *bifolia.*
Turdus sings in a spruce thicket, but is it *musicus?*
That must remain the subject of dispute.
And the botanist laughed at a little perky bird
For ever Troglodytes troglodytes L.

He arranged three kingdoms into a system.
Animale. Vegetale. Minerale.
He divided: classes, orders, genuses, species.
"How manifold are thy works, O Jehovah!"
He would sing with the psalmist. Rank, number, symmetry
Are everywhere, praised with a clavecin
And violin, scanned in Latin hexameter.

We have since had the language of marvel: atlases.
A tulip with its dark, mysterious inside,
Anemones of Lapland, a water lily, an iris
Faithfully portrayed by a scrupulous brush.
And a bird in foliage, russet and dark blue,
Never flies off, retained
On the page with an ornate double inscription.

We were grateful to him. In the evenings at home
We contemplated colors under a kerosene lamp
With a green shade. And what there, on earth.
Was unattainable, over much, passing away, perishing,
Here we could love, safe from loss.

May his household, orangery, the garden
In which he grew plants from overseas
Be blessed with peace and well-being.
To China and Japan, America, Australia,
Sailing-ships carried his disciples;
They would bring back gifts: seeds and drawings.
And I, who in this bitter age deprived of harmony
Am a wanderer and a gatherer of visible forms,
Envying them, bring to him my tribute—
A verse imitating the classical ode.

Here the hypertext engages the hypotext explicitly. Milosz depicts
Linnaeus, the great taxonomist, as a child completing the task that Adam
began but could not finish: happy in his childhood, "he would set out
with his botanic box / to gather and name, like Adam in the garden / who

did not finish his task, expelled too early." It was a necessary task: since Adam left off, "nature [had] been waiting for names ever since." Linnaeus took up the charge, arranging kingdoms into a system, dividing the world into "classes, orders, genuses, species." Whereas the other children "lived every day in hymn, in rapture, / not finding words," Linnaeus's songs had words. He would sing the praises written by the psalmist and add to them his own language of marvel: "rank, number, symmetry."

Milosz's linking of Linnaeus to Adam is multifaceted. The two figures begin life innocent, "happy in [their] childhood." Like Adam, Linnaeus is the namer of animals; he also has dominion over them, arranging them into "classes, orders, genuses, species," pressing them "on the page with an ornate double inscription." The bitter age after him is "deprived of harmony"; the generation that follows is condemned to wander.[168] Milosz's Linnaeus is like a new Adam, too:[169] his "disciples" travel the earth, going "to China and Japan, America, Australia"; he plants a garden "blessed with peace and well-being." The shifting of the characteristics of Adam(s) onto Linnaeus is a heterodiegetic transposition.

In terms of form, the poem is a self-described imitation. The speaker of the poem, a self-professed "wanderer and gatherer of visible forms" brings to Linnaeus this tribute, "a verse imitating the classical ode." The archetypal ode being imitated is the psalm, particularly Ps 104, which contains the intertext "How manifold are Thy works, O Jehovah!" That psalm is a litany of the wonders of creation; this psalm is a litany of the wonders of Linnaeus's cataloguing of creation. The "tribute," then, is twofold: Milosz's poem is a holding up of the scientist and the Bible both. The taxonomies of Adam and Linnaeus are exulted, and so by extension is the very creation both figures seek to name. Despite its apparent distance from the Bible, then—its resetting in a new time and a very different space, its valorizing the scientist—the poem is an affirmation of God's creation.

Equally affirming, less removed from Genesis is Nathaniel Tarn's 2002 poem "Before the Snake." It is a poem set now (thus a diegetic transposition), but also never. The setting of the poem recalls the moments just after creation: two people sit, "facing the sun, eyes closed,"

---

168.   Cf. Gen 4:13–14: "Cain said to the Lord, 'My punishment is too great to bear! Since you have banished me this day from the soil, and I must avoid your presence and become a restless wanderer on earth—anyone who meets me may kill me." Linnaeus, unlike Milosz's Cain-like narrator, is hardly banished from the soil; rather, in his planting of his garden, he embraces it.

169.   "It is in this sense that scripture says, 'The first man, Adam, became a living creature,' whereas the last Adam has become a life-giving spirit" (1 Cor 15:45).

listening to the birds fluttering, "singing in this luminous fall." The world of the characters is filled with elements formed in Gen 1—sun, space, birds, trees. The people of the poem are a new Adam and a new Eve, "so alone in this garden desert." They are "[f]orgotten, but remembering / ourselves as no one will ever remember us." The world of this poem is a new paradise: hesitantly, the speaker of the poem wonders whether this could in fact be so. "I can tell you, I think this may be / Eden." Resolutely, he recognizes it. "I think it is."

Although this is Eden, it is a different Eden. It is Eden transposed, and the glimmer of other people is there too: "beyond the birds there are persons carrying their names like great weights." Whatever the man called each living thing, that would be its name. The permanence of this fact is difficult to contemplate: as Tarn marvels, "Just think: / carrying X your whole life, or Y, or Z. / Carrying all that A and B and C around with you, / having to be A all the time, B, or C." But to be named something may not in fact be the same as to be it. There is the hope of name-lessness: "here you can / be the sun, the pine, the bird. You can be the / breathing." To be able to be self-name, to misname as the young son does, or to rename, like the garlanded Eve, is somehow liberating. For as both Louise Glück and Susan Donnelly's poems tell us, names are not only constricting, they may also be misleading. To name something is not always to reveal what it is. Genette's taxonomy gets us closer to precision, but not all the way there.

Hypertexts Generate Hypertexts

Beginning with the Renaissance understandings of influence and invention and arriving at Genette's vocabulary, we have come closer to the descriptive words for which we have been searching than we had by adopting the looser postmodern theoretical construct intertextuality, so often offered up as a response to the question, "How do we describe one text's use of another?"

Genette's extensive investigation is propelled by a sense that there is something more to a text that makes direct (or indirect) recalls to a foretext. At the close of *Palimpsests*, he proclaims: "Let me simply say that the art of 'making new things out of old' has the merit, at least, of generating more complex and savory objects than those that are 'made on purpose'; a new function is superimposed upon and interwoven with an older structure, and the dissonance between these two concurrent elements imparts its flavor to the resulting whole."[170] In the dissonance

170. Genette, *Palimpsestes*, 398.

between the telling and the retelling (to return us to our familiar words), lies the savor/ flavor of reading. Or, as he concludes, "one who really loves texts must wish from time to time to love (at least) two together."[171] The pleasure of the text lies in the relational reading, that *palimpsestuous* activity.

Genette goes on to assert that "the pleasure of hypertext is also a *game*... Every form of hypertextuality entails some kind of game, inherent in the very practice of reusing existing structures; at bottom, whatever its urgency, tinkering[172] is always a game, at least to the extent that it processes and uses an object in an unforeseen, unprogrammed, and thus 'unlawful' manner—true play[173] always entails some degree of perversion."[174] The retellings with which we concern ourselves are not merely perversions, however—some are inversions, some subversions. We can imagine an extended vocabulary, not dissimilar from Genette's, in which there would also be reversions and conversions, extroversions and introversions.

The taxonomy proffered in *Palimpsests* is extensive, but it remains incomplete. It tells us the very many ways that one text might approach another, but it offers little about what happens to the hypotext once it gives rise to the hypertext.[175] This is the question of stance. Genette verges on it when he talks about genres—the move to parody or travesty, for instance. But he does not ultimately address the attitude of the hypertext to the hypotext. Despite his attention to detail, Genette only brings us *closer* to the missing taxonomy; he does not provide it. He offers thoughts on the two axes we are calling approach and stance, yet does not pinpoint the intersections of these. He asks what one text does to another, but not what becomes of the text done to. Is it exalted? Exterminated? Revered? Rejected? Rendered dated? Obsolete? Timeless?

171.   Ibid., 399.
172.   French *bricolage*, as with Claude Lévi-Strauss. See Genette, *Palimpsestes* (original French edition), 452.
173.   That a text plays does not mean that it is enjoyable: "texts that are 'purely playful' in their purpose are not always the most captivating or even the most amusing. Premeditated and organized games (those that are played with a deliberate 'purpose') sometimes induce a deadly boredom, and the best jokes are often unintentional. The hypertext at its best is an indeterminate compound, unpredictable in its specifics, or seriousness and playfulness...of intellectual achievement and entertainment" (Genette, *Palimpsestes*, 400).
174.   Ibid., 399.
175.   Possible exceptions are his categories of complement, supplement, murderous continuation and suppression.

As I noted at the outset of our discussion, Genette is not working with a canon—or rather, he is working with an un-canon of his own making, derived from his "hasty and sketchy reading" of some un(der)determined "Dictionary of Works from All Times and All Countries."[176] He asserts that literature is prolific and self-perpetuating: "hypertexts, as it is well known, generate hypertexts"[177] to the point that there are very few hypotexts *per se*. Rather, the hypertexts become hypotexts; interpretation becomes scripture.

We are engaged in a discussion about canon, about the relationship between scripture and interpretation. How do text and tradition relate to one another? In what way does the interpretive afterlife have an impact on the life of the canon? Where does text leave off and interpretation begin? When does interpretation become canon? Commentary literature? The retelling simply a telling? These questions are linked to the ones that Genette's thorough and admirable taxonomy does not quite address. These are questions that will be most satisfactorily explored when we treat translation theory, but to some degree they will also be broached as we move to Jewish hermeneutics and a further discussion of the problems of telling and retelling, scripture and interpretation, canon and commentary.

176.   Genette, *Palimpsestes*, 399.
177.   Ibid., 373.

Chapter 5

IS IT IN HEAVEN?

Midrash and Literature

There is considerable precedent for offering up the language of midrash, rabbinic interpretation, in what is, for the most part, a literary-theoretical investigation. As we will see, literary theorists Jacques Derrida and Geoffrey Hartman, among others, have been drawn to midrash, to its apparent openness, its tolerance of multiple meanings, and its focus on the interaction between reader and text. Jewish literary critic David Jacobson has used the term midrash to "refer to the Jewish tradition of the interpretive retelling of biblical stories that began within the Bible itself, developed in the rabbinic periods and...has continued to the present."[1] Critic and poet David Curzon has even put the term forth to describe retellings of biblical stories by non-Jewish writers.

To determine to what degree these applications of the term actually reflect midrash, we begin this chapter with an examination of traditional rabbinic midrash.[2] How did it work? What was its approach? What was it doing? What was its stance? In exploring the nature of midrash, we will look specifically at midrash about the binding of Isaac (Gen 22). We will next consider the ways in which the vocabulary of midrash has already entered the field of literary studies, weighing the applicability of what is ultimately a theological construct (midrash) for describing what is generally a secular enterprise (literature).[3] We will look first at the intersection of midrash and literary theory, detailing how the two fields came to be in conversation, and assessing the ways that literary theory has understood midrash in its own image. We will ultimately find that in championing

---

1. Jacobson, *Modern Midrash*, 1.
2. Particularly as read through the lens of contemporary academics, including: Isaac Heinemann, Judah Goldin, David Weiss Halivni, James Kugel.
3. Susan Handelman, David Stern, Jacques Derrida, Roland Barthes, and Jorge Luis Borges are among those who have put midrash in dialogue with literary theory.

midrash, literary theory has distorted the concept. Likewise, when we consider the way that midrash has entered the vocabulary of readers and critics of popular literature, we will find that it has also been transformed.

Although midrash has entered the fields of literary theory and criticism, its definition has been (unrecognizably?) redefined and expanded. Thus I will ultimately reject the ways that midrash has so far been upheld as illuminating literature. In the chapter that follows this one, however, I will go beyond the broad term midrash and introduce us to some of its specifics (its own vocabulary), ultimately using the *middot*—rabbinic principles of exegesis—to explore whether there is in midrashic hermeneutics a potential language for describing non-rabbinic biblical retellings. Both Chapters 5 and 6 will be organized around the story of the binding of Isaac, forging a link between them.

What is Midrash?
The Two Faces of Midrash: Halakhah and Aggadah

Midrash, from the Hebrew *darash*—"to search or investigate"—is the ancient Hebrew word for interpretation. While it has come to reflect a specific mode of Jewish exegesis, as distinct from, say, *pesher* (interpretation that consists of an explicit citation of scripture followed by an explanation) or *piyyut* (a liturgical poem that may expand upon a scriptural verse), its original meaning was simply "interpretation." For the rabbis of antiquity, interpretation was not merely an entirely intellectual or even entirely theological pursuit. Rather, argues Gerald Bruns, "we ought to think of midrash as a form of life (in Wittgenstein's sense) rather than simply as a form of exegesis (in the technical sense); midrash is concerned with practice and action as well as with (what we think of as) the form and meaning of texts."[4] We can parse Bruns's assessment in such a way that it reflects the two categories into which midrash is customarily divided: Halakhah and Aggadah. The former, from the Hebrew *halakh*—"to go"—is legal, dealing with what Bruns calls "practice and action." The latter, from the Hebrew *l'haggid*—"to say or to tell"—is literary, treating "form and meaning."

Also reflecting a binary understanding, Judah Goldin considers midrash in literary and somewhat romantic terms. For him, "the two parts, Halakhah and Aggadah, are an articulation of the fundamental, universal,

---

4. Gerald Bruns, *Hermeneutics Ancient and Modern* (New Haven: Yale University Press, 1992), 104.

interminable combat of obedience and individual conceit."[5] Jacob Neusner is somewhat less poetic in his defining their respective roles, but nonetheless views the two modes as reflecting opposing and complementary aspects of Jewish life and thought. Neusner's understanding is useful for thinking about how the disparate forms work in tandem. In his description, neither Halakhah nor Aggadah is ever

> subject to confusion with the other. But, both in theory and in practice, the Aggadah and the Halakhah work out of the logic of a single generative conviction. It is that one and only one God is engaged in creating the world and sustaining a perfect world order based on justice and Israel shares in this task.[6]

The two forms are bound by a common principle, a notion not only of God as creator and creator of Israel, but of God as maintainer of justice and Israel as his adjutant in that role. From this position of co-sustainer, "the generations of loyal practitioners of Judaism, from antiquity forward, have received the Halakhah and the Aggadah as a single, seamless statement."[7] According to Neusner, the way that the two types of exegesis, so different in style and scope, form a "seamless statement" is by addressing two distinct facets of the life of Israel. The Aggadah is, to his mind, exterior; the Halakhah interior. Or, as he contends, "the Aggadah speaks in large and general terms to the world at large, while the Halakhah uses small and particular rules to speak to the everyday concern of ordinary Israelites."[8] The first retells the story of Israel, situating it among the nations; the second treats Israel "in its household, in the land, in eternity, out of all relationship with the nations but in a timeless realm of unchanging perfection or aspiring thereto."[9] The Aggadah, which faces outward to all humanity, comprises the exteriorities of Israel in her relationship to God; the Halakhah—which concerns itself with the relationships of Israel with God, of Israelites with one another, and of "the interior life of the individual Israelite household on its own with God"[10]—its interiorities.

What Goldin and Neusner do not make explicit in their finessing of the categories is the generic division between the two forms. Aggadah,

5. Judah Goldin, "The Freedom and Restraint of Aggadah," in Budick and Hartman, eds., *Midrash and Literature*, 69.

6. Jacob Neusner, *The Halakhah and the Aggadah: Theological Perspectives* (Lanham, Md.: University Press of America, 2001), vii.

7. Ibid., vii.

8. Ibid., 1.

9. Ibid., 1.

10. Ibid., 3.

which may take the form of homilies, parables, puns, fables, stories is, as Heinemann describes, all the "material in the Talmudic-midrashic literature which does not fall into Jewish law."[11] In light of the dichotomies outlined above, we can hone the distinction somewhat: Aggadah—the exterior, rebellious form—is lore; Halakhah—the interior, obedient form—is law. We must acknowledge that to a considerable degree the two forms set out to accomplish different things. That said, and the dichotomies and affinities between the two now established, we must also be aware that the goals of the two are not entirely distinct. Due to Halakhah and Aggadah's readily discernable styles and subject matters, readers frequently divorce the two interpretive modes from one another. They are, however, inextricably bound up together. Joseph Heinemann argues that there is a close link between Aggadah and Halakhah; they were, after all, created by the same sages. He notes that the two "coexist intimately in the halakhic midrashim"[12] where the rabbis used Aggadah to make their halakhic discussion interesting to their audiences. While Heinemann concedes that "there is a great distance between the two [forms]"—a chasm he illustrates by calling the Halakhah the bread and the Aggadah the wine[13]—he insists nonetheless that "aggadic thinking nourishes the Halakhah, and the Halakhah gives the Aggadah permanency by evolving from it legal norms."[14] The two modes go hand in hand.

In an intriguing appendix to *Peshat and Derash: Plain and Applied Meaning in Rabbinic Exegesis*, David Weiss Halivni describes the interpretive activity involved in both halakhic and aggadic midrash:

> Midrash Halakhah's cues overwhelmingly come from within the text. The text is the principal guide in determining what constitutes proper Halakhah, the mode of behavior. The reader's (the interpreter's) role is much more limited. He interacts with the text, but what he brings to bear on it is much more impoverished. The hermeneutic principles at his disposal are fewer in number; his maneuverability is restricted. The halakhist confronts the text; the aggadist joins the text. The halakhist submits to the text; the aggadist plays with it, as it were. The aggadist cooperates with the text (actively); the halakhist listens to the text (often passively)—except when reading into the text. Then, he is a determiner, a sharer in the making of

---

11. Joseph Heinemann, "The Nature of the Aggadah," in Budick and Hartman, eds., *Midrash and Literature*, 42.

12. Ibid., 50.

13. A point echoed by Judah Goldin, who refers to Halakhah as "the staff of life and its study ensures a place in the world to come" ("The Freedom and Restraint of Aggadah," 68).

14. Heinemann, "The Nature of the Aggadah," 51.

the law; a co-author. He interacts with the text as an equal. What he brings to bear is weighty, decisive. He is not a passive recipient but an active begetter—a creator. In religious language, he is a partner in the divine creation of the law.[15]

What we see throughout this description of approach is the profound level of engagement both the halakhists and the aggadists had with the text. What drove all ancient Jewish interpretation—halakhic and aggadic both—was a sense of the Bible's ability to communicate continuously with an ever more remote community of readers.

The Nature of the Aggadah

When we focus on Halivni's description of the aggadists, as against the halakhists, we cannot but notice how much they manipulated the text. J. Heinemann corroborates Halivni's assessment: "the aggadist could add, deviate from, change or permute the tradition he had received."[16] The sages maneuvered, joined, played, cooperated; their approach was always active. And yet they do not want to be original: "precisely what they seek is to prove that all innovation and invention of their tradition can already be found in the text of the Bible."[17] Through their interpretation, the rabbis elicit new readings that speak in the tradition of the divine text. They seek to reinscribe, not replace, the received divine text.[18] The rabbis clearly do not suffer from Bloom's anxiety of influence. As David Stern notes, they consciously—happily, we might even say—assume the stance of belatedness. They would have seen their interpretive activity, which seems to the modern eye often to read against scripture, as wholly consonant with "holy writ."

The literature resulting from this rabbinic approach is a mixture of stories, legends, parables, and homilies. Many of the sages' stories are fanciful, and most push the limits of the text. (Or, they push what we as

15. David Weiss Halivni, *Peshat and Derash: Plain and Applied Meaning in Rabbinic Exegesis* (New York: Oxford University Press, 1991), 159.

16. Heinemann, "The Nature of the Aggadah," 53.

17. David Stern, *Midrash and Theory: Ancient Jewish Exegesis and Contemporary Literary Studies* (Evanston, Ill.: Northwestern University Press, 1997), 34.

18. Did the rabbis know what they were doing? This is an unanswerable question, but Halivni weighs in: "De facto, the rabbis did give the reader-interpreter great leeway in shaping the meaning of a text. If asked, however, they would admit to little. They would most likely have sided with the opponents of the modern theorists and would have insisted that authorial intention is the sole criterion for true and reliable meaning, especially when that text is the Bible, whose divine authorship was universally accepted" (Halivni, *Peshat and Derash*, 160).

contemporary readers generally given to an understanding of the plain sense would consider the limits of the text.) While the aggadot appear in the various genres just listed, Isaac Heinemann makes a compelling case that they can be divided into two broad generic categories: creative historiography and creative philology.[19] The purposes of the former in midrash are exegetical (clarifying the text) and homiletical (giving it contemporary relevance); the purposes of the latter were to draw out the text's hidden meanings.[20] Heinemann contends that two principles governed both the aggadic and halakhic reading of Torah: one must interpret even the most minute details in scripture and one may explain all parts of the Bible as being simultaneously in dialogue with all other parts of the Bible *and* entirely autonomous.[21]

Addison Wright describes how these two principles play out. Letters, words, verses, and divisions in the Bible "retain an independent significance as well as unlimited possibilities of combination with each other."[22] Consequently, the rabbis occupied themselves endlessly with the letters of words, calculating their numerical values, turning them into acrostics, making anagrams from them. Disassembling and reassembling words yield new words, each with new connotations. At the next lexical level, they rearranged sentences and revocalized verses, which they assigned alternate meanings. Other hermeneutical maneuvers included interpreting entire sections allegorically or in conversation with apparently unrelated sections from elsewhere in the Bible.[23] Decontextualizing and recontextualizing allow—as we have seen—extant phrases or verses to gain new meaning. The canonical text, though fixed, is hardly immutable. The rabbis worked from within the confines of the text to push its boundaries.

In sharp contrast to Halakhah, which governed Jewish life, the Aggadah was frequently received as a lesser literature,[24] a frivolous diversion. We

---

19. Isaac Heinemann, *Darkhei ha-Aggadah* (2d ed.; Jerusalem: Hebrew University Press, 1954).

20. This is more true of the Halakhah, which is largely creative philology. Halakhah also involved deduction from the biblical text; this deduction was based in *middot*, principles of exegesis (which will be discussed later in the chapter.)

21. Heinemann, *Darkhei ha-Aggadah*, 96–101.

22. Addison Wright, *The Literary Genre: Midrash* (Staten Island: Alba House, 1967), 63.

23. Wright, *The Literary Genre*, 63.

24. Goldin traces a history of its reception, noting that from the time of Saadia Gaon through to the modern age, Aggadah has not been held to be fundamental to the Jewish faith. Nachmanides called aggadot "no more binding than the sermons of a bishop" ("The Freedom and Restraint of Aggadah," 59). Goldin traces this suspicion of Aggadah to the rabbinic rule of *ein somkhin al divrei Aggadah*—one may not

can ascribe this view, in some degree at least, to the simultaneous nar-
rowness and openness of aggadic midrash. On the one hand, it focuses
on the minutiae of the biblical text. And yet, as Heinemann describes it,
"Aggadah as a way of thinking is fluid and open,"[25] contingent on the
biblical text yet not bound to it.

To arrive at their understandings of scripture, the sages engaged in
considerable punning and wordplay that brought (out) new meanings to
the biblical text. In his discussion of aggadic midrash, Goldin stresses
the words "free" and "original." He notes that because "Aggadah is not
restricted by ancient legacy of practice, [the exegete] can draw cheerfully
on [his] intellect and imagination."[26] This is not to say, however, that
"when the sages indulge in haggadic speculation or teaching, all thought
of tradition is expelled":[27] rather, the sages immersed themselves in
tradition. They moved across the Bible with ease and fluidity, playing
disparate parts against each other, calling on Exodus, for instance, to
illumine Ecclesiastes.[28] Whereas Halakhah treats legal rulings, Aggadah
treats everything else, focusing occasionally on entire narratives but,
far more often, on particular verses and words, sometimes—as we have
seen—on individual letters and even occasionally on the dots and tittles
that adorn a letter.[29] For the most part, though, aggadic midrash is the
exegesis of biblical verses, and in this respect—that it treats the verse
unit rather than the book unit—it is markedly different from most literary
retellings.

What does it mean that midrash is the exegesis of biblical verses?
There are two key components to this assertion. First, *midrash interprets
the Bible*. Rabbinic attention is fixated on the Bible, on holy writ; there is
no comparable exegesis of other books. William Scott Green cautions
against over-emphasizing *Bible* here. He concedes that "the Hebrew
Bible had a fundamental place in rabbinic Judaism and constituted an

invoke haggadic sayings as support for a particular view. The Geonim, the heads of
the main Talmudic academies in the early medieval period (up to the eleventh
century), who in their denunciation of Aggadah opted for the establishment, elabo-
rated on the rule: *ein somkhin, ein lemedin*—base nothing on nor bring any proof
from aggadic statements; further, raise no questions because of them.

25. Heinemann, "The Nature of the Aggadah," 53.
26. Goldin, "The Freedom and Restraint of Aggadah," 63.
27. Ibid., 63.
28. See the midrash on Eccl 12:11 discussed in greater detail later on in this
chapter.
29. Here I turn my attention primarily to Aggadah. I will return to Halakhah later,
however, when I consider the vocabulary of midrash rather than the general concept
of it.

important component of its conceptual background,"[30] but notes that the rabbis' concern with the Bible was not all-embracing. Because their "interest in scripture was hardly comprehensive, and vast segments of it, including much of prophecy and the Deuteronomic History, escaped their interpretation...[we have to conceive of the] Bible's role in rabbinic literature as more complex and fluid than the book-religion model suggests."[31] Green suggests that while the Bible was the major source of rabbinic exegesis, "scripture neither determined the agenda nor provided the ubiquitous focus of rabbinic literary activity and imagination. Rather, it was a major—but certainly not the only—source the rabbis used to produce their literature."[32] As Green points out, the rabbis also "drew extensively on their own materials,"[33] expounding on previous interpretation. That prior interpretation, and the subsequent interpretation of it, however, was understood to have been given—alongside the written Torah—by God at Sinai. And although the rabbis may not have placed equal emphasis on all parts of the Bible, and while they may have turned to their own interpretation as well as to the Bible to inform their readings and writings, the Bible remained central to rabbinic exegesis.

This brings us to another essential point about midrash and midrashic activity: for the rabbis, the Bible is a sacred text—the "revealed word of God,"[34] no less—and thus there is a necessarily a theological underpinning to midrash. In their searching into the meaning of the text, the rabbis are searching for further divine revelation. In their view, the Bible is not only eternally valid (and therefore constantly revealing itself), its very language was revelatory: it "transcends the ordinary medium of human communication."[35] Every word—be it a proper name or a preposition, a command or a cliché—"was regarded as [a container] of deeper meanings which the interpreter was required to unlock."[36] The act of reading is an act of decoding the divine. The Bible was the rabbis' link to God.

---

30. William Scott Green, "Writing with Scripture: The Rabbinic Uses of the Bible," in Jacob Neusner with William Scott Green, *Writing with Scripture: The Authority and Uses of the Hebrew Bible in the Torah of Formative Judaism* (repr. Minneapolis: Fortress Press, 1989), 8. I am grateful to John Huddlestun of the College of Charleston for pointing me to this essay.
31. Ibid.
32. Ibid., 9.
33. Ibid.
34. Irving Jacobs, *The Midrashic Process: Tradition and Interpretation in Rabbinic Judaism* (Cambridge: Cambridge University Press, 1995), 4.
35. Ibid.
36. Ibid.

How do the rabbis forge that link? This brings us to the second component of the assertion above: *midrash is the interpretation of verses*. It is not an exposition of books, or stories, or even entire sentences. Wright identifies midrash as the interpretation of phrases, words, letters. In James Kugel's account, "the basic unit of the Bible, for the midrashist, is the verse: this is what he seeks to expound, and it might be said that there is simply no boundary encountered beyond that of the verse until one comes to the borders of the canon itself."[37] The rabbis jump from verse to verse, reaching beyond the verse in question, often across the entirety of the Hebrew Bible, for illumination. To elucidate the unconventional use of a word, for instance, they move to other verses that contain the same word, turning to them to explicate a confusing usage. Their method of reading across books, of drawing from all parts of the canon, suggests that they saw the biblical text as a continuum, in which any part could illuminate any other part.[38] Thus, when they encountered a sequence of words, or the juxtaposition of a particular word with another that recalled a similar combination elsewhere in the Tanakh, they would put the two texts in dialogue with one another. They viewed midrash as "linking up words of Torah with one another."[39] Bruns notes that linking could mean counting occurrences of particular words in scripture, attending to the varied contexts in which a word appears. It could also mean "using one text (a letter, a word, a phrase, a verse, a piece of narrative, in principle a whole book like the Song of Songs) to elucidate another."[40] The rabbis understood the Tanakh to be a "self-interpreting text," which means that they used verses or narratives where the meaning was easily grasped to clarify obscure occurrences.[41] This reading across the span of scripture came out of a notion that "words of Torah need each other. What one passage locks up, the other discloses" (*Midrash Rabbah*, Bemidbar, 19, 7).[42]

For the present discussion of midrash, of the method of rabbinic exegesis, it is important to consider what stirs the rabbis to comment, and how the clarification—this unlocking—takes place. Of the first, Judah Goldin has a light but important take based in his own extensive study of midrash:

37. Kugel, "Two Introductions to Midrash," 93.

38. Kugel, in his description of midrash as the exegesis of verses, is pointing to this notion.

39. *Midrash Rabbah*, Hazita [Song of Songs], 1.10.2

40. Bruns, *Hermeneutics Ancient and Modern*, 109.

41. Ibid.

42. Ibid.

> There is always a reason for a midrashic comment. I don't say that I always find the reason; indeed often I don't. But I still insist that a midrashic comment, even when so-to-speak playful, is the result of some provocation... I simply state what I always assume, that midrashic expression is the result of something specific pressing on the *ba'al midrash*, the midrashic spokesman, and if I can't find that specific cause it's my tough luck. But there *is* a cause.
> At times the provocation is lexical, growing directly out of the biblical text; at times the lexical is not the immediate provocation, but some idea or mood or speculation or resentment, for which the midrash accommodatingly provides the biblical idiom—a phrase, a clause, even a singular term if need be—to confirm, as it were, *dekula ba*, that everything is either in the Scriptures or under their surface.[43]

There is nothing new under the sun. One need not turn to outside ideas to unlock the meaning of the Bible, for everything one needs to understand the Bible is in the Bible itself. *Words of Torah need each other.* And once the reader recognizes this, he will soon find that there is nothing—either within the Bible or without—that scripture does not explain. Everything is either in the biblical text or under its surface.

The Inner Logic of Aggadic Midrash

How, then, does one access the meaning(s) within scripture? The rabbis begin with a prooftext—a biblical verse or part of a biblical verse (down to the diacritical markings)—and expound upon it. Sometimes their discussion works from their immediate concern back to the text. As Stern notes, "the essential preoccupation of Midrash is with finding in the biblical text a source for every law and belief in the Rabbinic tradition."[44] In this articulation, rabbinic ideas are bolstered by—not derived from—scripture. A rabbi has an exegetical point he wishes to make, and seeks to find the scriptural peg on which to hang it. The finding of the peg can happen in a number of ways. For the purposes of a particular reading, a rabbi might take a common word and ascribe to it an obscure definition, or even arrive at a new definition based on its immediate context. Irving Jacobs calls this latter tactic "climatic exegesis." This unusual method of reading is "based on the assumption that a scriptural expression, regardless of its usual connotation, or plain meaning, can absorb a new and quite unrelated meaning from the context or climate in which it occurs."[45]

---

43. Judah Goldin, "From Text to Interpretation and From Experience to Interpreted Text," in *Studies in Midrash and Related Literature* (ed. Barry L. Eichler and Jeffrey Tigay; Philadelphia: Jewish Publication Society, 1988), 275.

44. Stern, *Midrash and Theory*, 37.

45. Jacobs, *The Midrashic Process*, 4.

For example, when attempting to explain the significance of the term
מאכלת, the word for the knife Abraham takes to slaughter Isaac, the
rabbis seek to domesticate a peculiar usage. A relatively obscure word,
מאכלת appears four times in the Hebrew Bible: twice in Gen 22, where it
is the knife Abraham intends to use for the sacrifice of Isaac (vv. 6 and
10); once in Judg 19:29, to designate the knife used by the Levite to
cleave his dead concubine; and once in Prov 30:14, to describe the teeth
of a generation of men who devour the needy and the poor, who bring a
curse upon its fathers and no blessing to its mothers. The contexts for the
word give it an especially violent connotation. R. Hanina, however,
asserts that this unusual word is used in the Abraham story "because it
renders food (אוכלים) fit to be eaten"[46] (*Gen. Rab.* 56:3). (The consonants
appearing in the Hebrew word for "knife" recur in the word for "food.")
The midrash goes on to tell us that "the Rabbis said: All eating
(AKILOTH) which Israel enjoys in this world, they enjoy only in the
merit of that MA'AKELETH (KNIFE)."[47] What does this imply? An
ongoing connection between Abraham and the future generations of
Israel. The descendants repeatedly promised to him will benefit from his
obedience in fulfilling God's commandment: they will continue to be
sustained because of his willingness to wield that מאכלת. The lesson—
the ongoing connection between the generations, the eternal value of
Abraham's obedience—is rooted in a discussion of the meaning of a
single, somewhat obscure word.

Rabbinic exegesis also works in the reverse fashion. Rather than find a
scriptural hook on which to hang their homiletic point,[48] at times the
rabbis build from the prooftext outward. In these cases, the rabbis
address an aspect of the text that strikes them as problematic in some

---

46. R. Hanina understands מאכלת to be a present participle of the hiphil of אכל—
which would be "to cause to eat," or "to feed."

47. *Gen. Rab.* 56:3. *Midrash Rabbah: Genesis* (ed. H. Freedman and Maurice
Simon; New York: Soncino, 1983).

48. The suggestion in Kugel's "Two Introductions to Midrash" is that the activity
I have here described is the dominant mode of exegesis. Neusner takes strong exception to this characterization of midrash. In *Midrash as Literature: The Primacy of
Documentary Discourse* (Lanham, Md.: University Press of America, 1987), his
book-length response to Kugel's 27-page article, he writes: "Kugel imagines that the
verse of Scripture forms the precipitant and the generative category of what he calls
midrash. Everything starts (he maintains) from the character and contents of the
particular verse under discussion. I can show that *nothing* starts from the character
and contents of the verse under discussion, since different people read the verse out
of a different set of questions to produce different groups, then we cannot impute to
the base-verse a determinative role in midrash-exegesis" (ibid., 14–15).

respect. Perhaps the meaning of a phrase is not immediately evident, or a word is used in an unconventional way, or a verb is declined irregularly. Faced with these "surface irregularities,"[49] the rabbis attempt to explain the text, smoothing over the problem.

"Surface irregularities" include such mundane problems as apparent redundancy. The rabbis grapple with the recurrence of words: what, to the contemporary reader, would seem self-evidently to be repetition for emphasis was, to the rabbinic mind, new revelation. Each new appearance of a word reflected a new meaning. Thus, for instance, the description in Gen 22:6 of Abraham and Isaac walking up the mountain together (יחדו) is understood to mean together physically—the two walked with one another. With the repetition of יחדו two verses later, however, comes a new understanding—the two must have been together psychically as well as physically. As *Genesis Rabbah* records, "THEY WENT BOTH OF THEM TOGETHER: one to bind and the other to be bound; one to slaughter and the other to be slaughtered." The repetition of "together" suggests that Isaac was complicit in his father's mission, not merely its unwitting object. For if the word did not have two meanings, why would it have been repeated?

This is a question that plagues the rabbis again in their reading of Gen. 22, with the angel's repetitive call, "Abraham! Abraham!" In *Gen. Rab.* 56:7, R. Hiyya teaches that the two calls signify two distinct sentiments: "This is an expression of love and [this is an expression of] encouragement." R. Liezer pushes the understanding: "[The repetition indicates that He spake] to him and to future generations: There is no generation which does not contain men like Abraham, and there is no generation that does not contain men like Jacob, Moses, and Samuel."[50] The doubled "Abraham! Abraham!" is a sign, as in the earlier example, of the rabbinic conviction that God will maintain ties with the future generations of Israel, all of which will contain their share of great men. The promises made to Abraham are everlasting.

All these *derashim* derive from the rabbinic view that the text is perfect and perfectly harmonious. Nothing is redundant; nothing is superfluous. At its extreme, this conviction meant that accessing the multiple revelations of the text yielded tremendously convoluted readings. The early Tanna, Nahum of Gimzo, aspired to give meaning even to the prepositions and articles in the Tanakh. He applied rabbinic *middot* (hermeneutic

---

49. Kugel, "Two Introductions to Midrash," 93.

50. R. Jacob Moses Ashkenazi, in his *Yede Moshe*, notes that these figures "represent especially the spirit of philanthropy, service of God, study of the Torah, and civil justice, which may be regarded as the fundamentals of civilization."

principles) and read every גַּ ("also") and אֵת ("with") as a *ribui*, an amplification of the scope of the text or an allusion to something not specifically mentioned in it, and every אַך ("but") and רק ("only") as *miyyut*, a restriction or limitation of it.

The rabbis, however, were as attentive to what is *not* in the text as they were to what is there. As Erich Auerbach asserts in "Odysseus' Scar," his renowned essay on biblical poetics,[51] the biblical authors were laconic, their stories terse and "fraught with background."[52] So, as much as the rabbis were spurred on by "surface irregularities" in the text they had received, they were also motivated by the "background," by all those things that were not to be found in their text. As Auerbach notes, the opening of the Akedah (the basis for his characterization of biblical style) "does not, as Homer would, locate the speakers in space nor give them motives… The [biblical] narrator is not interested in what Abraham was doing when he was called."[53] With "everything…left in obscurity except for that which is necessary for the narrative,"[54] the rabbinic task becomes the illumination of the opaque narrative, the bringing into the foreground of all that has been recessed. Thus the rabbis set about to fill gaps and holes, to expand upon the elliptic narratives. At times, this entails fleshing out the Bible's skeletal characters, imbuing them with personal histories, thoughts, desires and motivations. Why, for instance, did God choose Abraham in the first place, single him out, and direct him to the new land? A popular midrash, taught in all Hebrew schools, offers the missing background as well as the missing motive: as a young man, Abraham decried idolatry and smashed his own father's idols—repeating "The Eternal He is God! The Eternal He is God!" to himself as he did so.[55] This is but one of dozens and dozens of stories that fill in gaps about the life of Abraham before God calls him to go to the appointed land, about his upstanding character and his piety, his trials by foreign leaders and his triumphs as the first embracer of monotheism.

The terseness of the biblical text, its tremendous silences, allowed the rabbis ample space to speak themselves. They could read the text in such a way as to explain apparent discrepancies between biblical Judaism and

---

51. Which he reads against Homeric poetics, setting the literary sensibility of Jerusalem against that of Athens.

52. Erich Auerbach, "Odysseus' Scar," in *Mimesis: The Representation of Reality in Western Literature* (Princeton: Princeton University Press, 1953), 12.

53. Ibid., 8.

54. Ibid., 11.

55. Louis Ginzberg, *Legends of the Bible* (Philadelphia: Jewish Publication Society, 1992), 94.

their own, so as to ensure that the biblical text continued to speak to readers of their day. With centuries between the revelation at Sinai and their own time, a major concern of the rabbis became the bridging of the gap between the religion of the Bible and the religion of rabbinic Judaism. This was both a halakhic and aggadic concern—and at times the two overlapped: the rabbis were often concerned to show that the biblical stories were in concert with the post-biblical understanding of biblical laws. If, as was commonly held to be true, Abraham was the father of the Jews and a pious and righteous follower of God, how could he not have been Torah-observant? Yet, they had to ask, why is there no mention of him observing the commandments? Marking the holidays? Why would he have taken "curds, and milk, and the calf which he had prepared" (Gen. 18:8)—an unkosher meal—and set it before his heavenly visitors? That the giving of the commandments to Moses at Sinai took place long after Abraham's death was of no consequence to the rabbis: they declare him to be a loyal follower of the Torah. In the rabbinic account, Abraham celebrated the Passover,[56] knew the sacrificial laws,[57] kept the whole Torah. How do the rabbis know this?

> Rab said: Our father Abraham kept the whole Torah, as it is said: *Because of that Abraham hearkened my voice.* R. Shimi b. Hiyyi said to Rab: Say, perhaps, that this refers to the seven laws?[58]—Surely there was also that of circumcision![59] Then say that it refers to the seven laws and circumcision [and not the whole Torah]?—If that were so, why does Scripture say: '*My commandments and My laws*'? Raba or R. Ashi said: Abraham, our father, kept even the '*erub* of the dishes,[60] as it is said: '*My Torahs*', one being the written Torah and the other the oral Torah.[61]

The idea is that the litany in Gen. 26:5—"because Abraham listened to my voice and kept my watch, my commandments, my laws and my instructions (*Torotai*)"—is not a series of synonyms. Rather, each term designates a different thing: Abraham not only observed the commandments given to him, but those given to Noah, *and* the Oral and Written "Torahs" given to Moses as well. Here, then, the rabbis deal with two

---

56. *Gen. Rab.* 42.

57. *Gen. Rab.* 44.

58. The seven laws given to Noah as the ark alit (Gen 9:1–7); these Noahide commandments were held by the rabbis to be binding to all people, not just to Jews.

59. This was clearly commanded of Abraham (Gen 9:7–14).

60. A reference to post-biblical legislation about preparing foods on fast days before the Sabbath; the suggestion is that Abraham knew the minutia of the Oral Law as well as the Written.

61. *b. Yoma* 28b.

problems: the apparent redundancy of the biblical text (the fact that
"watch," "commandments," "laws," and "instruction" all appear to
designate the same thing) and the patriarch's apparent lack of piety. This
rabbinic solution to a textual and theological problem clearly evidences
many of the traits of aggadic midrash outlined above: an attempt to
reconcile the world of the rabbis with the world of the Bible, a desire to
harmonize problematic passages, and an understanding of the Hebrew
Bible as perfect and perfectly harmonious (and therefore without
redundancy or superfluity).

What is intriguing about all the rabbinic explanations, motivations,
and clarifications we have seen is how far they reach beyond the written
text. Ibn Ezra dismissed those exegetes who understood Isaac to have
been slaughtered, resurrected, and come back to life, asserting that they
"[have] said the opposite of the Scripture."[62] Biblical scholar Jon Levenson counters, "Ibn Ezra understood better than most Jews of his generation or ours [that] to say the opposite of the Scripture is often precisely
what midrash does."[63] "*Derashic*" readings that read against the biblical
text stand in sharp contrast to more modern modes of reading that adhere
strictly to the *peshat* of the text, that attempt explanation and illumination by delving deep into a passage, pressing not its boundaries but its
depths. Focusing only on the Torah as it appears on the page (rather than
as read allegorically or through the lens of tradition), Auerbach tells us
that "Abraham's actions are explained not only by what is happening to
him at the moment, nor only by his character, but by his previous history:
he remembers and is always conscious of what God has promised him
and what God has accomplished for him already."[64] For the rabbis, this
text-based reading will not suffice. Rather, they use the biblical story as a
springboard for more stories. By fleshing out narratives or reconciling
apparent inconsistencies, they both myth-make and meaning-make.

The midrashic features delineated in this introduction are the ones
embraced by the secular literary communities that championed midrash
as both a form of interpretation and a form of literature. When the secular
scholars—Derrida, Lacan, Bloom[65]—first turned their attention to midrash, they were drawn to rabbinic midrash. Its appeal lay in the very
characteristics we have seen above: the freedom and openness of its

---

62. Ibn Ezra on Gen 22:19 in Jon D. Levenson, *The Death and Resurrection of
the Beloved Son* (New Haven: Yale University Press, 1993), 196.

63. Ibid., 196.

64. Auerbach, "Odysseus' Scar," 12.

65. Derrida and Bloom are, of course, Jewish, but they come to midrash by way
of their intellectual rather than spiritual commitments.

interpretation, the primacy it gives to text, the blurring of the lines between text and commentary. The following sections explain how and why midrash entered the language of literary theory, and what it became once it got there.

What is the Midrash of the Literary Theorists?

The dialogue between midrash and literary theory began in the late 1970s and early 1980s. In 1983–84, a group of literary theorists and rabbinicists convened for a year-long seminar on midrash and theory at Hebrew University in Jerusalem; it was a gathering that resulted in the 1986 publication of the seminal book, *Midrash and Literature*, edited by Sanford Budick and Geoffrey Hartman.[66] The dialogue, as epitomized in the seminar, is the product of a very specific moment in intellectual history.

The American academy of the late seventies and early eighties, with its

> breakdown of strict boundaries that previously had separated distinct academic disciplines and departments; the shifting of attention away from the centers of 'high' culture…toward the various 'others' that formerly inhabited only the peripheries and margins of academic study; and, perhaps most prominently, the emergence of critical theory…as a kind of new academic lingua franca[67]

allowed previously unrelated fields to "engage in genuine dialogue, often in the service of creating a kind of new critical metadiscourse. And among all of these shifting realignments, none, perhaps, was more surprising that the midrash-theory linkage."[68] Whereas literary attention had previously fallen squarely on the traditional canon, its gaze now shifted to the periphery, where it encountered not only the Jewish other with its own literary canon, but the "other" within that other: Halakhah's lesser sibling, Aggadah.

---

66. The book marks the first major intersection of midrash and literature. It has had considerable influence, but its reception has not been wholly positive. Jacob Neusner, who (as noted) devoted one of his many books to a refutation of the ideas put forth in *Midrash and Literature* notes, "The papers assembled in the volume edited by Hartman and Budick seem to me remarkably prolix and verbose, using a great many fancy words to say a few simple things, most of them wrong. But we shall not dwell on trivialities, though admittedly, it is no joy to read the circle represented by Kugel [whose "Two Introductions to Midrash" spurred Neusner's response]. Still, his paper is by no means the worst of the lot" (Neusner, *Midrash as Literature*, xi).

67. Stern, *Midrash and Theory*, 2.

68. Ibid., 3.

G. Douglas Atkins traces the impetus for this particular "realignment" to a dehellenizing trend among American literary scholars.[69] Turning away from the formalism of the New Critics and what Atkins calls the genteel[70] civility of their predecessors, they began to question the very assumptions of the study of literature, to the point of questioning what literature is. The result was a break away from the canon, and an embrace of texts that were not male, white, classical, or Christian. The scene thus set, midrash entered the world of literary studies.[71]

In *The Slayers of Moses*, Susan Handelman situates this entrance within a larger discussion of exegetical modes. Setting up an opposition between patristic and rabbinic modes of exegesis, she notes that recent critics like Derrida, Bloom, Lacan, and Freud responded against the Greco-Christian mode of interpretation seen in the chain from Augustine to Luther to Frye.[72] She contends that by and large, though, "little attention has been paid to the Rabbinic interpretive tradition"[73] in the predominantly Christian world of letters. She attributes this to three historical conditions: the Church's stigmatization of rabbinic interpretation; the inaccessibility of Jewish sources to those unfamiliar with Hebrew; and the exclusion of Jews from European intellectual life until the Enlightenment.[74] Two developments altered the trend, however: the birth of psycho-analysis and the rise of literary theory. With Freud's references to dreams as Holy Writ and Lacan's conception of psychoanalysis as midrashic,[75] and with the notion of Text replacing that of a Book of Books, there arose a place for the unsuspecting rabbis in the academy.

69. G. Douglas Atkins, "Dehellenizing Literary Criticism," *College English* 41 (1980): 769–79.

70. And, as Stern notes in a comparable slur, Gentile.

71. David Stern describes "the institutional and intellectual context in which the midrash-theory was forged. Essentially, two types of scholars were involved in making the connection: on the one side were a few younger students and scholars in Jewish studies, many of whom had entered the field with academic backgrounds in either English or comparative literature; on the other were several critics and theorists from the general literary world (many though not all of them Jewish), a number of whom were very distinguished figures, thus lending a kind of immediate prestige to the new interest in midrash that it otherwise would never have possessed. For all their differences, both groups of scholars found themselves fascinated by precisely the same wayward, antic features of midrashic interpretation that had been considered scandalous in the past" (Stern, *Midrash and Theory*, 3).

72. Susan Handelman, *The Slayers of Moses* (Albany: SUNY Press, 1982), xiv.

73. Ibid.

74. Ibid.

75. Ibid., xv.

Like Atkins before her, Handelman attributes this opening to the academy's move away from Hellenism. Outlining the opposition between Greco-Christian and rabbinic thought, she accounts for the Hebraic mode's attractiveness to literary theorists who had begun to think about rabbinic exegesis. Where "one of Christianity's central interpretive axioms was the distinction between spirit and letter,"[76] rabbinic thought "called for more intense concentration on the words and their relations, including even the physical shape of the letters and punctuation."[77] Imbuing the letter with spirit, rabbinic thought "always gave primacy to the text, the word."[78] This emphasis on the word in and of itself—on the text alone—held great appeal for literary theorists.

Beginning with the American New Criticism, which emerged in the 1920s and was prevalent through the 1950s, through the Geneva School of criticism of the 1940s and 1950s, theorists slowly and surely turned their attention to the word, honing in on the text itself. The New Critics focused on the internal coherence of a poem as against its historical situatedness,[79] while the Geneva School, influenced by Husserl's phenomenology, bracketed off the historical context of the literary work and focused instead on "a wholly 'immanent' reading of the text, totally unaffected by anything outside it."[80] And even as theory branched off in different directions, with reader response criticism insisting that the reader determines the text's meaning and deconstruction undermining the very possibility of stable meaning,[81] the theoretical emphasis remained on the text in and of itself. The author disappeared, to be replaced by the reader, who turned his gaze exclusively on the text, which was a reality in and of itself, existing to be interpreted. As Derrida had it, "there is nothing outside the text."[82]

---

76. Ibid., 16.

77. Ibid., 17.

78. Ibid., 22.

79. New Criticism did not understand the poem to be entirely divorced from reality, merely as independent of the (psychological) reality of both its creator and its reader.

80. Terry Eagleton, *Literary Theory: An Introduction* (Minneapolis: The University of Minnesota Press, 1995), 59.

81. Handelman argues that deconstruction is inherently Jewish; she describes Derrida as "intent on (Judaically) deconstructing the entire tradition of Western thought" (*The Slayers of Moses*, 16) and "(being his most Rabbinic) try[ing] to unmask the whole metaphysical basis on which thought about metaphor takes place" (ibid., 17).

82. Derrida, *Of Grammatology*, 158.

Similarly, "for the rabbis...the primary reality was linguistic: true being was a God who speaks and creates texts, and *imitatio dei* was not silent suffering but speaking and interpreting."[83] The rabbis moved through the biblical text, playing with it, drawing out its many meanings. Midrash was "a tradition that regenerates through disruption";[84] the movement of its writers was "a movement into the text, not out of it."[85] Likewise the movement of many literary theorists, who delved deep into text, tugging at its very fabric, probing its every meaning.

While some sought meaning in text, for many theorists the true pleasure[86] of the text lay in its ambiguity; the quest for a text's meaning had (d)evolved into a quest for its *meanings*. Thus, for those—Derrida, Hartman, Bloom among the luminaries—who turned their gaze to (aggadic) midrash, the draw was clear.[87] They were pulled to the rabbinic mode because of what they perceived as "the typical midrashic predilection for multiple interpretations, rather than for a single truth behind the text; its irresistible desire to tease out the nuances of Scripture rather than use interpretation to close them off; and, most of all, the way midrashic discourse mixes text and commentary."[88] Throughout his discussion of the intersection of midrash and literature, Stern stresses this latter point. As he tells it, the "new literary study of midrash aimed to demonstrate that midrash *was* a literature of interpretation, that its literary character was bound up with its exegetical dimension."[89] Thus a forgotten corpus— interpretative not literary, Hebraic not Hellenic, polysemic not monolithic—came under the aegis of postmodern theory.

83. Handelman, *The Slayers of Moses*, 4.

84. Daniel Boyarin, *Intertextuality and the Reading of Midrash* (Bloomington: Indiana University Press, 1990), 28.

85. Handelman, *The Slayers of Moses*, 21.

86. The term is from Barthes, of course, who equates readerly bliss and orgasm.

87. It is important to note the emphasis on aggadic midrash. As David Weiss Halivni states, "legal comments in general are closer and more tightly bound to the text, more grounded in it than in nonlegal midrash. It is worthwhile noting here that the textual examples cited in the rapidly accumulating literature of the new literary theorists as illustrations of their position overwhelmingly come from the nonlegal writings. Legal texts do not lend themselves so easily (despite recent attempts) to the new modes of interpretation. Authorial intention will always play a more significant role in legal texts than in nonlegal texts. Midrash Halakhah remains less susceptible to modern theory than midrash Aggadah" (*Peshat and Derash*, 159).

88. Stern, *Midrash and Theory*, 3.

89. Ibid., 8. Emphasis in original.

Postmodern Midrash

Midrash's encounter "with contemporary literary studies—structuralism, semiotics, deconstruction, cultural studies, indeed virtually all the modes of postmodernism as they have come into fashion and gone out of it"[90]— entailed a change not only in the ways that midrash is read, but in the very understanding of what midrash is. Stern notes that "under the impact of theory, midrash has gone through a veritable sea change. The focus of the field, its methods, its conceptual premises, have all experienced a fundamental, radical transformation."[91] It is important that we take note of the flow of influence: for the literary theorists who began to consider the intersection of midrash and literary theory, midrash was a literature to which theoretical constructs could be applied. This is a fundamentally different concern from ours here. We are not asking *In what way does midrash prove to be a literature that reflects the concerns of theory?* but rather, *In what way can the concerns of midrash be put towards a theory of literature (specifically, literary retelling)?*[92] There are obvious reasons to consider midrash and retelling alongside one another, but literary theory may not make these evident. In fact, while what Hartman, Derrida and the rest did with midrash—that is, appropriate the methods and conceptual premises of the genre—has some bearing on our own investigation, their understanding of midrash demands considerable manipulation and recasting of the form.

In the opening essay of *Midrash and Literature*, Hartman lays out the significance of midrash for literary theory:

> While midrash must be viewed as a type of discourse with its own rules and historical development, and while we cannot assume that its only function was exegetical, little is more important today than to remind secular literary studies of the richness and subtlety of those strange rabbinic conversations which have been disdained for so long in favor of more objective and systematic reading.[93]

90. Ibid., 1.
91. Ibid.
92. This project also deviates from David Stern's: he states in his introduction to *Midrash and Theory* that "the time has arrived to reap the fruits of the original linkage [between midrash and theory] and to begin the real work of reading midrash theoretically, as literary discourse—that is, to use the theoretical sophistication appropriated from literary studies to describe midrash's literary forms in their specificity and full complexity" (ibid., 9).
93. Geoffrey Hartman, "The Struggle for the Text," in Budick and Hartman, eds., *Midrash and Literature*, 3.

Hartman's comment echoes Stern's points about the appeal of those "strange," "disdained" rabbinic conversations—they were, when they surfaced in the secular academy, entirely "Other."[94] In addition, the rabbis' departure from "more objective and systematic reading" also held appeal for the theorists. The freedom and openness of thought allowed for a corollary freedom and openness of form: "in terms of content the Aggadah includes wise sayings, expressions of faith, expositions and elaborations of scripture and stories; in terms of form, epigrams, anecdotes, wit, humour, terse explanations of words in scripture, and stories of epic length."[95]

This listing of the many styles and forms midrash takes underscores yet another essential element in our understanding of the genre: it is literature as much as it is interpretation of literature. As Michael Fishbane notes, "Judaism has sought to dignify the status of religious commentary."[96] Thus the oral Torah, the law of the rabbis, is said to have been given to Moses at Sinai alongside the written Torah. And when prophecy ceased in Ancient Israel, revelation continued through exegesis. This attempt to afford equal status to the text and the commentary on the text—in this case, *Torah mi-Sinai* and *Torah she'b'al peh*—sets midrash apart from other modes of interpretation.[97] As Stern emphasizes, midrash blurs the line between text and commentary. In his view, it "epitomizes the types of discourses to which much critical writing has recently aspired: it avoids the dichotomization of literature and commentary, and focuses on the relationship between text and interpreter."[98] As we are mostly concerned with ways to talk about literature that revisits the Bible—with fictions that sustain scripture—the blurring of the line between literature and commentary is utterly relevant to us: how we

94. Stern notes that "with the demise of deconstruction, literary theorists…seem to have lost interest in midrash and in other aspects of classical Judaism and its literature… More sadly, Jewish studies, no longer understood as the repressed or suppressed 'other' of Western culture, is now perceived as part of the hegemonic cultural imperialism that has suppressed and continues to suppress all the minority voices within that culture, the supposedly authentic voices of multiculturalism and pluralism" (Stern, *Midrash and Theory*, 8–9).

95. Heinemann, "The Nature of the Aggadah," 42.

96. Michael Fishbane, "Inner Biblical Exegesis: Types and Strategies of Interpretation in Ancient Israel," in Budick and Hartman, eds., *Midrash and Literature*, 19.

97. Further, Stern points to midrash's commingling of text and commentary as one of the bases of its appeal for literary theorists.

98. David Stern, "Midrash and the Language of Exegesis: A Study of Vayikra Rabbah, Chapter 1," in Budick and Hartman, eds., *Midrash and Literature*, 132.

describe various acts of retelling will signal whether we are discussing commentary that takes the form of literature or literature that functions as commentary.

In the absence of terms that make evident these distinctions, let us shift our focus to the relationship between text and interpreter. In his treatment of the connections between midrash and modern literary theories, Halivni plays up the relationship between text and interpreter. He notes—as we did earlier—that structuralists and deconstructionists both give the reader a significant role in the formation of meaning. The reader does not passively receive the text, but participates actively in it, giving it coherence and structure. In fact, the reader determines meaning: an unread text is meaningless. However, readings can be more or less responsible. Halivni cautions, "The reading, however, has to be disciplined to comply with the prevailing conventions and be circumscribed by the interaction with the content, the mode of expression and genre of the text (even by the authorial intention)."[99] Herein comes the analogy to midrash, "which although it everywhere cites Scripture is often not motivated or set in motion by Scripture, and is rarely supported by the 'natural' meaning of the text."[100] Rather, midrash comes from the scriptural hermeneut, who responds to "the text—against the text's natural meaning—to indulge his imaginative comments. In midrash the reader is not passive. Most of his cues come from outside the text; the reader actively brings these cues to bear on the text and interacts with it."[101] Midrash and modern literary theory both turn on what transpires in the interaction of text and reader.

In Halivni's view, the parallels between reader response or reception theory and rabbinic readings are the most cogent—and least explored—link between theory and midrash. As he sees it, the existing literature treating the connection between the two fields

> pays insufficient attention to the reader's role in forming meaning. The reader's role represents the strongest similarity between midrash and modern literary criticism... All the other similitudes are problematic either because they are not expressive of the literary school as a whole,[102] or because they are not accurately describing the nature of midrash.[103]

99.   Halivni, *Peshat and Derash*, 158.
100. Halivni, *Peshat and Derash*, 158–59.
101. Halivni, *Peshat and Derash*, 159.
102. This could be said of Halivni's understanding of reception theory as well. Wolfgang Iser's reception theory claims to be about the individual reader bringing himself or herself to a text. Thus, there should be as many readings as there are readers. And yet, in Iser's theory, there are correct readings. As Eagleton explains, "textual indeterminacies just spur us on to the act of abolishing them, replacing them

Halivni takes issue with the misrepresentations of theory and of midrash by structuralists and deconstructionists both. In his view, neither stripe of theorist understands how midrash works, yet both assert their affinities with it.

Midrash and Indeterminacy?

Foregrounding their ability to read multiple interpretations coherently, Handelman readily positions the rabbis as Derridean post-structuralists, rejecting binary oppositions in favor of polysemy. She states that "the movement of Rabbinic interpretation is not from one opposing sphere to another, from the sensible to the nonsensible, but rather from sense to sense."[104] The way the midrashim have been preserved seems to underscore this perspective: "the Talmud and Midrashim are a polyphonic choir of hundreds of rabbis from the most varied times and places and thus represent an open process of discussion of all kinds of questions of faith and life."[105] The reading of one rabbi is placed immediately after the reading of the one before; the first does not seem to be first because it is correct, not because it is incorrect and needing to be rectified by the ensuing reading. The second reading may contradict the first; it may agree with it. It may finesse the point just made; it may seem not to have even heard it. The form is unhierarchical: no redactor intervenes to tell us who is right or who is wrong; the presentation does not indicate whose opinion is to be followed and whose dismissed. Implicit in the polysemy is an assertion of the validity of multiple interpretations.

Let us consider a midrash—one on the nature of midrash itself—that illustrates the potential for many readings. In his chapter on rabbinic hermeneutics, Bruns offers a midrash on Eccl 12:11, "The words of the wise are as goads, and as nails well fastened (literally, 'planted') are those that are composed in collections; they are given from one shepherd." The midrash begins with a discussion of the first part of the verse: it first likens the words of the Torah to the goad that directs the cow

with a stable meaning. They must, in Iser's revealingly authoritative term, be 'normalized'—tamed and subdued to some firm structure of sense. The reader, it would seem, is engaged in fighting the text as much as interpreting it, struggling to pin down its anarchic 'polysemantic' potential within some manageable framework" (Eagleton, *Literary Theory*, 81).
103.   Halivni, *Peshat and Derash*, 228.
104.   Handelman, *The Slayers of Moses*, 21.
105.   Karl-Josef Kuschel, *Abraham: Sign of Hope for Jews, Christians and Muslims* (New York: Continuum, 1995), 53.

along the furrows so as to bring life into the world, and then moves on to the image of the nails well planted, drawing a comparison between the Torah and a plant which both bear fruit and multiply. For our purposes, it is after this point that the conversation becomes most interesting:

> "*Those that are composed in collections (ba'ale asufoth)*." '*Ba'ale asufoth*' applies to the scholars, who sit in groups and study the Torah, some of them declaring a thing unclean, others declaring it clean; some pronouncing a thing to be forbidden, others pronouncing it to be permitted; some disqualifying an object, others declaring it fit. Lest a man should say, Since some scholars declare a thing unclean and others declare it clean; some pronounce a thing to be forbidden, others pronouncing it to be permitted; some disqualify an object while other uphold its fitness, how can I study Torah in such circumstances? Scripture states, "*They are given from one shepherd*": One God has given them, one leader (Moses) has uttered them at the command of the Lord of all creation, blessed be He; as it says, *And God spoke all these words* (Ex. XX.1). Do you then on your part make your ear like a grain-receiver and acquire a heart that can understand the words of the scholars who declare a thing unclean as well as of those who declare it clean; the words of those who declare a thing forbidden as well as those who declare it permitted; the words of those who disqualify and object as well as those who uphold its fitness.[106]

Bruns' reading of the midrash reflects an understanding first, of the text as divine—"given from one shepherd"—and second, of the interpretation of that text as communal.[107] Some members of the community interpret (and rule) one way, others another. According to this midrash, however, this is not a problem. It is the practice of midrashic exegesis that is authoritative, not any given interpretation.[108] The act of interpretation is significant; the content is not.

The midrash above advocates that readers "acquire a heart that can understand the words of the scholars who declare a thing unclean as well as of those who declare it clean." In this view, what is ultimately to be desired is not a definitive reading, but an understanding of how it is that the variant readings are arrived at. God, after all, "spoke all these words": *all* suggests to the rabbis not just the words of the Torah itself, but the words of the interpreters as well. Thus interpretation is a divine act, one to be undertaken by *all* Israel. According to I. Jacobs,

---

106. Bruns, *Hermeneutics Ancient and Modern*, 108. The passage is from *Midrash Naso* (Numbers) 14.4. Bruns also treats this midrash in his essay "Midrash and Allegory: The Beginnings of Scriptural Interpretation," in *The Literary Guide to the Bible* (ed. Robert Alter and Frank Kermode; Cambridge, Mass.: Harvard University Press, 1987), 630–34.

107. Bruns, *Hermeneutics Ancient and Modern*, 113.

108. Ibid., 117.

the midrashic process...did not consist purely of an interaction between a divinely inspired text and its authoritative interpreters. There was a third, equally indispensable component, the people for whom the text was intended. Consequently, the interpretation and exposition of Scripture were never regarded as exclusive activities, to be confined to the circle of scholars and their disciples in the *Bet Ha-Midrash*.[109]

Every Israelite had a relationship with the text; each one was entitled to interpret it.[110]

Herein, for Derrida and the deconstructionists—who, like Fish and the reader response critics, insist on the indeterminacy of the text—lay the appeal of midrash. In midrash, "the infinity of meaning and plurality of interpretation are as much the cardinal imperatives, even the divine virtues, for Rabbinic thought as they are the cardinal sins for Greek thought."[111] The affinity between midrash and theory is apparent. In fact, Stern goes so far as to trace an intellectual lineage between midrash and theory, arguing that "midrash is an antecedent (or counterpart) to the indeterminacy of recent literary theory."[112] The concept of indeterminacy appears to be built right into the midrash, behind which is "the underlying belief that there are manifold meanings of scripture."[113] The rabbis come to embrace "a readiness, better still [an] eagerness for sweeping association, for welcome multiplicity of interpretations, of what might almost be regarded as infinite variety, seven times seven faces of the Torah";[114] they seem to extol indeterminacy. And thus the rabbis' conception of meaning, to the theorists at least, seems wholly postmodern.

It Is Not in Heaven:
The Problems with the Midrash of the Literary Theorists

It goes almost without saying that Jacques Derrida, the patriarch of deconstruction, should have been attracted to midrash—or at least to midrash as he construed it. Derrida's critical project was devoted to

109.   Jacobs, *The Midrashic Process*, 13.
110.   Bruns describes midrash as "a form of life lived with a text that makes claims on people. A text that makes claims upon people turns them into respondents: they are answerable to the text in a way that is qualitatively different from the answerability of disengaged observers to the scenes they wish to depict" (Bruns, *Hermeneutics Ancient and Modern*, 118).
111.   Handelman, *The Slayers of Moses*, 21.
112.   David Stern, "Midrash and the Language of Exegesis: A Study of Vayikra Rabbah, Chapter 1," in Budick and Hartman, eds., *Midrash and Literature*, 134.
113.   Heinemann, "The Nature of the Aggadah," 48.
114.   Goldin, "From Text to Interpretation," 272.

breaking down the binary oppositions insisted upon by structuralism; in his deconstructing "the opposition between what is the proper meaning and what is not, between essence and accident, intuition and discourse, thought and language, intelligible and sensible are overthrown."[115] Overthrowing involves undermining the text by way of the text itself. Derrida's deconstructionist method lingers on something at the edge of a text, on a "symptomatic" point, teasing it until it frays the entire fabric of the text itself. He tugs the binary oppositions that ostensibly order the text and shows that they cannot, in fact, offer an organizing principle. The text spills over itself, disseminating, uncontainable: in every text resides a surplus of meaning. The binary oppositions do not stand opposite one another; they are contained within each other. At every turn, the text undermines itself.

Derrida's method, his searching for the loose threads in the fabric of a text, has its parallels to that of the rabbis. Hartman describes their mutual interest in "the fault lines of a text; the evidence of a narrative sedimentation that has not entirely settled; and the tension that results between producing one authoritative account and respecting traditions characterized by a certain heterogeneity."[116] This tension is what most fascinates the theorists, but from the rabbinic point of view, the problem is overstated. The Bible, ostensibly a unity, is a multiplicity of voices, a collection of stories all fraught with their share of "surface irregularities"; the midrash, though multiple and multiply contradictory, nonetheless represent a unified stance toward text. They all understand the text to be divine in origin. Thus, for the rabbis, as opposed to the deconstructionists, the search for frayed material was not conducted in the interest of finding the thread that, when pulled, would unravel the cloth. Rather, they were darners, patching—strengthening, even—the fabric with whatever material they had at hand.

In this respect, midrash is fundamentally conservative, attempting to preserve what the rabbis perceived as the integrity and meaningfulness of the text often at the expense of its literal sense. The rabbis want to uphold a text that continues to speak with authority, so they become its co-authors, disclosing in the text aspects the reader might not have otherwise seen, but that now seen cannot be ignored. The multiple interpretations, the drawing out of many and varied readings, seems to be as much about celebrating the possibility of meaning as it is about asserting the depth and breadth of the word of God. With every new reading—every *davar acher*—the rabbis underscore that this *davar*—word, thing, matter,

115. Handelman, *The Slayers of Moses*, 20.
116. Hartman, "The Struggle for the Text," 11.

affair—*is* most certainly in the text itself, *is* one of its possible readings. The underlying supposition is, as we have seen, that the Bible has said everything that can be said. To contain the totality of all possibilities means to contain infinite contradictions. Neither is this problematic for the rabbis: each reading is put forth without negating other possible readings.

The Babylonian Talmud preserves a now-famous debate in the rabbinic academy: the question of the purity or impurity of the oven of Akhnai,[117] which is made of burnt clay cut into tiles, layered upon one another with sand between them. R. Eliezer alone argues that the vessel is incomplete and therefore unable to be declared impure; as proof of the truth of his claim he performs a series of miracles. R. Yehoshua, his adversary in the debate, remains unimpressed, rebuking the material objects that have corroborated R. Eliezer's view for daring to partake in the rulings of the disciples of the law. At last R. Eliezer seeks confirmation of his stance from on high, saying:

> If the law is as I say, let it be proven from heaven. A voice went out and said, What are you next to R. Eliezer, according to whom the law is in every place? R. Yehoshua stood on his feet and said, "It is not in heaven!"[118] What is "It is not in heaven"? Said R. Yermia: Since the

---

117.   An annulated serpent; the oven is so named because "on that day [the sages] encompassed [R. Eliezer like a coiled serpent] with [irrefutable] arguments and pronounced the oven unclean... On that day R. Eliezer brought forward all the arguments in the world to prove his claim, but [the sages] would not accept them." (*b. Baba Metzia*, 59a, b.)

118.   R. Yehoshua is, of course, citing his biblical prooftext here: "For this commandment which I command you today is not too difficult for you or too remote. *It is not in heaven*, that one should say, Who will arise to the heaven, take it and make it heard that we might do it. And it is not over the sea, that one might say, Who will cross to the other side of the sea and take it for us, and make us hear it, that we might do it. Rather, the word [thing] is very close to you in your mouth and heart, to do it" (Deut 30:11–14). As Daniel Boyarin points out, Yehoshua's use of the verse is an inversion of it; the sage "transforms the verse through his citation into meaning that the Torah is beyond the reach, as it were, of its divine author. The nature of R. Yehoshua's hermeneutic speech act here is vital to understanding the text. If we do not perceive what he is doing with the verse from Deuteronomy, we could misunderstand him to be making precisely the opposite claim, namely that the text is autonomous and sufficient in itself, not requiring the author to guarantee its true interpretation—a version of the New Criticism. By performing the act of tesseration of the language, however, the rabbi disables any such reading of his statement. Without fanfare, R. Yehoshua creates radical new meaning in this verse, simply by reinscribing it in a new context. 'It is not in heaven' means not only that the Torah is not beyond human reach, but that it is beyond divine reach as it were" (Boyarin,

Torah has already been given from Mt. Sinai, we do not pay attention to heavenly voices, for You have written already at Mt. Sinai, "Incline after the majority." R. Natan found Eliahu[119] and asked him, What was the Holy One, Blessed be He, doing at that moment? He said to him: Laughing and saying, My children have defeated Me. My children have defeated Me.[120]

In many respects, our modern theorists offer a relatively accurate account of midrash. They understand the second part of the story; they appreciate fully the notion that the text has arrived in human hands, is interpretable by human minds, and is thereby multiple in its meaning. There remains, after its going forth from heaven, no single reading: the text is polysemic not univocal. And yet the theorists leave unexamined the questions of motive and meaning to which we perpetually return. The first part of the story—the backdrop of it, really—cannot be effaced. The Torah may have left heaven, *but it came from there.*

The theorists are right in perceiving indeterminacy in rabbinic exegesis: the Torah, like God, was seen to have many faces, and revealed those faces at different moments, making infinite reading possible. Moshe Idel links midrash and God: "the nature of the hermeneutic enterprise reflects the dynamic nature of God. In lieu of one, frozen type of information that can be extracted from a biblical verse…the biblical text now remains open for novel interpretations."[121] Kugel sums up the rabbinic view in a similar fashion: "in short, a text is a text, and whatever hidden meaning one is able to reveal in it is there from divine plan."[122] And yet, if we stop for a moment to focus on Idel's comment about God, to linger over the second part of what Kugel has said, we find ourselves entirely outside the purview of postmodern theory.

Intertextuality and the Reading of Midrash, 35). Boyarin's concern here is to point to the direction in which the text is taken—and the way that the text itself is seen to give license to that direction—rather than to focus on what the rabbis perceived as its origin. Throughout his writing, however, he reflects the rabbinic view of divine authorship. "God, the implied author of the narrative of the Torah, has willingly, as it were, encoded into His text the very kinds of dialogue that all His epigones were destined willy-nilly to encode into theirs. As with all literature, so with the Torah, it is precisely the fault lines in the text, the gaps that its author has left, which enable reading," he asserts (ibid., 40); this is hardly a statement that Derrida would make.

119. The prophet Elijah.

120. *b. Baba Metzia*, 59a, b.

121. Moshe Idel, "Midrash vs. Other Jewish Hermeneutics," in *The Midrashic Imagination: Jewish Exegesis, Thought and History* (ed. Michael Fishbane; Albany: SUNY Press, 1993), 50.

122. Kugel, "Two Introductions to Midrash," 79.

For Derrida and the other literary theorists introduced here, there is no notion of a divine plan, or even of the divine. Which brings us to the theological assumptions behind the rabbis' writing of midrash, and the concomitant reasons for rejecting the term "midrash" to describe secular retellings of biblical stories. In his appendix on midrash and literary theory, Halivni notes "another dissimilarity that may disturb the resemblance between the rabbis of the Talmud and the modern literary theorists [is that]…the rabbis may not have applied their mode of interpretation to any text other than the biblical one."[123] Midrash arose as a response to the Bible, not as a response to text generally.

There is clearly a theological reason for this: the biblical text had a status unlike any other. In Jewish tradition, it is understood to be the word of God. Hence, as Irving Jacobs claims, "the determining factor in early Jewish scriptural exegesis was the rabbis' perception of the Bible itself. They saw it as the revealed word of God, not only in terms of its eternal validity, but also with regard to the uniqueness of its languages, which transcended the ordinary medium of human communication."[124] Handelman pushes the description further, noting that "for the Jews, God manifested Himself through words in a divine text."[125] Moreover, because God manifested himself through the text, access to God came through the words themselves.[126] Given the notion of the Bible as containing "Divine Language," for the rabbis,

> the most common-place terms and expressions…were to be regarded as 'containers' of deeper meanings, which the interpreter was required to unlock. Consequently, the main challenge of the Bible as perceived by the ancient Jewish exegetes, was to decode its messages, to reveal the inner significance of the text.[127]

123.   Halivni, *Peshat and Derash*, 160.
124.   Jacobs, *The Midrashic Process*, 4.
125.   Handelman, *The Slayers of Moses*, 32–33.
126.   Handelman notes that "in Hebrew thought, the word is reality in its most concentrated, compact, essential form" (ibid., 32). Consider the rabbinic understanding of the connection between Torah and the world: the Torah is the blueprint for the universe; the universe itself is the product of Torah. In many respects, this perspective is akin to New Criticism's notion of a poem as the locus of reality. As I mentioned earlier, New Criticism did not see the poem as divorced from reality, merely as independent of the (psychological) reality of both its creator and its reader. Rather, the 'coherence' of the poem, its internal unity, was thought to correspond to reality itself. For the New Critics, as important as 'coherence' was 'integration,' the "belief that the poem's discourse somehow included reality itself" (Eagleton, *Literary Theory*, 47).
127.   Jacobs, *The Midrashic Process*, 4.

That reading involves unlocking a deeper meaning has a theological consequence. Kugel asserts that "proper understanding is inseparable from prophecy itself":[128] the rabbis used interpretation as a means of bringing themselves closer to God. Equally, as the well-known dictum about the Shekhina alighting whenever two or more people sit together to study Torah, they perceived God as bringing himself closer to those who engage his word.

At this point, let us revisit one of Handelman's comments, shifting our emphasis in the reconsideration. She notes that "for the rabbis, however, the primary reality was linguistic: *true being was a God who speaks and creates texts,*[129] and *imitatio dei* was not silent suffering but speaking and interpreting." Behind the midrashim, as multivalent as they are, lies one basic presupposition: God is the author of the text expounded.

In light of this fundamental aspect of midrashic exegesis, the appropriation of the construct of midrash by literary theorists seems to have been ill-conceived. Midrash is not as multivalent as the theorists would have us believe; it is driven by its approach. In "The World of Ancient Biblical Interpreters," his introduction to *The Bible as It Was*, Kugel puts forth four assumptions he asserts were commonly held by early interpreters: to begin, the Bible is a fundamentally cryptic document.[130] As Robert Alter describes it:

> The Bible…is artfully contrived…to open up a dense swarm of variously compelling possibilities, leading us to ponder the imponderables of human character, human nature, historical causation, revelation, election, and man's encounters with the divine. If all literary texts are open-ended, the Bible, certainly in its narrative aspect, is willfully, provocatively open-ended: that, indeed, is why there is always room for more commentary.[131]

The text lends itself to interpretation; it is gapped, laconic, ambiguous, even obscure. And yet this is not all. "The Bible has invited endless exegesis not only because of the drastic economy of its means of expression but also because it conceives of the world as a place full of things to

---

128. Kugel, "Two Introductions to Midrash," 84. Kugel's view on this point stands in sharp distinction to Stern's, who states that "the act of interpretation in midrash is almost completely severed from prophecy or revelatory experience" (Stern, "Midrash and the Language of Exegesis," 152).

129. Emphasis mine.

130. James Kugel, *The Bible as It Was* (Cambridge, Mass.: The Belknap Press of Harvard University Press, 1997), 18.

131. Robert Alter, *The World of Biblical Literature* (New York: Basic, 1992). 152.

understand in which the things of ultimate importance defy human understanding";[132] the Bible comes from beyond us. We must dig deep into the text to understand it, while knowing that we will also never understand it.

This special status of the Bible gives the text another significance: as the second assumption has it, the Bible is an ongoing source of guidance,[133] the word of God and the way for humans. In midrash, "the major assumption is that the authoritative text is an independent entity, to be encountered as a sacred text, which can be interrogated to answer religious questions;[134] the boundaries between God and Torah have become delineated, and the Torah stands in for God in his historical absence.

The third assumption is that the Bible is "perfect and perfectly harmonious,"[135] a characteristic that is closely linked to the fourth basic assumption: the Bible is "somehow divinely sanctioned, of divine provenance, or divinely inspired."[136] Kugel concedes that this last point is perhaps least obvious to the reader of ancient interpretation, particularly given the practice of Greek interpreters to refer to human authors of biblical texts.[137] However, he points to Judith's prayer (which begins with an invocation of Simeon's avenging his sister's defilement[138] and builds to an assertion of God's presence and hand in all human drama) as evidence that the early exegetes understood God to have been the author of all scripture, including "the ordinary narrative fabric of biblical books."[139] Kugel's contention that the God to whom Judith appeals is the omniscient narrator of Genesis is based in her declaration:

> For you have done these things and those that went before and those that followed. You have designed the things that are now and those that are to come. What you had in mind has happened; the things you decided on presented themselves and said, 'Here we are!' For all your ways are prepared in advance, and your judgment is with foreknowledge.[140]

132.   Alter, *The World of Biblical Literature*, 22.
133.   Kugel, *The Bible as It Was*, 19: "Scripture constitutes one great Book of Instruction, and as such is a fundamentally *relevant* text."
134.   Idel, "Midrash vs. Other Jewish Hermeneutics," 49.
135.   Kugel, *The Bible as It Was*, 20.
136.   Ibid., 22.
137.   Moses as author the Torah, David and Solomon as authors of the Psalms, Qohelet as author of Ecclesiastes, for instance. Ibid.
138.   Jdt 9:2: "O Lord of my ancestor Simeon, to whom you gave a sword to take revenge on those strangers who had torn off a virgin's clothing to defile her, and exposed her thighs to put her to shame, and polluted her womb to disgrace her; for you said 'It shall not be done'—yet they did it."
139.   Kugel, *The Bible as It Was*, 22.
140.   Jdt 9:5–6.

This post-biblical understanding of God's role has its biblical forerunners; Isaiah also spoke of God as knowing and announcing history.[141] For interpreters from biblical times forth, the notion of God as author and knower of Torah was prevalent.

What precisely this understanding of God entails is less than clear. As Moshe Idel notes, "the Midrash was informed by a theology that has never been presented explicitly."[142] In contrast to other Jewish exegesis, "it is expressly dominated by a personalistic view of God, conceived of as deeply concerned with the human affairs: a changing entity, endowed with power and able to interfere in the course of history."[143] This perspective in which there is a "theological identification of God with the vicissitudes of Jewish history"[144] is borne out of the exile experience of the rabbis, Idel claims. The God of Isaiah, the one who ruled history, has become, in the rabbinic world, a God who "willingly accepts the tragic *fatum* of his elected people."[145] The writer of the biblical text has given it to his people that they may make sense of their situation. The sense-making is the proliferation of exegesis.

Thus, past its openness and freedom, midrash is driven by a single rule, by one theological principle: God is the divine author of the text. The text could not be pushed such that it was made to say anything that defied this basic principle, and its corollary, that the biblical text is therefore perfect and perfectly harmonious.[146] The midrashic enterprise was, as illustrated above, an attempt to harmonize apparent imperfections. The attempt was always made from within the bounds of a theological perspective, one which held God as the author (if not current owner) of the text.

Thus, in strong opposition to the theorists who argue for the infinite multiplicity of rabbinic readings are scholars who assert the theological underpinnings of rabbinic readings. William Scott Green goes so far as

---

141. Isa 44:6–8: "Thus says the Lord, the King of Israel, and his Redeemer, the Lord of hosts; I am the first and I am the last; besides me there is no god. Who is like me? Let them proclaim it, let them declare it and set it forth before me. Who has announced from of old the things to come? Let them tell us what is yet to be. Do not fear, or be afraid; have I not told you from of old and declared it? You are my witnesses! Is there any god besides me? There is no other rock; I know not one."

142. Idel, "Midrash vs. Other Jewish Hermeneutics," 49.

143. Ibid.

144. Ibid.

145. Ibid.

146. Thus every transcription of the Torah had to be completely faithful; *b. Erubin* 13a tells us that a letter missing from or added to a *Sefer Torah* could "destroy the world."

to argue that the rabbinic task extended even beyond limiting any reading that countered notions of the perfection of divine writ, to limiting reading *period*. As Green notes, the Hebrew of the Torah was written without vowels, and thus "could not be read by itself because its writing was indeterminate script."[147] The vocalization of the text by the rabbis was a means not only of making the Torah discourse, it was a means of "imposing a determinate discourse on it."[148] The rabbis could not read the text without the vowels; with the vowels, however, the text they could read was, to some degree, one that they themselves had created. In their claiming that the writing and discourse of scripture were part of oral Torah handed from God and possessing the same authoritative status as the written Torah, the rabbis asserted their exclusive right to interpretation and manipulation of the sacred text. Thus they became the determiners—and hence limiters—of meaning, and midrash itself became determinate.[149] Green refutes the theorists' notion that

> in their use of scripture, rabbis confronted the 'undecidability of textual meaning'... [Rather] as heirs and practitioners of a levitical piety, rabbis could afford little tolerance of ambiguity, uncertainty, or unclarity. The holy writ on the sacred scroll that was the stable center of their system could not appear to speak, as it were, with a forked or twisted tongue.[150]

So, in their controlling the text, in their giving it the vowels that allowed it to speak, the rabbis had the Torah speak in their voice, and echo their concerns.

Here Green points to the problems with the literary theoretical consideration of midrash. Midrash is not indeterminate; it cannot be made to say everything. It is itself a part of the sacred tradition, and it reflects an understanding of the relationship between Israel, its sacred text, and that text's divine author. As Green puts it, "the rabbinic interpretation of scripture, therefore, was anything but indeterminate or equivocal. Rather, it was an exercise—and a remarkably successful one—in the dictation, limitation, and closure of what became a commanding Judaic

---

147.   Green, "Writing with Scripture," 15.

148.   Ibid., 15.

149.   The rabbinic determination of meaning through vowels was quite deliberate: there are, however, ten passages in the Torah that the tannaim marked with a dot, indicating a suspect or uncertain reading. The *Abbot deRabbi Natan* preserves a midrash about the dotted passages: "Ezra the Scribe said, If when Elijah comes, he protests to me, Why did you adopt the doubtful readings, I'll say to him, Notice I put dots over them; and if he says to me, You've copied well, I'll then remove the dots" (Goldin, "From Text to Interpretation," 272).

150.   Green, "Writing with Scripture," 21.

discourse."[151] It seems that midrash may not be the thing the theorists thought it was.

And yet, despite the constraints that Green is so careful to articulate, midrash has nonetheless come to be synonymous with indeterminacy (and deconstruction) within the fields of literary theory. To speak now of midrash in the context of literary theory, or studies in literature generally, is to conjure up theorists like Derrida or Barthes and their respective (and inter-related) concepts of text. These concepts, as this section should make clear, reflect a pervasive misunderstanding (or, in Bloom's terms, misreading) of midrash. Nonetheless, because midrash has entered the field of literary study, any further co-opting of the vocabulary in the context of literary study has to happen in full awareness of this intellectual history, openly acknowledging the currency the term has had among postmodern theorists.[152]

What is Modern Midrash?

Reconsidering the term midrash in the context of literary studies cannot simply entail exposing the shortcomings of the literary theoretical understanding of midrash. The term has gained currency in other literary circles as well. It has had a (third) incarnation as describing post-biblical story-telling. This has been particularly—although not exclusively—the case in Jewish literary circles.

Modern creative writers have sometimes been explicit in their equation of "midrash" and "Jewish." In her short story "Sarah," Allegra Goodman describes a classroom of adult students at the Washington Jewish Community Center all writing creative *midrashim*: stories, poems, and reflections based in the Bible but betraying their authors' own personal histories.[153] The story, ostensibly *about* midrash, is itself a midrash—it is a reflection on the biblical Sarah's having a child in her old age,[154] a

151. Ibid., 21–22.

152. Admittedly, my thinking here is influenced somewhat by the rules of scientific nomenclature—specifically, the naming of new species—that dictate that, in order to avoid confusion, once a name has been used it can never be re-used. I do recognize the profound irony in my hesitation to recycle a term.

153. Allegra Goodman, "Sarah," in *The Family Markowitz* (New York: Washington Square Press, 1997), 208–33.

154. In the short story, the child of old age is a metaphoric one; the protagonist, Sarah, a writer, laughs at the thought of conceiving (of) a new novel so late in her life. She ends up bringing Rose, her increasingly dependent mother-in-law, into her home, thus taking on mothering duties in her mid-age. In this respect, Goodman is inverting the biblical story of Sarah in which it is the mother who is advanced in years; here it is the child.

commentary on the relationship of Ruth and Naomi. As a story about
Jews who write *midrashim* about Jewish experience, as a story written by
a Jew, it thus falls squarely within the popular understanding of "midrash." What is captured in Goodman's fiction also occurs in the real
world: in Philadelphia, a (self-described) "remarkable group of writers,
artists and scholars have created The Institute for Contemporary Midrash
(ICM) to promote the development of contemporary midrash on biblical
and liturgical texts."[155] In practice, modern midrash has not only emerged
as a popular genre but, thanks in part to the wild successes of books like
The Red Tent, comes to be almost synonymous with Jewish creative
writing.

Curiously, however, the idea of midrash also sometimes escapes its
Jewish context. In describing his own poems on biblical themes, and in
introducing *Modern Poems on the Bible: An Anthology*, his collection of
poetry based in the Bible, poet David Curzon notes that he "view[s]
modern poetry on the Bible as an extension of Midrash, the tradition of
rabbinical commentary, which shares with contemporary criticism a
belief in the multivalent meaning of texts."[156] In Curzon's anthology,
"whether the poets knew it or not, and some of them did,"[157] all of William Butler Yeats, Marianne Moore, Rainer Maria Rilke, Jorge Luis
Borges, Dan Pagis, Paul Celan, Edna Aphek, and Yevgeny Vinokurov—
non-Jews and Jews alike—engaged in the making of midrash. Here
Curzon uses midrash as the collective term for the "rabbinic flights of
interpretive imagination,"[158] which he describes as having three characteristics: midrash is "a response to a specific and very short biblical
text, the response is imaginative, and it makes a point."[159] According to
Curzon, the imaginative responses of the twentieth-century writers in his
collection share the hermeneutic concerns of the rabbis they may or may
not know they are echoing. Like the rabbis, most of Curzon's authors
"respond to the terse and archaic narrative style of the text with elaborations and anachronisms";[160] they often "report the thoughts and talk
omitted in the text";[161] they "use the technique of an omniscient narrator
to elaborate on matters left up to the imagination by the terseness of the

---

155.   Institute for Contemporary Midrash homepage, online: http://www.
icmidrash.org/about/about.htm
156.   David Curzon, ed., *Modern Poems on the Bible: An Anthology* (Philadelphia: Jewish Publication Society, 1994), 2.
157.   Ibid., 3.
158.   Ibid.
159.   Ibid., 4–5.
160.   Ibid., 5.
161.   Ibid., 6.

text."[162] Further, both the rabbis and the contemporary writers deal with apparent problems in the non-narrative aspects of midrash that "come from the historic development of new circumstances, ideas and values that, from at least the Hellenistic period onward, have appeared incompatible with much of the ancient biblical writing."[163] In short, interpretation can renew or make relevant texts that are chronologically remote. In terms of approach, the rabbis draw on prooftexts from disparate parts of the Bible to underscore their points; the contemporary version does not use what Curzon calls "the verse from afar"[164] but its close relative: the modern "implicit prooftext."[165] The poets "present an understanding of biblical texts in the light of something else that is introduced in evidence. In twentieth-century midrashic poems, such implicit proof-texts are drawn from virtually all domains of knowledge, including science, mathematics, history, other religious traditions, and personal experience."[166] Contemporary writers find their verses from afar outside the Bible, possibly even from beyond the text and instead from experience, from the poets' own worlds. And, in Curzon's view, these worlds may be Jewish or non-Jewish.

The Jewish Question

Curzon has made clear the many ways that biblical retelling and midrash are analogous. The retellings that concern us are literary and aesthetic; like the aggadot they are legend or lore (rather than law). Their connection to their *Urtexts* parallels the aggadot's to the Bible: retellings are selective in their use of the text, offering not a line by line commentary but impressions, imitations, or expansions. Thus the retellings and the aggadot share a freedom and originality which are not only conceptual but formal. Where the aggadot take many forms, retellings too span genres. Finally, while allusion (according to critic Christopher Ricks, at least) succeeds only when it turns the reader back to the original text (wherein lies the greater glory), midrash (or at least, midrash as understood by Stern and Fishbane) puts text and commentary on equal footing. Thus, like the aggadot, the retellings strive to be an independent literature, though they often live in the shadows of the texts that bore them.

162. Ibid.
163. Ibid., 7.
164. Ibid., 15.
165. Ibid., 12.
166. Ibid., 14.

In *Modern Midrash*, a book that grew out of a doctoral dissertation on modern Hebrew writers' retellings of Hasidic tales, David C. Jacobson uses the term midrash to "refer to the Jewish tradition of the interpretive retelling of biblical stories that began within the Bible itself, developed in the rabbinic periods and...has continued to the present."[167] To illustrate this ongoing tradition of interpretive retelling, Jacobson points to recastings of the Akedah—a story we have already touched on in this chapter and to which we will return again shortly—tracing a development in the depictions of Isaac through centuries of Jewish lore. In the biblical account, Isaac is the unwitting child, the object in a story about another's devotion to God. He is the innocent, offered as a sacrifice and rescued at the last moment. In the rabbinic tales, he is cast as complicit adult, not only offering himself on the altar, but asking his father to tie him there tightly. In medieval Jewish legend he is the favorite son, slaughtered and then resurrected. And in the post-Holocaust poetry of modern Hebrew poet Amir Gilboa, he is the child again, watching in helpless horror as his own father is slaughtered. For Jacobson, the authors of these retellings "created new works out of the Biblical text in significantly different ways that reflect each period's literary norms and attitudes towards the Bible."[168] Thus the three post-biblical depictions reflect their authors' own concerns with piety and obedience; suffering and martyrdom; and senseless decimation and loss, respectively. Their differences aside, Jacobson contends that they "share a common midrashic impulse to use the Bible as a source of characters, plots, images and themes in order to represent contemporary issues and concerns. For authors of midrash, the way that a biblical text can serve as a meaningful vehicle for the representation of contemporary reality is by transforming it, sometimes even to the point of turning it on its head."[169] This is particularly true of Gilboa, whose poem reacts against—rather than builds upon—a longstanding Jewish tradition valorizing (self-)sacrifice. The ideal of boundless devotion found in rabbinic midrash is absent in his modern midrash.

And yet, in terms of literary heritage, or awareness of the midrashic tradition at least, Jacobson can somewhat reasonably trace a line of influence from the Bible to the rabbis to the medievalists directly to Amir Gilboa and just about any other twentieth-century Jew of his choosing. But even Jacobson is aware of the limits to which he can press the nomenclature. Midrash is a mode of exegesis. In the case of the binding

---

167. Jacobson, *Modern Midrash*, 1.
168. Ibid.
169. Ibid., 3.

of Isaac, both the rabbis and the medieval poets draw their readings from the biblical text. But this is not always the case; as Jacobson himself points out, "at other times rabbinic and medieval retellers of biblical tales make no real claim that there is an exegetical basis for their retold stories."[170] All the more so modern writers like Gilboa or Dan Pagis,[171] who eye the biblical text with suspicion and subvert it through their rewritings.

Recognizing this problem, Jacobson turns to Alan Mintz's work,[172] drawing from it the term "figuration," which Mintz uses to describe the transformation of characters from the past "into new types that reflect the values and experiences of the present."[173] This move towards the language of literature opens up the fields of literary criticism and theory for Jacobson. He avails himself of both. He turns first to the notion of mythopoesis, as described by Northrop Frye and Harry Slochower, noting that mythopoetic writers "discover in the myths of the past a set of cultural values superior to the currently accepted ones. [They] therefore see the mythic world of the past as a source of revolutionary values more appropriate to the current needs of their time than are the values of the present."[174] The use of the voices of the past to speak to the readers of the present is commonplace in Jewish literature, particularly literature with overt biblical allusions. History is brought to bear on the present; through the creation of counterhistories, Jewish writers respond to contemporary crises. The crisis of modernity spurs a particularly Jewish type of retelling. According to Jacobson, in addition to seeing modern Jewish retelling in light of midrash and mythopoesis, "it is also helpful to note its relationship to the literary phenomenon of 'intertextuality' that has received so much recent attention by critics."[175] In his view, Julia Kristeva and Harold Bloom, about whom he comments briefly, "are analyzing a process of literary creation which is analogous to that of the modern

170. Ibid.

171. Dan Pagis is another contemporary Israeli poet, a survivor who uses biblical characters, passages, and themes to jarring effect, often revisiting them in poems about the Holocaust.

172. Specifically, to Mintz's *Hurban: Responses to Catastrophe in Jewish Literature* (New York: Columbia University Press, 1984).

173. Ibid, 4.

174. Ibid., 5.

175. Ibid. I came to Jacobson's work relatively far into my thinking on the topic, and when I arrived at this sentence wondered whether I was about to discover that he had already written this book for me. As it turns out, he pays only cursory attention to the concepts of midrash and intertextuality: his concern is with close readings of specific works rather than with the theoretical underpinnings of these readings.

writer retelling the narratives of his cultural tradition."[176] Midrash, mythopoesis, and intertextuality all inform the Jewish retelling.

Jacobson draws from these three literary phenomena because

> the reteller of traditional Jewish narratives shares with the midrashic exegete, the mythopoetic writer, and the poet engaged in an intertextual struggle with a precursor an attempt to appropriate a text from the past and transform it in order to better understand the experiences of the present.[177]

Yet while he entertains all three modes, Jacobson ultimately describes the retellings as midrash. The designation both lacks precision and carries with it significant extant connotations.

At no point does Jacobson attempt to explain what is traditionally meant or entailed by midrash. Rather, as indicated, he traces a spectrum of Jewish revisitations of traditional literature. Within this frame, he offers "a system for categorizing Hebrew works related to traditional narratives according to the nature of their relationship to the traditional narratives on which they are based and the contemporary cultural context in which they are written."[178] At one end we find Buber's *'Or Haganuz*, a collection of Hasidic tales that preserves the plot, characterization, and style of the traditional narratives, while making "some adjustments to meet contemporary literary norms."[179] At the other, we find poems, plays, and novels that make sustained allusion to traditional Jewish narrative in their descriptions of contemporary experience. Between these two poles, says Jacobson, lies modern midrash. It "maintains much of the plot and characterization in the traditional narratives on which it is based, but it takes great liberty in adding and subtracting aspects of the narratives' content and imaginatively retells the narratives in a more contemporary

---

176. Ibid., 6. I find this comment contentious. Jacobson's treatment of intertextuality is only a paragraph long; the concept is by no means central to his discussion. However, while he does note that "theories of intertextuality do not generally focus on the specific phenomenon of the retelling of traditional narratives" (ibid.), he in no way indicates that theories of intertextuality are not in the least concerned with authorial intent or even with writing as a conscious act. For both Kristeva and Bloom, texts seem merely to happen. Intertextuality is a fact, because every text by definition refers to every text before it, not because any given author seeks to emulate, transform, revisit etc. his literary forerunners. (This perception reminds me of Foucault's notion of power: power is not exerted; it is not contingent on subject or object. Power itself deploys.) I treat this problem in my discussion of intertextuality proper.

177. Ibid. Given intertextuality's effacing of the author, a third of this sentence rings false.

178. Ibid., 7.

179. Ibid.

style."[180] Most significant, for the present purposes at least, modern midrash "is a particularly illuminating source of information about the relationship of the modern Jew to the Jewish cultural past and present."[181] According to these criteria, biblical retellings by non-Jews are not midrash, despite being based in a Jewish telling.

Although David Curzon is quite willing to extend the understanding of midrash to include non-Jewish writing, for Jacobson, midrash is an exclusively Jewish mode of exegesis. By this he means that midrash is not merely written by Jews, but by Jews immersed in the Jewish exegetical tradition.[182] James Kugel describes midrash as a Jewish mode of exegesis, although this characterization earns him the wrath of Jacob Neusner, who rails:

> Some imagine that *midrash* for Jewish exegetes generically differs from *exegesis* for non-Jewish ones. My sense is that Kugel and his colleagues wish to think so, though they do not prove it in concrete ways. What hermeneutics characterizes *all* exegeses produced by Jews (everyone, everywhere, in all Judaisms, all canonical constructions), but *no* exegeses produced by non-Jews (anywhere, in all Christianities and among all their canonical compositions), who presumably do not produce *midrashim* on verses but do produce exegeses of verses, of the same Hebrew Scriptures no one has said. So as a category, *midrash* meaning simply all "Jewish" or "Judaic exegesis" but no gentile exegesis rests upon self-referential, therefore essentially inherent (that is, racist) lines. Appeals to innate traits, whether of race or religion or ethnic group, settle no important questions for reasonable people.
>
> Accordingly, the first usage seems so general as to add up to nothing, or so racist as to add up to an unacceptable claim to private discourse conducted through inherently ethnic or national or religious modes of sensibility not shared with the generality of humanity. If *midrash* is what Jews do while *exegesis* is what gentiles do when each party, respectively, interprets the same verses of the same Holy Scripture with (in modern times) essentially the same result as to the meaning of the passage at hand, then in my mind it follows that *midrash*, a foreign word, simply refers to the same thing—the same activity or process of thought or intellectual pursuit—as does *exegesis*, an English word. Then the word *midrash* bears no more, or less, meaning than the word *exegesis*.[183]

180.   Ibid.
181.   Ibid., 8.
182.   Jacobson is not alone in this view. Consider this comment by David Weiss Halivni: of one of the great Jewish thinkers, Moses Mendelssohn, Halivni notes "[he] and his entourage…were so influenced by the outside world, by the non-Jewish world, that they may no longer count as a bona fide link in the chain of traditional biblical exegesis" (Halivni, *Peshat and Derash*, 30). If Mendelsohn is not Jewish, than there is no arguing for Milton or Rilke.
183.   Neusner, *Midrash as Literature*, 4.

Bracketing the ethnic question, one could argue that there are in fact theological underpinnings to midrash that make the term inapplicable to many secular writers of biblically themed literature—Jewish and Christian both.[184] As we saw in our questioning of the literary-theoretical understanding of midrash, one might reasonably argue that midrash is marked not by Jewishness, but by a belief in the divinity of the biblical text.[185]

David Stern, in his introduction to Bialik's *Sefer Ha-Aggadah*, underscores the difference between the modern poet and the ancient rabbis. For the latter, biblical interpretation was "an intrinsically religious pursuit; a path to worshipping God."[186] "If you wish to know Him by whose word the world came into being, study *Aggadah*; you will thereby come to know the Holy One, blessed be He, and hold fast to his ways," a famous Rabbinic statement declares.[187] Obviously, as Neusner is arguing, the criterion of belief in the divine origin of the Bible alone does not make Jews the only ones able to write midrash. But an understanding of interpretation as a way of coming to know God—and, particularly, a conviction that interpretation is the site where God is to be found—has a distinctly Jewish ring.

Two other factors push midrash into the wholly Jewish category, and they need to be considered here. The first, not specifically Jewish trait, is its provenance as a response to crisis.[188] The second, a more generally

---

184.   Conversely, one would then have to argue that a Christian re-writer of scripture who is familiar with ancient Christian exegesis (which aligns closely with early rabbinic hermeneutics) and who writes from a conviction that scripture is divine is without doubt writing midrash. As Peter S. Hawkins has made clear, a figure like Dante certainly fits the description.

185.   Interestingly, in her treatment of the use of scripture in twentieth-century Hebrew poetry, Ruth Kartun-Blum speaks not of midrash, but of "profane scripture," signaling her sense that "the confrontation of modern Hebrew literature with the biblical text is distinct from the traditional Jewish posture towards the Bible." Ruth Kartun-Blum, *Profane Scriptures* (Cincinnati: Hebrew Union College Press, 1999), 4.

186.   David Stern, "Introduction," in *The Book of Legends—Sefer Ha Aggadah* (ed. Hayim Nahum Bialik and Yehoshua Hana Ravnitzky; trans. William G. Braude; New York: Schocken, 1992), xxi.

187.   Ibid.

188.   As Mintz, Fishbane, and Heinemann all point out, midrash is very much a literature of crisis. Heinemann asserts, midrash "represents an attempt to develop new methods of exegesis to yield new understandings of Scripture in times of crisis and conflict" ("The Nature of the Aggadah," 42). This is particularly true after the fall of Jerusalem in 70 C.E.: "With the Temple's destruction, the main avenue of Jewish worship, the offering of sacrifices, along with many other religious practices and observances connected to the Temple cult, were all rendered impossible. How

theological theme, is its role as didactic literature. Neither characteristic alone makes midrash specifically Jewish. Narrowed and intertwined, however, they become inherently Jewish. The crises to which midrash responds are distinctly Jewish: it attempts to bridge time and tradition at moments of historical and religious uncertainty. The function of midrash becomes teaching about tradition at the very moments that the tradition seems most in danger of losing either its footing or its relevance.

In the time of transition "following the destruction of the Temple, the text of Torah itself became the primary sign of the continued existence of the covenantal relationship between God and Israel."[189] The rabbis "recentered Judaism, shifting its forms of worship from a particular place, a special class of religious functionaries, and a specific type of worship dependent both upon that place and its functionaries...to a complex of newly important institutions"[190] that included the synagogue, the Torah (and study thereof), and the Halakhah as a legal code. It was a period of transition from the Temple to the Torah; from the priests and prophets to the sages; and from the sacrificial cult to deeds of loving-kindness.[191] The Aggadah was the locus for much of the remaking of Judaism, for "the words of the Torah, its text, were also the lens, the prism, through which the sages viewed their own world."[192] They looked to Torah to make sense of their own situation, and they brought the biblical world to their own world.

Characteristic of rabbinic midrash is an effacing of the contemporary situation and a foregrounding of the biblical present; the rabbis collapse time and history, "unselfconsciously portray[ing] figures from the distant past like the patriarchs in their own image."[193] The function of this deliberate anachronizing is symbolic: "By bringing their own experiences to the interpretation of the words of Torah, and taking back from the Torah the language that allowed them to articulate their own experiences, the rabbis created a kind of mythical, timeless realm removed from the travails and injustices of contemporary history."[194] In this a-chronic realm, everything that the rabbis valued and believed (even everything

---

could Jews now worship God?" asks Stern (Stern, "Midrash and the Language of Exegesis," xx). Many of the givens of Judaism eradicated, it fell upon the rabbis not only to make sense of this catastrophe, but to ensure an uninterrupted line of tradition despite the evident fissure.

189. Stern, "Midrash and the Language of Exegesis," 153.
190. Stern, "Introduction," xx.
191. Heinemann, "The Nature of the Aggadah," 42.
192. Stern, "Introduction," xx.
193. Ibid.
194. Ibid.

that they feared) "could take shape, unimpeded by hostile forces, and be realized, however complexly so."[195] This perfect realm would then impart the knowledge and experiences necessary for living in this imperfect world.[196] The Bible served the rabbis not merely as an example by which to live: through creative transposition in aggadic midrash, the Bible gave the rabbis a place *to* live. The biblical world became the present; anxiety over the current state of exile was subsumed into a concern with propagating the ongoing validity and presence of the biblical story.

The crises to which midrash was able to attend were not exclusively historical. As the introduction to midrash above makes clear, they were also textual. As Fishbane notes, "exegesis arises out of a practical crisis of some sort—the incomprehensibility of a word or a rule, or the failure of the covenantal tradition to engage its audience."[197] This latter crisis— the failure of tradition—is directly related to the final concern about using the term midrash. As Judaism shifted from Temple to Torah, it also moved into the synagogue. Thus many of the midrashim have a homiletic function; they are tales told in synagogue.[198] Heinemann argues that aggadic interpretation had a theological undercurrent. The writers of the aggadot stood at a juncture between past, present, and future: they looked back to the Bible to uncover its full meaning and they looked forward from there to the present and the future. This location afforded them a vantage "to give direction to their own generations, and to guide them out of their spiritual complexities."[199] Aggadic interpretation was not as concerned with working on the surface irregularities of the Bible as it was grappling with contemporary problems, providing moral instruction, and bolstering faith.[200] Thus the rabbinic Aggadah was the product of the sages themselves, created "not for entertainment [but with] a strong and self-conscious didactic function, [of] clarif[ying] scripture and draw[ing] from it moral points."[201] The sages wrote Aggadah in the service of the Bible, wherein, in their view, was contained the answer to every contemporary problem.[202]

Just as the literary theorists are selective in their understanding of midrash, appropriating only those facets that reflect their theoretical concerns, so the literary critics present a version of midrash that does not

195.   Ibid.
196.   Ibid.
197.   Fishbane, "Inner Biblical Exegesis," 34.
198.   Heinemann, "The Nature of the Aggadah," 47.
199.   Ibid., 48.
200.   Ibid., 49.
201.   Ibid., 47.
202.   Ibid., 49.

wholly do justice to the traditional definition of the term. Midrash is a literature that takes as divine the focus of its inquiry (the Bible), and proceeds from a crisis in the text or in the community to interpret in ways that appear indeterminate and polysemous. The theological component seems entirely to have fallen out of the literary theorists' (and, in Curzon's case, the literary critics') renewed definition of midrash. Does this failure of "modern midrash" to reflect faithfully traditional midrash mean that the language of midrash cannot be used to illuminate literature?

Chapter 6

THE WORD IS VERY NEAR

From Aggadah to Halakhah:
Co-opting the Vocabulary of Midrash

Our entire discussion of midrash so far has been focused on the meaning of the term. What is midrash? Who has used the term and how? Is contemporary understanding of midrash at all representative of what midrash once was? When we use the term now, do we refer to the midrash of the rabbis; the midrash of the post-structuralists, the deconstructionists and the reader response critics; or the midrash of the David Jacobsons and David Curzons? The term, as we have seen, is quite open, and in itself does not get us too far in our thinking about how the language and presuppositions of midrash might be put towards a theory of literature. This question is altogether different from those of the literary theorists, who asked in what way midrash proves to be a literature that reflects the concerns of theory and in what ways the concerns of literary theory reflect those of midrash.

One of the closest connections between midrash and retelling has to do with approach: as Halivni describes it, the rabbis "read in" to the Bible. They bring to the text a meaning other than the one that is overtly there, and this entails undoing the original, for, where allegorizing preserves the surface meaning of a text, "reading in" displaces it. As a number of medieval scholars—Maimonides among them—assert, "the rabbis of the Talmud knew, if not in all cases, at least in most of them, that reading in does not represent the genuine meaning of the text, that the content occasioned by reading in is either rooted in tradition or is rabbinically instituted."[1] We cannot, for instance, read the plain sense of Genesis as telling us that Abraham was a Torah-observant Jew. In fact, his preparation of an unkosher meal of curds, milk, and a calf (Gen 18:8); his deception of Pharaoh and Abimelech (Gen 12, 20); and his

---

1. Halivni, *Peshat and Derash*, 13.

lack of concern for Hagar, the alien in his midst (Gen 21) and his concubine (see Deut 17:17), all suggest that he is not conversant in Halakhah. Nor, of course, should we reasonably expect him to be. As we have seen, however, Rab contended that Abraham "kept the whole Torah"—down to observing the 'erub of the dishes. Rab's assertion demands a certain degree of "reading in" to the text, and it is a reading in that necessarily displaces the original. Abraham could not have kept kosher *and* prepared a *treyf* meal for his guests.

This issue of displacement raises the interesting question of the relationship between the Bible (telling) and the midrash (retelling). That (in the rabbinic imagination at least) Abraham knew the Oral Law as well as the Torah and that Rab's reading displaces Genesis raises interesting questions about the relationship between the Bible and midrash—and between the telling and the retelling more broadly. What the Rab example seems to suggest is that in midrash—which comes from a community that values Written Torah and Oral Torah equally—the original author's intent carries no more weight than the intent of the interpreting author. As Bruns notes, "what matters in midrash is not only what lies behind the text as an originating intention but what is in front of the text where the text is put into play. The text is always contemporary with its readers or listeners, that is, always oriented toward the time and circumstances of the interpreter."[2] Midrash always recontextualizes the Bible, making it relevant (and present) in the interpreter's context. Similarly, the movement in the retelling is toward the reteller and her audience; the reteller imports the original into her contemporary setting, rather than taking her audience back to the world of the original (biblical) author.

In this respect, the reteller can be seen as breathing new life into the telling, or as contributing to its afterlife. This is true of the midrashist as well. The rabbis were evidently concerned that the Torah not grow stale. The *Pesikta de Rab Kahana* (12.12) avers, "Let the Torah never be for you an antiquated decree, but rather like a decree freshly issued, no more than two or three days old… [Indeed,] Ben Azzai said: not even as old as a decree issued two or three days ago, but as a decree issued this very day."[3] If we assume that the writer of the retelling seeks to freshen the telling, to embrace it rather than conquer it, then we may find yet another area of overlap in midrash and retelling's approach and stance.

Finally, the preservation of multiple, often contradictory readings one alongside the other, none of them favored, all of them made legitimate by the very fact of their being preserved for generations, evidenced for

2. Bruns, *Hermeneutics Ancient and Modern*, 105–6.
3. Ibid., 106.

literary theorists a rabbinic belief in the indeterminacy of the text. For our purposes, the multiplicity is interesting as well. Bruns notes that the "rabbis did not think of interpretation as problem solving, settling things once and for all, or working toward a final agreement as to how the text is to be taken."[4] Equally we can say that even the reteller who seeks to usurp rather than enhance the original text will be aware that his retelling, in turn, will be susceptible to revision. If we use midrash as our model for considering rewritings, we allow not only that the new text, while not displacing the original, may be valued as much as the old, but further that the new new text may stand alongside the old new text without displacing *it*. Not only does the New Testament understanding of Abraham as the obedient servant of faith seen in Hebrews[5] stand along the stories of Gen 12–23, it depends on them to make its theological point. And alongside Paul's understanding we could place *Fear and Trembling*, Søren Kierkegaard's treatise on faith, without rendering Genesis or Hebrews obsolete. If this is the case with theological readings, all the more so literary ones.

As we have seen, in the realm of the literary, theorists such as Derrida, Hartman, and Handelman, and critics such as Jacobson and Curzon have all employed the term "midrash." In the view of the literary theorists, it is a word specific enough to suggest indeterminacy. By contrast, the literary critics point to the breadth of its possible meanings: after all, the word midrash is merely the ancient Hebrew term for interpretation generally. If we introduce literature to midrash a third time, it will have to be a different, narrower definition of literature and a different, narrower definition of midrash. In our context, the narrowed sense of literature is the retelling. And the narrowed sense of midrash? Within the arena of midrash is an entire glossary of terms—among them Halakhah and Aggadah, which we have already encountered—that could be useful for our discussion of retellings.

Given this inverted approach—the putting of the concerns of midrash toward a theory of literature—we turn not to Aggadah, which has been the locus of literary investigation of rabbinic interpretation, but to Halakhah. The idea is not to argue for an affinity between retellings of biblical literature and legal exegesis—a difficult proposition, to be sure—but

---

4. Ibid., 110.

5. Viz. "By faith, Abraham when put to the test, offered up Isaac, and he who had received the promises was ready to slay his only son, of whom it was said, 'it is through Isaac that offspring shall be continued for you.' He reasoned that God was able to raise even from the dead, and he received Isaac back as a symbol" (Heb 11:17–19).

to mine Halakhah's more developed hermeneutical vocabulary. We look to the *middot*, the clearly defined principles that guide the ways legal interpreters (generally rabbis) have gained access to scripture. In turning to this dimension, we can engage midrash without also having to engage midrash as re-presented in literary theory and criticism. More significantly, however, by considering exegetical principles—all turning on the question of approach—we can find in the vocabulary of midrash the very precision it lacked in the accounts of Derrida, Curzon and Jacobson.

The Middot: *Principles of Rabbinic Exegesis*

How the rabbis approached the biblical text is of prime significance to the present discussion. We cannot, of course, know what they thought they were doing as they interpreted. This ignorance is perhaps helpful; if we accept our inability truly to discern how they conceived of themselves, we by extension rescue ourselves us from attempting to imagine what John Milton, Cecil B. DeMille, or Barbara Kingsolver thought they were doing to Judges when they produced *Samson Agonistes*, "Samson and Delilah," and *The Poisonwood Bible* (respectively). That said, we can gain insight by speaking generally about the broader hermeneutical questions of approach and of stance. To reiterate: by approach, I mean the method by which the retelling gains access to the telling; by stance I mean the relationship of the retelling to the telling.

Rabbinic midrash derives rulings from biblical texts using a set of interpretive principles. Both the halakhic and aggadic midrashim follow *ha-middot she-ha-Torah nidreshet bahen*—the principles through which the Torah is expounded. In rabbinic literature, we find different lists of these hermeneutic principles—Hillel's seven principles, Rabbi Ishmael's thirteen,[6] Rabbi Eliezer the son of Rabbi Yose HaGelili's thirty-two[7]—which outline some, but never all, of the rules of aggadic and halakhic midrash.

---

6. R. Ishmael's thirteen principles have the greater status in terms of tradition: they are part of the daily morning prayers and are understood to have been given by God at Sinai. Hillel's seven are found within Ishmael's thirteen; the thirteen develop with greater specificity those principles we will examine here, with subclassifications creating the additional six tenets.

7. The Malbim (R. Meir Loeb ben Yehiel Michael 1809–1879) went so far as to compile a list of 613 principles of halakhic midrash, mirroring the 613 commandments given to Moses at Sinai.

The base set of seven, those compiled by Hillel, presents us with a fundamental vocabulary that we can apply to our understandings of retellings. They consist of rules by which an exegete can gain entry into a text; they offer a way of defining relationships between Urtexts and texts (and, in fact, between tellings and retellings). The seven principles are: inference from major to minor; inference from a similarity of phrases; deduction from one verse; deduction from two verses; inference from general and particular/inference from particular and general; similarity elsewhere; deduction from context.

These seven rules offer approaches that can be seen in literary retellings as well as in legal expositions. Finding their application for literature requires a certain contortion of the *middot*; for our purposes here the concise rules will come to take on less than literal meanings. In turning to the principles, we are perpetuating the afterlife not only of halakhic rulings, but of the rules themselves: we are participating in the very activity with which this exploration concerns itself. Beyond the apparently mimetic or self-reflexive nature of this conscious transformation of tradition, however, is a genuine concern with what lies behind each rabbinic principle. Thus we will begin by examining what each rule means in the context of traditional interpretation. We will then read beyond the tradition, expanding the definition so as to consider the understanding of approach—of entry into the text—that drives the rule. This consideration will allow us to determine whether and how we might be able to use the *middot* to encompass contemporary retellings, as we test out the applicability of the newly redefined principle on a particular retelling.

Kal vahomer (קַל וָחֹמֶר)

The phrase *kal vahomer* refers to an inference from minor to major. We see in Deuteronomy, for instance, rules about the burial of a criminal: "If a man is guilty of a capital offense and is put to death, and you impale him on a stake, you must not let his corpse remain on the stake overnight, but must bury him the same day" (Deut 21:22–23). What we have here is the harder case—the treatment of the criminal. The logical argumentation of *kal vahomer* would thus go: "If this is the respect we show to the corpse of a criminal, all the more so would we act this way in the case of the ordinary (innocent) person." Similarly, the laws about slaves in Exodus command that the man who marries a second slave girl "must not withhold from this [first] one her food, her clothing, or her conjugal rights" (Exod 21:10). And, accordingly, the *kal vahomer* reading would be: "If this is how a man is to conduct himself with regard to a slave girl, all the more so with regard to a second wife." Put simply, this principle is an "explicit or implicit inference *a minori ad maius* and vice versa":[8] *kal vahomer* tells us "if even in this case…all the more so in this other."

This principle, which appears in all standard lists of exegetical rules, has the following premise: "If the law is stringent in a case where we are usually lenient, then it will certainly be stringent in a more serious case; likewise, if the law is lenient in a case where we are usually not lenient, then it will certainly be lenient in a less serious case."[9]

What drives the principle, what lies at its root, is the question of degree, of movement from lenient to stringent—*kal vahomer, a minori ad maius*. What appears in the lesser case holds true in the greater; what is true of the greater may also be applied to the lesser. It is useful to think about the question of degree in a discussion of retelling: frequently a new writing shifts the emphasis of a biblical text. A retelling may exert force, making a statement where the scriptural story did not, or it may shift the limelight, backing away from a question or issue at the core of a biblical narrative.

What kinds of retelling might reflect the principle of *kal vahomer*? Ones that shift the emphasis of the text, fleshing out a minor figure or minor event in scripture and making it the central concern of the re-scripting. There are abundant examples of this phenomenon in later literature: in the case of Isaac, who is overshadowed in the Bible by both his father and his sons, post-biblical narrative interest in him begins in antiquity and continues, as we will see, through modernity. The ancient interpreters' takes on Isaac evidence *kal vahomer*, the movement from lesser to greater.

The biblical story is very much about Abraham—he receives the command from God to take his son, his only son, whom he loves, Isaac, up the mountain for a sacrifice. He is the subject of thrity-two active verbs. By contrast, God, who is the hero of Genesis and the prime mover who sets the action in motion (Gen 22:1–19), has only three active verbs. He "put[s] Abraham to the test" (22:1), he "[says] to him, 'Abraham'" (22:1), and he "[says] take your son…" (22:2). Isaac, for his part, is all but inactive: he is the direct object of God's command and the recipient of Abraham's action. He himself merely does two things: he says, "My father" (22:7), to which Abraham replies *"Hineni,"* and he says, "Here is the firestone and the wood, but where is the sheep for the burnt offering?" Isaac's whole contribution to the drama is to make two tentative remarks. The telling itself foregrounds Abraham's presence, making him

8. Budick and Hartman, eds., *Midrash and Literature*, 363–67.
9. Adin Steinsaltz, *The Talmud: The Steinsaltz Edition.* Vol. 1, *A Reference Guide* (New York: Random House, 1989), 153.

the main actor. Three times he asserts himself, saying הנני. *Hineni*: "I am here; I am ready."[10] *I am present. I am at the center.*

And of course he is. When the story was written, and for the generations that first heard it, Abraham was in fact the indisputable hero of the story, the faithful and obedient servant who will do anything for his God. His willingness to sacrifice his son is a perfect defining myth for a religion establishing itself. His legacy continued in early interpretation—later books of the Bible have him as an exemplar of faith and obedience. Paul too, turns to Abraham as the father of faith.

During the Second Temple period, however, Abraham's hold on the story begins to slip, as the interpretive focus shifts from father to son. It is a strange development given Isaac's virtual absence in scripture. In Genesis, he is the innocent—perhaps, the fool—never the actor, always the acted upon. In this period, however, Isaac becomes not merely a prop in the story of his father's faith, but complicit in his own story. According to interpretation preserved in the apocryphal book of Judith, Isaac too was tested:

> In spite of everything let us give thanks to the Lord our God, who is putting us to the test as he did our forefathers. Remember what he did with Abraham, and *how he tested Isaac*, and what happened to Jacob in Mesopotamia in Syria, while he was keeping the sheep of Laban, his mother's brother. For he has not tried us with fire, as he did them, to search their hearts, nor has he taken revenge upon us; but the Lord scourges those who draw near to him, in order to admonish them. (Jdt 8:24–27, emphasis added)

The language of the test has shifted from father to son. Genesis 22 begins, "God tested Abraham" (Gen 22:1). In the apocryphal account, God "*did* with Abraham," but he *tested* Isaac.

Other pseudepigraphic sources have Isaac not merely tested, but unafraid of his father's obeying the commandment:

> Remember that it is through God that you have had a share in the world and have enjoyed life, and therefore you ought to endure any suffering for the sake of God. For his sake also our father Abraham was zealous to sacrifice his son Isaac, the ancestor of our nation; and *when Isaac saw his father's hand wielding a sword and descending upon him, he did not cower.*[11]

The second-century Jewish historian Josephus, writing after the fall of Jerusalem and the destruction of the Temple, has Isaac not only unflinching under the knife, but willing himself to the altar:

10. He responds thus to God (Gen 22:1 and 22:11) as well as to Isaac (Gen 22:7).
11. *4 Macc* 16:18–20.

Isaac, however, since he was descended from such a father, could be no less noble of spirit [than Abraham] and *received these words with delight*. He said that he would never have been worthy of being born in the first place were he not now to carry out the decision of God and his father and submit himself to the will of both.[12]

Here is a reading that seems to run directly counter to the biblical text. For, if Isaac did in fact know what was to happen, that he was to be the sacrifice, why would he ask his innocent question: "Father, here is the fire and here is the wood, but where is the lamb for a burnt offering?"[13]

We now see how the ancient interpreters arrive at the idea that Isaac is a willing participant. Convinced that the text is perfect and perfectly harmonious, that nothing in it is superfluous, they proceed under the assumption that repetition within the biblical text indicates new information. Thus, as we have seen, when Genesis tells us twice that father and son walked on together, יחדו ("together") comes to mean together physically and psychically: "The two of them walked together—the one to slaughter, the other to be slaughtered."[14] Likewise Philo asserts that יחדו indicates that Abraham and Isaac were "going at the same pace—no less with regard to their thinking that with their bodies, down the straight path whose end is holiness, they came to the designated place."[15] The impulse here is to show that father and son were of one mind.

In making Isaac complicit, these accounts place equal emphasis on Abraham and Isaac. Other versions shift the emphasis from father to son. *Midrash Rabbah* and *Targum Pseudo-Jonathan* both contend that Isaac was not only offered for the slaughter, not only that he agreed when he heard of the plan, but that he in fact offered himself up to God:

> Isaac and Ishmael were engaged in a controversy. Ishmael said to him, "I am more beloved than you, since I was circumcised at the age of thirteen, but you were circumcised as a baby and could not refuse." Isaac retorted, "All that you gave to the Holy One, blessed be He, was three drops of

---

12. Josephus, *Ant.* 1.232.

13. In fleshing out the biblical dialogue, *Targum Neofiti* gives us an answer. Abraham responds: "The Lord will provide a lamb for himself for burnt offering, my son—and if not, you will be the lamb for the burnt offering. And the two of them walked together with firm intention" (*Neofiti* 22:8). And *Genesis Rabbah*, again placing increasing emphasis on Isaac's role, has the son counter, "I will do all that the Lord has spoken to thee with joy and cheerfulness of heart. As the Lord lives, and as thy soul lives, there is nothing in my heart to cause me to deviate either to the right or to the left from the word he has spoken to thee" (*Gen. Rab.* 56:11).

14. *Gen. Rab.* 56:4.

15. Philo, *Abr.* 172.

blood. But behold, I am now 37 years old,[16] yet if God desired of me that I be slaughtered, I would not refuse." The Holy One, blessed be He, said, "This is the moment!"[17]

Why the shift in emphasis? What is at stake in showing that Isaac himself wanted to be a sacrifice for God? We see that Isaac not only becomes, for the rabbis, a martyr, but he gives martyrdom a precedent in Torah. And thus, the move from Abraham to Isaac as the hero of the Akedah is a response to the phenomenon of martyrdom—the exemplar of faith becomes not the one who kills but the one who is killed.[18]

Thus midrash is the new process by which the biblical text gets read against what it says, and the Bible is able to take on new meaning, to undergo a shift in emphasis without itself changing. To read as the rabbis do here, to move from the lesser figure and make it the greater, to draw out what is only latent in the scriptural narrative, allows us into the text in a way that simultaneously affirms the text alongside the contemporary response to and need for the text. The change in emphasis represents a shift from the minor to the major, increasing the lesser point, we thus make the move from *kal l'homer.*

Gezerah Shavah (גְּזֵירָה שָׁוָה)

Literally meaning "equal ordinance" or "statute,"[19] *gezerah shavah* is an argument based in analogy. The construct, broadly speaking, indicates that when a word means something in one place, it means the same in another. Like the principle of *clal ufrat* ("the fifth principle"), *gezerah shavah* operates not on the level of the verse but on that of the narrative as a whole. Here a passage is expounded by inference to a similar passage. If a word appears in two places in Torah, and a law is derived in one of those places, we can understand the law to apply in the other place also.

16. The number comes from the fact that the report of the death of Sarah, who bore Isaac at 90, immediately follows the Akedah. If Sarah died at 127, then Isaac would have been 37 at the time. (Other accounts, based on the amount of time Abraham spent in Hebron, calculate Isaac's age at the Akedah to be 26). While the biblical story takes on a radically different tenor when we read the sacrifice as a middle-aged man rather than a young boy, the *aggadot* about his complicity in the sacrifice become somewhat more comprehensible.

17. *Gen. Rab.* 55.4.

18. The idea of Isaac as the willing sacrifice appears in the Christian tradition as well: "Why was our father Abraham blessed? Was it not because he acted righteously and truthfully through faith? Isaac, knowing full well what was to happen, was willingly led to be sacrificed" (1 Clem 31:2–4).

19. H. L. Strack and Günter Stemburger, *Introduction to the Talmud and Midrash* (trans. Markus Bockmuehl; Minneapolis: Fortress, 1996), 18.

Inference from similarity elsewhere is a useful concept when considering literature whose relationship to the Bible is allusive—for instance, when an individual phrase in a retelling brings the telling to mind.[20] (The use of allusion is not strictly a literary device. The bringing to mind of a passage or story through an echoing phrase also has a halakhic function too: the concept of *zekher ladavar* [literally "remembrance of something"] is used to note that "even though there is no proof of this matter, there is an allusion to the matter."[21] Again, the divide between how we read literature and how we derive law was blurred long before our appropriation of halakhic principles for the service of literary analysis.)

A. B. Yehoshua builds an entire short story around God's command to Abraham to take his beloved son Isaac to the land of Moriah. Unlike "The Sacrifice" or "The Parable of the Old Man and the Young," which we will examine presently, Yehoshua's "Three Days and a Child" makes no overt references to the biblical tale. It is the story of Dov, a middle-aged Jerusalemite, who receives a phone call from an ex-girlfriend asking whether he would mind her three year-old son, Yahli, for three days while she and her husband prepare for university entrance examinations. The child is described as the ex-girlfriend's "only child, whom she loves":[22] this is the phrase on which we can build the analogy to the biblical text.

Once the phrase is identified and the biblical hook thereby established, the reader will find that the story of the binding of Isaac ripples through Yehoshua's text. The three days mirror the three days of Abraham and Isaac's walk up the mountain; the protagonist's desire for the death of the child Yahli reflects Abraham's own willingness to sacrifice his son Isaac. We can read these signs because the story provides us with the clue, the one verse, the variant on Gen 22:2, that tells us to look for Abraham and Isaac in the story of Dov and Yahli. The story could be understood as an instance of *gezerah shavah* in contemporary retelling.

---

20. Adele Berlin has also invoked the concept to describe literary readings of the Bible that highlight parallels among disparate narratives. She says that finding innerbiblical allusions and parallels can be an undertaking similar to *gezerah shavah*. Adele Berlin, "Literary Exegesis of Biblical Narrative: Between Poetics and Hermeneutics," in *"Not in Heaven": Coherence and Complexity in Biblical Narrative* (ed. Jason P. Rosenblatt and Joseph C. Sitterson, Jr.; Bloomington: Indiana University Press, 1991), 124.

21. Steinsaltz, *The Talmud*, 152

22. A. B. Yehoshua, "Three Days and a Child," in *The Continuing Silence of a Poet: The Collected Short Stories of A. B. Yehoshua* (Syracuse, N.Y.: Syracuse University Press, 1998), 37.

Binyan Av MiKatuv Echad (בִּנְיָן אָב מִכָּתוּב אֶחָד)

A principle of interpretation based on deduction, *binyan av mikatuv echad* arrives at rulings based on analysis of a lone verse: it takes into account the verse's various parts. The term literally means, "'founding of a family' (*ab* short for *bet ab*[23]) 'from a single Scriptural text.'"[24] Thus, "by means of this exegetical norm, a specific stipulation found in only one of a group of topically related biblical passages is applied to them all."[25] (Unlike *gezerah shavah*, the principle is applied when two cases are not precisely analogous to one another.[26]) The crux of this *middah* is that rulings based on related verses may be applied, so that other verses are made to harmonize with the one in question.

While, for the rabbis, causal reasoning (by which I mean their finding the cause of a problem and then predicting comparable outcomes in similar contexts) is at the heart of *binyan av*. What is potentially interesting for our discussion of approaches into the text is less the "building of the family" than that building's being based on *katuv echad*—one verse. We can use the principle of *binyan av mikatuv echad* to designate retellings which are built on one (explicit) scriptural verse, and which then use that verse to create something extending well beyond the biblical text.

By way of accounts derived from the Abraham cycle, which has been our "prooftext" throughout this chapter, we can turn to Leonard Cohen's song "Story of Isaac," which has as its scriptural point of departure the progression of Isaac and Abraham up the mountain ("so we started up the mountain"). Cohen's song recounts the Akedah from the perspective of a nine year-old Isaac. The song begins without agency: Isaac recalls, "the door it opened slowly." Abraham enters, his blue eyes shining, his voice cold, to tell his son, "I've had a vision / and you know I'm strong and holy, / I must do what I've been told." There is a distance in the account, a passivity: Abraham does not open the door; God does not test Abraham. Only Isaac is active: once Abraham tells him his vision, the two figures "started up the mountain," Abraham walking but Isaac running. Although Cohen seems to let the reader determine whether the child is running to keep up with his father or to get away from him, once the altar

---

23. *Lit.* "father's house."
24. Strack and Stemburger, *Introduction to the Talmud and Midrash*, 19.
25. Ibid.
26. The most basic type of *binyan av, mah mazinu*, asks us "What do we find?," and invariably tells us, "Just as we find in case A that law X applies, so too we may infer that in case Bible, which is similar to case A, law X should apply" (Steinsaltz, *The Talmud*, 149). Having a more complicated structure than *mah mazinu, binyan av mikatuv echad* "is used when the two cases being compared are not fully analogous, and so an objection is raised to the comparison" (ibid., 150).

is built, Cohen's Abraham is confident the child will obey: he looks "once behind his shoulder" but Isaac asserts, "he knew I would not hide." A sustained biblical allusion, built on the sole phrase "started up the mountain," the song becomes a commentary on peace and war. Cohen adjures his listeners to cease building altars on which to sacrifice children, to resist confusing human schemes with divine visions, to have mercy on all men at war. Cohen's Isaac reproaches those fathers who stand over their sons, "hatchets blunt and bloody," and reminds them that they "were not there before." The present cannot be compared to or seek to emulate a past in which a boy "lay upon a mountain / and [his] father's hand was trembling / with the beauty of the word." Cohen's song is not a call to peace,[27] although it has been appropriated as one, but a lament "about those who would sacrifice one generation on behalf of another."[28]

One might read Cohen's poem as a corrective to the biblical account; here the story is told from another perspective (Isaac's), and, moreover, presents a counter-perspective (condemning rather than celebrating Abraham's willingness to sacrifice). The truth of the Bible is not, in fact, universal: Abraham's story was unique, unimportable. The schemes of moderns do not compare to the visions of ancients; the altars built to hold the sons can no longer be justified. Despite the fact of the poem's recourse to the biblical moment—its building on a single verse—its very message is that the biblical moment is not to be repeated.

Binyan Av MiShnei K'tuvim (בִּנְיָן אָב מִשְׁנֵי כְּתוּבִים)
Deduction from two verses, the hermeneutic principle at work in *binyan av mishnei k'tuvim* is the same as in the above situation, except that the analogy is drawn between two verses. Thus, what we find in case A also applies to case B, which is similar to case B. Like *binyan av mikatuv echad*, it is used when "the two cases being compared are not fully analogous."[29] We can stretch the understanding of this rule so that it describes literature in which more than one telling underlies the retelling. In such cases, just as with the halakhic principle, the building from two verses, the truth (or, in these narratives, the truth of the story) is established by plurality of testimony. A conclusion cannot rest upon one passage alone.

27. The song ends: "When it all comes down to dust / I will kill you if I must, / I will help you if I can. / When it all comes down to dust / I will help you if I must, / I will kill you if I can."
28. This is how Cohen introduces the song on the album, *Live Songs*. Leonard Cohen, *Live Songs*, Columbia Europe, 1973.
29. Steinsaltz, *The Talmud*, 149.

In the case of Allegra Goodman's short story, "Sarah," which we encountered earlier, one character is best understood when read in light of her two literary foremothers. "Sarah" is the story of a middle-aged writer, Sarah Markowitz, whose publishing of one novel years ago provides her with the necessary credentials to teach creative writing—midrash, specifically—at the local Jewish Community Center. Her own children out of the house, Sarah is faced with the possibility of having dependents again when her aging mother-in-law, Rose, becomes unable to care for herself. The story stands on its own—as do all good retellings—but the main character gains depth when we read her against the matriarchs of Israel. Like Sarah, her namesake, our Sarah is old and imagines herself to be barren; she cannot picture producing (another novel) at this advanced age, and, like the biblical Sarah, laughs at the very idea. She does, however, bear in her old age—if not a novel or a child then a mother-in-law, who will enter her home and for whom she will have to care. The themes of the biblical book of Ruth echo throughout the story; Sarah's own ambivalence about tending her mother-in-law stands in contrast to Ruth's devotion and willingness to go with Naomi. There are explicit recalls to the scriptural novella; one of Sarah's students writes a midrash about losing her own daughter:

> My daughter and I are like Ruth and Naomi, but with a twist. When my husband passed away, may he rest in peace, and we went on the way, as it says in the Bible, I said to Ellen, "Don't stay with me, go and live your life." "I want to stay with you and take care of you," she said. "No, you need to live your own life," I said. "Okay," she said, so she went back to New York where she was attending NYU film school.[30]

The daughter meets and moves in with a non-Jewish man, which pains the mother:

> This is what I want to ask her—"How do you think you can live in New York like a Ruth gleaning the alien corn? How do you think you can come to him and lie at his feet in the night so that one morning he will marry you? How can you go on like this living in his apartment for five years? If I had known this would happen when we went on the way I would not have told you to go. I would have said, 'Stay.'"[31]

Sarah reads the story of another woman, and this story recalls two more women—Ruth and Naomi. Thus, in addition to the evocation of the biblical Sarah, we must read the protagonist Sarah's own story in light of the foregrounded narrative of Ruth. Goodman asks us to do so, as does her character Sarah, who is moved by her student's story in a way that

30. Goodman, "Sarah," 219.
31. Ibid., 219–20.

she cannot understand. *She* cannot understand it, but we as readers know that her story is reflected in the biblical one, and we know her better for seeing her through the lens not only of the biblical Sarah, but of the biblical Naomi as well. Goodman's story is built not on one verse, but on two, and its truth is revealed through both.

Clal Ufrat (כְּלָל וּפְרָט)

This fifth principle—inference from general and particular—is expanded in later exegetical lists to include a number of hermeneutic rules that treat the relationship between the general and the particular. In some cases, the general statement is seen to be limited by the particular one that follows; in others, the particular is seen to be limited to the general.

Where applying the principle of *kal vahomer*, for instance, allowed us to think about retelling in terms of degree, *clal ufrat*, the question of the general and the particular, could allow us to think in terms of specificity. A biblical retelling may scrutinize the text, acting as a zoom lens which increases the scale of that which is hardly seen in the biblical story, or it may pull back from the scriptural details altogether, offering a panoramic shot. Two roughly contemporary European poems about the binding of Isaac reflect the two different approaches. The first, H. Leivick's poem, "Sacrifice," is a movement into the minutiae of the account of the Akedah. We could describe its approach with respect to the biblical text as *m'clal l'frat* (moving from the general to the particular). By contrast, Wilfred Owen's "The Parable of the Old Man and the Young," is a movement *m'frat l'clal* (from the particular to the general) in which the details of Abraham's sacrifice of his son come to light in the much broader context of the sacrifice of Europe's sons in World War I.

The son of a *cohen* and the descendant of a Minsk rabbi, H. Leivick (1888–1962), the Yiddish poet from Ihumen, Byelorussia, was educated in a local *heder* and then at a yeshiva in a larger town nearby. During the Revolution of 1905, after attending illegal meetings in the forests, he rallied against tsarist Russia and joined the *Bund*. While he had been trained in Hebrew, and had written poetry in the "clerical language," he quickly adopted Yiddish as his poetic language. "Sacrifice," written in Yiddish, is a retelling of the story of the binding of Isaac, a story that would have been well-known to Leivick from his religious upbringing:

Sacrifice
Bound hand and foot he lies
on the hard altar stone
and waits.

Eyes half shut, he looks
on his father standing there
and waits.

His father sees his eyes
and strokes his son's brow
and waits.

With old and trembling hands
the father picks up the knife
and waits.

A Voice from above cries, "Stop!"
The hand freezes in air
and waits.

The veined throat suddenly throbs
with the miracle of the test
and waits.

The father gathers up the son.
The altar is bare
and waits.

Ensnared in thorns a lamb
looks at the hand with a knife
and waits.[32]

Leivick inserts himself into the biblical narrative at Gen 22:9: "Abraham built the altar there, and laid the wood in order, and bound Isaac his son, and laid him upon the wood. And Abraham stretched forth his hand to slay his son." His account adheres closely to the biblical version. The details in the poem are more precise: the Bible's Isaac is bound, but Leivick's is bound "hand and foot." As the description becomes more detailed, it takes on a psychological tenor. Isaac is not merely bound, not merely "laid upon the wood"; rather, "he lies on the hard altar stone and waits." The discomfort and tension suggested in the biblical text are brought slightly to the fore in this retelling: "Eyes half shut, he looks on his father standing there and waits." In the Bible, the building of suspense comes through the rhetoric of God's command to Abraham—his movement to precision is so careful (as the rabbis have noted) that we practically hear Abraham's mental, emotional response: Take your son (Which son? I have two.), your only son (Both are the only sons of their mother.) whom you love (But I love them both.), Isaac (Oh.)[33] In "Sacrifice," we know which son it is who will be sacrificed; we have already

32. H. Leivick, "Sacrifice" (trans. Robert Friend), in *The Penguin Book of Modern Yiddish Verse* (ed. Irving Howe, Ruth R. Wisse, and Khone Shmeruk; New York: Viking, 1987), 238.

33. We see a version of this imagined conversation recounted in *Pesikta Rabbati* 40.3.

had our hearts sink and we have already been filled with dread. The suspense, the tension, comes through the recurring "and waits." What Leivick's poem accomplishes masterfully is the slowing down of an already deliberate pace, the insertion of time and suspense, the *waiting*. Where Genesis allows the reader to move from verse to verse, Leivick holds her back. Each action is punctuated not just with a passage of time, but with an excruciating passage of time. Isaac lies. And waits. He looks. And waits. Abraham sees. And waits. With each forward motion, the poem retracts. Action is marked by restraint, and the result for the reader is a choking sensation. The broader strokes of the biblical account are obsessively chronicled. What was general becomes specific. Each motion, and the interminable pause after it, is marked in detail. Leivick's "Sacrifice" is a zeroing in on the particular such that the horror of the general is cast into even greater relief.

By reaching beyond the biblical text, by giving it an application in the contemporary world, Wilfred Owen likewise highlights the horror of the sacrifice of the beloved son. What he also does, however, as he draws the particulars of the biblical text out to generalizations, is speak to the horror of the new setting in which he situates the story of Isaac. Owen's is a war poem, a condemnation of the so-called Great War in which the poet fought and was killed.

Roland Bartel has described the poem as a parable, that "like many other parables, withholds its meaning until the very end. Owen keeps the reader off guard by following the account in Genesis closely in the first thirteen lines of his poem, then changing the original story abruptly to create the shock."[34] The poem reads:

> *The Parable of the Old Man and the Young*
> So Abram rose, and clave the wood, and went,
> And took the fire with him, and a knife.
> And as they sojourned both of them together,
> Isaac the first-born spake and said, My Father,
> Behold the preparations, fire and iron,
> But where the lamb for this burnt-offering?
> Then Abram bound the youth with belts and straps,
> And builded parapets and trenches there,
> And stretched forth the knife to slay his son.
> When lo! an angel called him out of heaven,
> Saying, Lay not thy hand upon the lad,
> Neither do anything to him.

34. Roland Bartel, "Teaching Wilfred Owen's War Poems and the Bible," in *Biblical Images in Literature* (ed. Roland Bartel; Nashville: Abingdon, 1975), 199.

> Behold, A ram, caught in a thicket by its horns;
> Offer the Ram of Pride instead of him.
> But the old man would not so, but slew his son,
> And half the seed of Europe, one by one.

Bartel is only partially correct in asserting that the ending of the poem is a surprise. The attentive reader will notice the introduction of iron—foreign to Gen 22—in line 5; will see the poem wander in line 7 with the reference to belts and straps; and will recognize complete deviation from scripture with the mention of parapets and trenches in line 8. Through the introduction of new details—particulars—Owen is situating the story in a broader—generalized—context. This is his movement *mifrat l'clal.*

The poem takes on a new dimension with its movement across space and time, from the biblical Moriah to early twentieth-century Europe. It is at this moment that the general—the notion of child sacrifice—becomes most particularized. The poem is a commentary against the unprecedented carnage of World War I, and the hero of the Bible's localized family drama becomes the exemplar not of faith but of pride. As Bartel notes, Owen "converts the ram caught in the thicket to the Ram of Pride and makes Abraham into a war lord whose refusal to slay his pride causes him to slay his son, 'And half the seed of Europe, one by one.'"[35] In this conversion, the newly generalized also takes on particulars: the anonymous, undistinguished ram of the biblical account becomes the Ram of Pride and so within the broadening of the poem's application there is a narrowing of its signifieds. The movement *m'frat l'clal* also contains within it a movement *m'clal l'frat.*

Ke-yotsei Bo BiM'kom Acher (כְּיוֹצֵא בּוֹ מִמָּקוֹ אַחֵר)

Yet another principle based on similarity among verses, this sixth rule (which literally means "as it goes forth with this from another place") is less limited than *gezerah shavah*'s argument from analogy. In their *Introduction to the Talmud and Midrash*, Strack and Stemburger point to the opening of the *Mekhilta de Rabbi Ishmael*[36] for their illustration of the principle:

---

35. Ibid.

36. *Mekhilta*, the Aramaic equivalent of Hebrew's *middah* or *klal* ("rule," "norm"), means "the derivation of the Halakhah from Scripture according to certain rules; secondly also the halakhic exegesis itself and its result" (Strack and Stemburger, *Introduction to the Talmud and Midrash*, 250). In Geonic times it comes to mean halakhic commentary on the biblical books from Exodus through Deuteronomy.

> The beginning of Mekhilta (L. 1.1–3)…refutes the assumption that 'whatever is mentioned first in Scripture has precedence' by adducing for each case a corresponding Bible verse in which the order is different. In Exod 3.6 it says, 'the God of Abraham, the God of Isaac, and the God of Jacob' but Lev 26.4 states, 'I remember my covenant with Jacob, my covenant with Isaac, and my covenant with Abraham.'[37]

The two verses are equivalent, despite their reversed order: no precedence of Abraham over Isaac and Jacob can be asserted when other lists preserve different orders.

When we consider this ruling—yet another principle derived from analogy—in the context of literary analyses of retellings, what is most interesting is the very framing of the rule itself. The idea of a verse "go[ing] forth from another place" has significant application for us. The approaches we have considered here use the biblical text as their starting point, and while they may depart radically from it, inverting or subverting the meaning of the text to align it with a contemporary perspective, they draw us back to the Bible itself. These retellings have read the biblical text through the experience of the author's world, perhaps, but not through the lens or filter of another text.

With the introduction here of the idea of a filter, we touch on a concern secondary only to approach and stance for our thinking about retellings. Is there another text—another place from which the telling goes forth—that plays into the retelling and has implications for both approach and stance? There are Christian and Jewish texts that illustrate the way a retelling of the Abraham story might go forth from another place than merely the Genesis account. For orthodox Christian writers, that place—that filter through which the story flows—is the New Testament, and the sacrifice, death, and resurrection of God's own beloved son. For traditional Jews, the story filtered through the rabbinic midrashim.

The Epistle of Barnabas (c. 130 CE) for instance, reads the binding of Isaac as prefiguring Jesus: "Jesus was the fulfillment of that which was foreshadowed in Isaac who was offered upon the altar."[38] In *City of God*, Augustine draws parallels between Isaac carrying the wood and Jesus carrying the cross, between the ram caught in the thicket and Jesus bearing the crown of thorns, and between the blood of the ram and the blood of Christ. Abraham, who was willing to sacrifice his son, was the exemplar of faith, but the Hebrew story does not stand on its own: Abraham's willingness to sacrifice his son was the necessary precursor for the sacrifice of Jesus. Irenaeus makes explicit the link:

37. Ibid., 20.
38. Epistle of Barnabas 7:3.

> Since indeed Abraham, having followed, in keeping with his faith, the commandment of God's word, did with a ready mind give up his only begotten and beloved son, for a sacrifice unto God, that God again might well be pleased to offer unto Abraham's whole seed his only begotten and dearly beloved son to be a sacrifice for our redemption.[39]

In Irenaeus's view, in fact, it is only because Abraham was willing to sacrifice his beloved son, whom he loved, that God was able to offer his only son, whom he loved, as a sacrifice for the redemption of all the descendants of Abraham.

In the view of medieval poet Rabbi Ephraim ben Jacob of Bonn (b. 1132), Abraham's willingness to sacrifice his son also served as a forerunner to a later story: the tragedy of Jewish persecution during the Crusades. From the fortress of Wolkenburg, which was under protection of the Bishop of Cologne, the thirteen year-old poet heard among Jews— who, like his own family members, had fled there for their lives—the praises of those who had been more willing to martyr themselves than to renounce their faith. As an adult he wrote of the righteous who "sprayed their own blood and the blood of their dear children, and underwent many an Akedah, and built altars, and prepared sacrifices: [and prayed] O God, remember them to the good."[40] Unlike Wilfred Owen, however, R. Ephraim did not merely read the Bible through the lens of the bloodshed of his day;[41] he read it through the lens of rabbinic midrash. In his lengthy poem, "The Akedah," his description of the binding of Isaac reflects his familiarity with the rabbinic tropes I have outlined here:

The Akedah
The Pure One showed him the altar of the ancients.
A male without blemish you shall offer of your own free will.
Whispered the soft-spoken dove: Bind me as sacrifice
With cords to the horns of the altar.

Bind for me my hands and my feet
Lest I be found wanting and profane the sacrifice.
I am afraid to panic; I am concerned to honor you,
My will is to honor you greatly.

39. Irenaeus, *Against Heresies* 4:5.
40. Shalom Spiegel, *The Last Trial* (trans. Judah Goldin; Woodstock, Vt.: Jewish Lights, 1993), 138.
41. And even in his reading of the Bible against his contemporary situation, R. Ephraim's understanding of scripture is markedly different from later, secular readers: as Spiegel describes, "The writer of the memoirs explains from whom it was that the heroes who did His will in the Rhine region learned their lesson: from the haggadic lore about the sacrificer and the sacrificed on Mount Moriah" (Spiegel, *The Last Trial*, 134).

When the one whose life was bound up in the lad's
Heard this, he bound him hand and foot like the perpetual offering.
In their right order he prepared fire and wood,
And offered upon them the burnt offering.

Then did the father and the son embrace,
Mercy and Truth met and kissed each other.
Oh, my father, fill your mouth with praise,
For He doth bless the sacrifice.

I long to open my mouth to recite the Grace:
Forever blessed be the Lord. Amen.
Gather my ashes, bring them to the city,
Unto the tent, to Sarah.

He made haste, he pinned him down with his knees,
He made his two arms strong.
With steady hands he slaughtered him according to the rite,
Full right was the slaughter.

Down upon him fell the resurrecting dew, and he revived.
(The father) seized him (then) to slaughter him once more.
Scripture, bear witness! Well-grounded is the fact.
And the Lord called Abraham, even a second time from heaven.

The ministering angels cried out, terrified:
Even animal victims, were they ever slaughtered twice?
Instantly they made their outcry heard on high,
Lo, Ariels cried out above the earth.

We beg of Thee, have pity upon him!
In his father's house we were given hospitality.
He was swept by the flood of celestial tears
Into Eden, the garden of God.

The pure one thought: The child is free of guilt,
Now I, whither shall I go?
Then he heard: Your son was found an acceptable sacrifice
By myself have I sworn it, saith the Lord.

In a nearby thicket did the Lord prepare
A ram, meant for this mitzvah even from Creation.
The proxy caught its leg in the skirts of his coat,
And behold, he stood by his burnt offering.

R. Ephraim knows the midrashim. He knows that Isaac was the willing
sacrifice, that he asked to be bound hand and foot lest he flinch as Abraham lowered the knife and thus render himself blemished and unfit for
sacrifice. He knows that Isaac was in fact killed, and was resurrected.[42]

---

42. According to *Midrash Rabbah*, Isaac returns to life, revived by the heavenly
voice admonishing Abraham not to slaughter his son. Abraham loosens his bonds and

He knows that Isaac was killed again, and taken to Eden where he studied Torah for three years before returning to this life to marry Rebecca. What is most intriguing, however, is not R. Ephraim's knowledge of these *aggadot*, but his incorporation of them into his own telling. For him, as for the devout Christian reader, scripture does not stand on its own: it cannot be seen except through the lens of the revealed tradition. In his introduction to this translation of *The Last Trial*, Judah Goldin asserts that:

> R. Ephraim's interpretation of the biblical Akedah story is admittedly very far-fetched, and it illustrates clearly what happens when the literal meaning of texts is crowded out by the commentator's conviction that the ancient revealed formulation has anticipated every single detail of later events. However, regardless of the persuasiveness of this or any particular interpretation, that conviction lies at the heart of Midrash all the time: the Scriptures are not only a record of the past but a prophecy, a foreshadowing and foretelling, of what will come to pass.[43]

The oral Torah and the written Torah are here indistinguishable, both divine revelation and divine prophecy. The written text is read through the lens of the oral; as stated in the sixth hermeneutic principle, the word goes forth from another place as well.

Davar Halamed Mi-Inyano (דָּבָר הַלָּמֵד מֵעִנְיָנוֹ)

In this last case, *davar halamed mi-inyano*, the inference is drawn from the entire context, such that a symphonic verdict is reached. As Steinsaltz frames it, "an unclear verse should be interpreted in the context in which it appears."[44] A verse should not be read—or interpreted—in isolation.

Here, as I invert the places of the telling and retelling to make the principle usable for literary study, let us turn to Aryeh Sivan's poem about contemporary Israel. A commentary on the war-torn and fraught state of modern Israel, Sivan roots his poem in a biblical reference:

> *To Live in the Land of Israel*
> To be cocked like a rifle, the hand
> holding a revolver, to move
> in strict closed rank, even after
> the cheeks fill with dust
> and the flesh goes, and the eyes can't
> focus on the target.

Isaac stands up and speaks the benediction, "Blessed art thou, O Lord, who quickens the dead."

43. Spiegel, *The Last Trial*, xx
44. Steinsaltz, *The Talmud*, 151.

There's a saying: a loaded revolver
will fire in the end. False.
In the Land of Israel anything can happen:
a broken firing pin, a rusty spring
or an unexpected cancellation order
like what happened to Abraham on Mount Moriah.[45]

On its face, this is a poem about the conquest of the modern state of Israel, about the winning of it by war. The end of the poem, however, offers a twist, and we must read the poem not merely through the knowledge of this last line, but through the connotations that the allusion in the last line invokes. To speak of a cancellation order, of the uncertainty of the command, is simply to say that nothing can be predicted. To speak of a cancellation order in terms of "what happened to Abraham on Mount Moriah" is no longer to speak about flukes or unpredictability, it is to speak about divine caprice (at worst) or divine intention (at best). To invoke Abraham's order on Mount Moriah—the second command, not to slaughter his son—is to invoke the promise to Abraham—the promise of land and of offspring. The poem is an account of the conquest of the land, but the last line, with its resonances not merely of the recall of the command to sacrifice but of its affirmation of offspring places an even greater question mark over the conquest. Is the conquest to be undertaken at the cost of the children, who are the promised seed? And ultimately, do we not learn through Abraham at Moriah that God does not require the sacrifice of his children? Should we not then wait for the unexpected recall, the divine cease-fire? But how then to accomplish the reclamation of the land, the very land promised to Abraham along with descendants to populate it? Here Sivan's allusion conjures the whole of the Abrahamic legacy, uncovering the tensions within it and thereby carrying over those same tensions to the contemporary setting. The context of the original verse becomes grafted onto the context of the rewriting.

The Viability of Co-opting (Anew) the Vocabulary of Midrash

We have taken the basic vocabulary of midrash—Hillel's seven exegetical principles—and given them a literary twist. As this investigation illustrates, the *middot* can provide us insight into the relationship between telling and retelling. They have enabled us to explore the ways that a variety of later thinkers—rabbis, poets, and authors—have built on or returned to an ancient work. Is this set of seven rules sufficient? Can it be universalized?

---

45. Translated from the Hebrew by Linda Zisquist.

Let us begin with the second question. In a number of respects, midrash is a strictly Jewish enterprise. It rests on understandings of God as the author of the sacred text of the Jews; arises at moments when the sacred text seems an insufficient link between divine author and human readers; and functions as a bridge to connect God back to the Jews. More than this, the act of interpretation sanctifies the Jews; it is their route back to God. These characteristics make the grafting of the term midrash onto non-rabbinic, non-traditional, non-Jewish literature more problematic than Derrida would have led us to believe it would be. And yet, there remain reasons to consider using if not the term "midrash" then the vocabulary of midrash in describing the literary retellings that concern the present study.

Midrash may be premised on the acceptance of the divine origin of the text. It may well be an exclusively Jewish enterprise. It may be a literary response to national catastrophe. Nonetheless, various characteristics continue to draw us to midrash. It is a mode of literary expansion of the biblical text. It is creative, open, and free in its approach. It is able to bridge the distance between the world of the Bible and the world of its later readers.

The vocabulary of midrash, specifically of its exegetical principles, has suggested itself as a possible vocabulary for describing literary retellings of biblical tales. What renders this classification usable is the degree to which it enables us to speak about the retelling. To this end, we have seen the many ways that the *middot* can open up our reading of later texts. There are, however, some real limitations to the vocabulary I have introduced here.

The most significant restriction on the use of these terms—or our use of the redefinitions of these terms—is that they only describe approach, the means by which the retelling gains entry to the telling. They can tell us whether the author of the later work borrows the plot of the earlier, whether she fleshes out an under-developed biblical theme, whether she intertwines two tellings to construct her retelling. In some cases, these principles even describe a double approach: they can be used to explain the approach of the author of the retelling to the biblical text, and our own approach to the retelling.

What the principles do not do, however, is allow us to consider stance. What is the relationship of the retelling to the telling? Does it supplement the telling or attempt to displace it? Is it an embrace or a conquest of the original? A parody or an homage? If we are to borrow from the language of midrash, or the language of midrash outlined in this chapter, we will need to supplement with another vocabulary, one that allows us to consider what one text "thinks" of its *Urtext*, and allows us to do so without drawing us into the thorny area of authorial intent. To this end, let us turn our attention to the language of translation theory, where both approach and stance are given consideration.

Chapter 7

LET US CONFOUND THEIR LANGUAGE

The Literary Afterlife:
Where Retelling and Translation Intersect

In his *Preface to Sylvae: Or, the Second Part of Poetical Miscellanies,*
John Dryden comments that "For this last half Year I have been troubled
with the disease (as I may call it) of Translation."[1] It is a disease that has
him alternately in tedious "Cold prose fits of it" and in less frustrating
hot ones, which allowed him to compose these "Miscellanies." As old as
Babel, Dryden's disease might more accurately be described as an epi-
demic. The legions afflicted include those who have sought simply to
render a text in another language (Wycliffe, for instance, in his translating the Bible into English), those who have liberally translated (David
Rosenberg's *Book of J,* perhaps), those who have editorialized their
translations (the Targumim with their elaborate expansions of the biblical
text), and those who have unabashedly reconstituted the text in "translating" it (one thinks of Mark Twain's "translation," *The Diaries of Adam
and Eve*).

Not everyone would agree that a transformation like Twain's is translation: many would assert that any translation that is not faithful to the
original—that is, stylistically and semantically representative—is a mistranslation. This view reflects a particular valuation of translation that is
by no means universal; as this chapter will suggest, the ideas of translation vary tremendously across time and place. At its least "faithful"
(most transformative), it can come to be indistinguishable from retelling.
But the gradations even within what could be called faithful translation
are tremendous. In order for translation to be a viable category in our
context, we must be open to thinking about the very nature of translation,
and the many possible ways it can manifest itself.

1. John Dryden, *The Works of John Dryden,* Vol. 3 (ed. Earl Miner and Vinton
A. Dearing; Berkeley and Los Angeles: California University Press, 1969), 3.

It may not be terribly revolutionary to think of retelling as translation, for, as George Steiner asserts in *After Babel*, "translation is formally and pragmatically implicit in *every* act of communication, in the emission and reception of each and every mode of meaning, be it in the widest semiotic sense or in more specifically verbal exchanges. To understand is to decipher."[2] In this view, translation and interpretation are inextricably linked:[3] translation is an act of meaning-making, not merely meaning conveyance. This is particularly true when the interpreter stands at a temporal remove from the text he has received. Steiner argues, "when we read or hear any language-statement from the past, be it Leviticus or last year's best-seller, we translate. Reader, actor, editor are translators of language out of time."[4] All are involved in a process by "which a message from a source-language passes into a receptor-language via a transformational process."[5] With this final point, Steiner hits on the most compelling reason for thinking about translation in our context: *translation is not merely a carrying across of a text from one culture to another, but a carrying across in which the text undergoes a process of transformation.*

The image of translation as a carrying of text across cultures, rather than merely across languages, has been explored somewhat by translation theorists. As we saw earlier, J. Hillis Miller reads the afterlife of the book of Ruth as mistranslation. He contends—as discussed above—that "this book of the Hebrew Bible has been alienated from itself, translated from itself. It has been put entirely to new uses, uses by no means intended by the original authors or scribes."[6] Most notable among them is its inclusion in the Christian canon. The creation of the Old Testament out of the Hebrew Bible, Bloom calls "the most outrageous example of 'misprision' in the history of the West, that is, of 'mistakings' or takings amiss, translations as mistranslation."[7] The New Testament use of Ruth is only one of many subsequent misprisions of Ruth, a litany that includes the two Miller explores in detail: the folk tradition of *Sortes*

2. Steiner, *After Babel*, xii.

3. A note from Steiner here: "An error, a misreading initiates the modern history of our subject. Romance languages derive their terms for 'translation' from *traducere* because Leonardo Bruni misinterpreted a sentence in the *Noctes Atticae* of Aulus Gellius in which the Latin actually signifies 'to derive from, to lead into.' The point is trivial but symbolic. Often, in the records of translation, a fortunate misreading is the source of new life" (ibid.).

4. Ibid., 29.

5. Ibid.

6. Miller, "Border Crossings," 220.

7. Ibid., 221.

Sanctorum, and allusions to Ruth in "Ode to a Nightingale." The divination by Bible and key Miller describes as "a mistranslation if ever there was one";[8] Ruth "in tears amid the alien corn" he calls Keats's "translation, or mistranslation, of the story of Ruth for his own quite different purposes."[9] Miller's misprision, mistranslation, and translation all seem to fall squarely under the rubric of retelling. What we need to consider is whether these three are subsets of retelling, or whether retelling can be described as translation.

One could argue that to translate—on any level, from inter-linear crib to interpretive parallel—is to give a text an afterlife. Some of Steiner's thoughts on the subject resonate with our present concerns about how the telling and retelling relate. At one point in his lengthy description of modes and methods of translation, Steiner broadly sketches translation theory's three classes of (post-seventeenth century) translation. First is "strict literalism," which he defines as "the word-by-word matching of the interlingual dictionary, of the foreign-language primer, of the inter-linear crib." Second is "'translation' by means of faithful but autonomous restatement," a close reproduction of the original in which the translator "composes a text which is natural to his own tongue, which can stand on its own." Third is the imitation, which might also be called "recreation, variation, interpretative parallel." This class "extend[s] from transpositions of the original into a more accessible idiom all the way to the freest, perhaps only allusive or parodistic echoes."[10]

Imitation is the site where translation and interpretation overlap, where the faithful, autonomous reproduction becomes the recreation or variation, the allusion or parody. As Steiner tells it, *imitatio*, in the modern view "can legitimately include Pound's relations to Propertius[11] and even those of Joyce to Homer."[12] Biblically speaking, we find multiple examples of *imitatio* in the latter day psalms of poets such as Yehuda Amichai, April Bernard, Allen Ginsberg, Denise Leverton, Jacqueline Osherow,

---

8. Ibid.

9. Ibid., 222.

10. Steiner, *After Babel*, 266.

11. When asked whether he had translated Propertius, Pound replied "No, I have not done a translation of Propertius. That fool in Chicago took the *Homage* for a translation despite the mention of Wordsworth and the parodied line from Yeats. (As if, had one wanted to pretend to more Latin than one knew, it wouldn't have been perfectly easy to correct one's divergencies from a Bohn crib. Price 5/-.)" (J. P. Sullivan, "The Poet as Translator—Ezra Pound and Sextus Propertius," *The Kenyon Review* 23, no. 3 [Summer 1961]: 37). Clearly Pound was not doing what Jakobson calls 'translation proper,' but he may well have been doing translation.

12. Steiner, *After Babel*, 266.

Karl Shapiro, David Slavitt, and Mark van Doren. These range from poetic interlingual translation to sustained allusions to variations on a familiar form.

Walter Benjamin speaks to the (after)life-giving qualities of translation in "The Task of the Translator." His thinking about the function of translation also touches on the close connection between translation and retelling:

> Just as the manifestations of life are intimately connected with the phenomenon of life without being of importance to it, a translation issues from the original—not so much from its life as from its afterlife. For a translation comes later than the original, and since the important works of world literature never find their chosen translators at the time of their origin, their translation marks their stage of continued life. The idea of life and afterlife in works of art should be regarded with an entirely unmetaphorical objectivity...[13]

In Benjamin's view, texts are quite literally living entities, and to translate them is to transform them: "no translation would be possible if in its ultimate essence it strove for likeness to the original. For in its afterlife—which could not be called that if it were not a transformation and a renewal of something living—the original undergoes a change. Even words with fixed meaning can undergo a maturing process."[14] A fixed text like the Bible gains new life through translation and retelling alike.

The common ground in the two types of afterlife is compelling. The retelling, like the translation, must come *later*. Furthermore, according to Benjamin, it is dependent not only on the telling, but on the telling's having achieved some level of "fame." Thus the history of a work's reception, as well as the work itself, is bound up in the retelling—as in the translation. Just as translating the Bible is a wholly different enterprise from translating a bicycle repair manual, and not entirely because the one is (arguably) literary and the other technical, the condition of the retelling hangs on the status of the story it retells. Implicit in the very act of retelling—as in translation—is the affirmation of the worth (or former worth) of the telling.

Theories and Theoretical Vocabularies of Translation

If translation and retelling are fundamentally similar enterprises, we stand to learn much from translation. Moreover, unlike in literary criticism and

13. Walter Benjamin, "The Task of the Translator," in *Illuminations* (New York: Schocken, 1969), 69–82 (71).
14. Ibid., 73.

theory, or even midrashic studies, practitioners' and scholars' thinking about—or, possibly, theorizing—translation attends explicitly to the questions of stance and approach (although these terms are not used). Thus we will find that the language and theory of translation speaks directly to some of the questions of retelling.

In concert with his disdain for the "present-day, ubiquitous use of the term and rubric 'theory' in poetics, in hermeneutics, in aesthetics,"[15] Steiner holds that "there are, most assuredly, and *pace* our current masters in Byzantium, no 'theories of translation.' What we do have are reasoned descriptions of processes."[16] In preceding chapters, I have spoken of translation theory as though it were a single identifiable body of thought. Neither I nor Steiner is precisely correct. There is no translation theory, but there are translation theories. These theories are often incompatible with one another, and yet I will treat them in one (long) breath in order to get a full sense of the many possible terms the field offers. I will come to apply some of these to questions of retelling.

Just as there has been a history of understanding of literary influence and imitation, and a diversity of opinions about the nature and role of midrash, so too has translation been discussed, dissected, described, and defined in varied terms by a variety of translators and theorizers of translation. Since the 1960s, there has been some effort to develop translation studies as a recognizable discipline. Edwin Gentzler, who directs the Translation Center at UMass Amherst, notes that in the early sixties, "there were no translation workshops at institutions of higher learning in the United States";[17] translation was a marginal activity, subordinated to literary criticism and theory. It is only since 1983 that "translation theory" became a separate entry in the *Modern Language Association International Bibliography*.[18]

While the act of translation is as old as language itself, discussion about translation comes in and out of vogue. As we will see, Dryden and

15. Steiner, *After Babel*, xvi. Steiner regards this usage of the term "theory" as "spurious." He goes on to say that "It has no substantive status and radically obscures the subjective, imaginatively transcendental (in Kant's sense) tenor of all arguments, proposals and findings in literature and the arts (there *are*, unquestionably, authentic theoretical, which is to say 'formalizable,' elements in the analysis of music). There are no 'theories of literature', there is no 'theory of criticism.' Such tags are arrogant bluff or a borrowing, transparent in its pathos, from the enviable fortunes and forward motion of science and technology."

16. Steiner, *After Babel*, xvi.

17. Edwin Gentzler, *Contemporary Translation Theories* (2d rev. ed.; Clevedon: Multilingual Matters, 2001), 5.

18. Ibid., 1.

Goethe, Nietzsche and Rilke all reflected on the art of translation. But until relatively recently little attempt had been made to theorize translation. As Gentzler notes, "George Steiner characterized the history of translation theory until Jakobson as a continual rehashing of the same formal (consistent with the form of the original) versus free (using innovative forms to stimulate the original's intent) theoretical discussion."[19] Evidently, the parameters of the discussion were quite contained.

Since Roman Jakobson developed his structural linguistics in the mid-twentieth century, however, there has been an explosion of ideas concerning translation, and a corresponding proliferation of writing on the topic. Even a cursory scan of relevant bibliographies reveals that the number of works on translation published increases each year.[20] Gentzler links the explosion to a comparable explosion—which we have witnessed here—in literary theory: "'Modern' translation theory, like current literary theory, begins with structuralism and reflects the proliferation of the age."[21] Gentzler's own project, a survey of developments in translation studies since the 1960s, attests that the new "field" is in full bloom. He observes that there have recently been five major movements in translation studies, and he outlines and examines them in some detail, devoting a chapter to each.

First is the North American development of the *translation workshop*, courses and workshops begun in the late 1960s and early 1970s at selected universities across the U.S. The growth of these venues led to the establishment of a professional organization, American Literary Translators Association (ALTA), and the foundation of a journal, *Translation*. Gentzler notes that "for a while in the late seventies and early eighties, it looked as if the translation workshop would follow the path of creative writing, also considered at one time a non-academic field, and soon be offered at as many schools as had writing workshops;[22] the process of growth tapered off, however, despite the simultaneous increase in translation activity.

Unlike the anecdotal approach of the translation workshop, the *science of translation* sought an empirical entry into the topic. The subfield is

19. Ibid.
20. Gentzler observes, "If, as Ted Hughes argued, the sixties were a period that experienced a boom in literary translation, the nineties might be characterized as a period that experienced a boom in translation theory" (ibid., 187). His own bibliography is heavily weighted to current literature: the number of works written in the last twenty years is roughly equivalent to the number written in the preceding two hundred.
21. Ibid., 2.
22. Ibid., 6.

epitomized by Eugene Nida's *Toward a Science of Translating*, which is strongly influenced by Noam Chomsky's thinking about universal syntactic structures. Nida's concern with translation grew out of his experience with Bible translation;[23] initially he treated the practical aspects of conveying the gospel in other tongues. Aware that his anecdotal approach was unsystematic, Nida began to theorize translation in an "attempt to scientifically validate his methodology and apply it to translation as a whole."[24] He incorporated Chomsky's theory of syntax and generative grammar—which is not (nor intended to be) a theory of translation—because, in keeping with Nida's own beliefs, it assumes a single, coherent, fundamental structure underlying all languages. Happily for Nida, who has as his task the spread of the Word across the globe, Chomsky's theory suggests that all languages can be made to speak to one another. While Nida and Chomsky's objectives were notably different—with "one arguing the existence of universal rules of grammar and universal lexical forms; the other making metaphysical claims about an original divine message[25]—both sought to further a science of language.[26]

As against the scientists of translation, who focused on deep linguistic structure, practitioners of *early translation theory* treated the translated text itself. Early translation theory was an equal response to the literary and scientific approaches to translation, the two dominant modes of research through the seventies. It was developed by James Holmes and André Lefevere, both of whom we will encounter shortly, who sought to show that translation theory's two poles—which Lefevere calls the hermeneutic (interpretive or artistic) and the neopositivistic (scientific)—need not be oppositional, or even mutually exclusive. Rather, translation as a field can be seen as simultaneously literary and non-literary. This compromise allows new questions to be asked "regarding the subject of investigation, the nature of the translation process, how mediation occurs, and how the process affects both the original (redefined as source text) and received (redefined as target text) works."[27] Lefevere and his cohort even scrutinized the distinction between original writer and translator. The concern of early translation theory was "to produce a comprehensive theory which [could] be used as a guideline for the production of

23. Eugene Nida, *Toward a Science of Translating, with Special Reference to Principles and Procedures Involved in Bible Translation* (Leiden: Brill, 1964).

24. Ibid., 46.

25. Ibid., 47.

26. Nida turns to anthropologists, semanticists, psychologists, psychiatrists and philologists as scientists able to support his claims about language. (See the introduction to *Toward a Science of Translating*, 6–8.)

27. Gentzler, *Contemporary Translation Theories*, 79.

translations";[28] the intent, however, was not to be prescriptive. Rather than turning to extant theories of literature and linguistics and appropriating them for use in translation, early translation studies looked first at translations themselves and attempted to theorize them.

Polysystem theory likewise focused almost entirely on the translation—specifically on its impact on the target language. The theory was pioneered by Itamar Even-Zohar, who in 1978 introduced the term "polysystem" for "the aggregate of literary systems (including everything from 'high' or 'canonized' forms (e.g., innovative verse) such as poetry to 'low' or 'non-canonized' forms (e.g., children's literature and popular fiction) in a literary system."[29] In Even-Zohar's view, translated literature is a crucial part of the polysystem.[30] Translation here is understood to be a fact of the target system, rather than a product of the source. Even-Zohar asserts that the translation itself has an innovatory force, that it—as much as the original—can become part of major events in literary history. Building on these ideas, Gideon Toury isolated and defined translation norms, rather than simply translations themselves, as they play into the linguistic polysystem. The adequacy of a translation—which was once the primary locus of debate about translation—ceases to be a productive line of inquiry because the norms of the target are always shifting. What is of interest, rather, is "the 'acceptability' of the translation in the receiving culture, the ways in which various shifts constitute a type of equivalence that reflects target norms at a certain historical moment."[31] Polysystem theory was, in Lawrence Venuti's assessment, a significant development in translation study. Its focus on the target rather than on translation practice enabled polysystem theorists to examine and describe in detail what transpires in specific translation rather than prescribe practice (e.g. pragmatic, functional, communicative).[32]

Deconstruction, the last of Gentzler's five moves, stands in sharp distinction to the four previous categories. The theory has radically redrawn the boundaries and issues of translation. The translation workshop

28. André Lefevere, "Translation Studies: The Goal of the Discipline," in *Literature and Translation: New Perspectives in Literary Studies with a Basic Bibliography of Books on Translation Studies* (ed. James S. Holmes et al.; Leuven: Acco, 1978), 234.

29. Gentzler, *Contemporary Translation Theories*, 106.

30. Itamar Even-Zohar, "The Position of Translated Literature within the Literary Polysystem," in *The Translation Studies Reader* (ed. Lawrence Venuti; New York: Routledge, 2000), 193.

31. Lawrence Venuti, "1960s–1970s," in idem, ed., *The Translation Studies Reader* (New York: Routledge, 2000), 123.

32. Ibid.

assumes the same aesthetic experience in source and target language; the
science of translation assumes linguistic structural/dynamic equivalence
across languages; early translation theory assumes corresponding literary
function across cultures; and polysystem theory assumes similar formal
correlation governed by social acceptability in the target culture. Deconstruction, by contrast, assumes no equivalences.[33] Rather, it is based in
différance, and is arguably therefore "inexorably connected" with translation. Both deconstruction and translation, to the extent that it is possible, "practice the difference between signified and signifier."[34]

Each of these five courses has spawned a considerable body of
literature. Despite the movement of the study and activity of translation
from the periphery to the mainstream, in view of the proliferation of
works there remains considerable debate as to the nature of translation
studies. Is it an aesthetic? A formula? An art? A science? Is it about the
transmission of sense or the replication of equivalent words? And again,
with regard to our overarching concern, how might it relate to retelling?
What are the possible approaches and stances of translation?

The Science of Translation

How one views translation will to a great extent frame how one talks
about it. Eugene Nida, as we have seen, understands translation to be a
science. He puts forth four basic requirements of a translation: making
sense; conveying the spirit and manner of the original; having a natural
and easy form of expression; and producing a certain response.[35] These
four elements, however, can occasionally be at odds with one another.
Thus Nida attempts to identify scientific principles that will guide the
translator.[36]

Acknowledging that there can be no "absolute correspondence"
between languages, because "no two languages are identical, either in the
meaning given to corresponding symbols or in the ways in which such
symbols are arranged in phrases and sentences,"[37] Nida sets out to
explore what he calls "Principles of Correspondence,"[38] the ways that

33. Gentzler, *Contemporary Translation Theories*, 145.
34. Ibid., 146.
35. Nida, *Toward a Science of Translating*, 164.
36. Especially the Bible translator, for whom Nida—as a Bible translator himself—writes.
37. Ibid., 156.
38. Eugene Nida, "Principles of Correspondence," in Venuti, ed., *The Translation Studies Reader*, 121.

texts in different languages are found or made to align with one another. This method reflects a concern with equivalence that marked translation theory in the 1960s and 70s. One communicates the foreign text by "establishing a relationship of identity or analogy with it."[39]

He notes that three factors contribute to differences in translation. The first is the nature of the message, which may "differ primarily in the degree to which content or form is the dominant consideration."[40] In translating the Sermon on the Mount, Nida contends, the primary concern is with message; in translating acrostic Psalms, however, the main consideration is adherence to the formal principle. The second factor is "the purpose or purposes of the author, and, by proxy, of the translator."[41] Is the text intended to edify? To amuse? Will the reader's processing of the text be largely cognitive? Emotional? Is the translator conveying imperatives? Merely information? The third element is the type of audience. Nida isolates four types of target audience: children, "whose vocabulary and cultural experience are limited";[42] new literates, "who can decode oral messages with facility but whose ability to decode written messages is limited";[43] the "average literate adult, who can handle both oral and written messages with relative ease";[44] and "the unusually high capacity of specialists…when they are decoding messages within their own area of specialization."[45] Thus how one translates is determined to a considerable degree by the audience for whom one is translating.

With these specifics in mind, Nida maps out two basic orientations in translating. "Since 'there are, properly speaking, no such things as identical equivalents'…one must in translating seek to find the closest possible equivalent,"[46] which will be either formal or dynamic. The extent to which one opts for dynamic as opposed to formal equivalences will have to do with the extent to which source and target languages and cultures are related.

Formal equivalence centers on the message itself, both in terms of form and content. Poetry is made poetry; sentences, sentences; concepts, concepts: "the message in the receptor language should match as closely

39. Ibid., 121.
40. Nida, *Toward a Science of Translating*, 156.
41. Ibid., 157.
42. Ibid., 158.
43. Ibid.
44. Ibid.
45. Ibid.
46. Ibid., 159.

as possible the different elements in the source language."[47] To make formal equivalences, the translator may focus on the literal rendering of grammatical units, which would entail translating nouns as nouns and verbs as verbs; keeping phrases and sentences intact; and preserving punctuation, paragraphs, poetic indication and other formal markers. He may strive for consistency in word usage, drawing upon a concordance of terminology, and he may root meanings in terms of the context of the source rather than that of the target.[48]

Dynamic equivalence, by contrast, is based upon "the principle of equivalent effect";[49] the translator is "not so concerned with matching the receptor-language message with the source-language message, but with the dynamic message, that the relationship between receptor and message should be substantially the same as that which existed between the original receptors and the message."[50] Or, as Ezra Pound has it, "more sense and less syntax."[51] The goals of a translation with dynamic equivalence are naturalness for the receptor, who need not know anything about the culture in which the original text was created in order to appreciate it on his own terms.[52] There are three essentials in a dynamic-equivalence translation: it must be *equivalent*, thereby pointing back to the source-language message; *natural*, thus oriented to the receptor language; and *closest*, which is to say able to "bind the two orientations together on the basis of the highest degree of approximation."[53]

Even within the more flexible parameters of the dynamic-equivalence translation, the translator may encounter problems rendering a text as convincingly as he might like. As the next part of his science, Nida lays out a series of "techniques for adjustment" that "permit adjustment of the

47.   Ibid.

48.   Ibid., 165.

49.   A term Nida borrows from E. V. Rieu and J. B. Phillips's "Translating the Gospels."

50.   Nida, *Toward a Science of Translating*, 159.

51.   Ezra Pound, *Literary Essays of Ezra Pound* (ed. T. S. Eliot; London: Faber & Faber, 1954), 273.

52.   The distinction between formal and dynamic equivalence is made clear in examples of translations of Rom 16:16. Nida notes that a formal translation of the phrase "holy kiss" would render the idiom literally, and offer a note or gloss explaining that such a greeting was customary in New Testament times. J. B. Phillips, however, sought to offer the concept rather than the action to the readers of his Romans: he has Paul instruct his adherents to "give one another a hearty handshake all around." Nida describes the choice as "quite natural" (Nida, *Toward a Science of Translating*, 159–60).

53.   Nida, *Toward a Science of Translating*, 166.

form of the message to the requirements of the structure of the receptor language; produce semantically equivalent structures; provide equivalent stylistic appropriateness; and carry an equivalent communication load."[54] Like Genette's modes by which the hypertext may work with a hypotext, these include addition and subtraction.[55] Like Genette, Nida also breaks these three techniques into detailed subcategories, which I will outline here, and which may prove adaptable to our needs.

Nida outlines the nine most common and important types of addition for translation.[56] *Filling out elliptical expressions* allows the translator to fill a perceived lacuna. This may be entirely grammatical—"He is greater than I" may need to become "He is greater than I am great" in certain languages[57]—or it may be semantic as well: as noted in our discussion of midrash, the biblical text is often gapped. *Obligatory specification* is necessary when a text is vague; the use of proper names can elucidate the ambiguity that sometimes comes from using pronouns. *Additions required by grammatical restructuring* include shifts of voice and alteration from indirect to direct discourse: the passive "He will be condemned" needs an agent when the phrase is translated into a language without passive forms.[58] *Amplification from explicit to implicit status* may be used when the target language does not possess the same cultural norms as the source. For instance, "God of peace" (Phil 4:9) will need in some languages to become explicitly "God who brings (or causes) peace" so as to be distinguished from a "peaceful God."[59] *Answers to rhetorical questions*: as Nida points out, in some languages rhetorical questions always demand a response.[60] *Classifiers*, such as *the river* Jordan, or the Pharisee *sect*, and *connectives*, transitional words that repeat portions of the preceding text,[61] allow for clarity and specificity. Lastly, *doublets*, the addition of a synonymous expression—as is common in Biblical Hebrew

---

54. Ibid., 226.

55. As well as alteration, which has mostly to do with sounds and word classes. In his consideration of adjustments, there is also some discussion of the usefulness of footnotes, and the need at times to make adjustments based on experience, neither of which is as central to the present concerns as the first three techniques.

56. I will outline eight here; the ninth, *categories of the receptor language* seems wholly grammatical and without application to this discussion.

57. Nida, *Toward a Science of Translating*, 227.

58. Ibid.

59. Ibid., 229.

60. Ibid.

61. "He went up to Jerusalem. There he taught…" in some languages would require a connective: "He went up to Jerusalem. Having arrived there, he taught…" (ibid., 230).

poetry, for instance—add no semantic content but may be used to emphasize an idea in languages where doublets are common.[62]

As we found in our discussion of Genette's hypertexts, it is more common that a later interpretation adds to a text than takes something away. Similarly, subtractions are "neither so numerous nor as varied"[63] in translation as are additions. Nida outlines seven types of subtraction, all self-evident enough to go without comment. They are *repetitions, specification of reference, conjunctions, transitionals, categories, vocatives,* and *formulae.*[64] In narrowing the elements of translation, Nida supplies us with a series of words and terms that could be of use for describing retelling.

Early Translation Studies

Early translation studies, with its effort to negotiate between the aesthetic and scientific perspectives, saw itself as a social science. In 1972, at the Third International Congress of Applied Linguistics, James Holmes presented the now oft-cited "The Name and Nature of Translation Studies,"[65] in which he promotes translation studies as an empirical discipline, as defined by social scientist Carl G. Hempel.[66] The charge of an empirical discipline is "to describe particular phenomena in the world of our experience and to establish general principles by means of which they can be explained and predicted."[67] Holmes takes Hempel's model, stating that to "describe the phenomena of translating and translation(s) as they manifest themselves in the world of our experience, and establish general principles by means of which these phenomena can be explained and predicted"[68] are the objectives of translation studies as a field. In proposing the field—one of pure research—Holmes "envision[ed] a full-scale scientific discipline which could apply to the whole 'complex of problems clustered round the phenomenon of translating and translations.'"[69]

62.   Ibid., 231.
63.   Ibid.
64.   Ibid.
65.   The work existed only as a mimeographed pre-publication for years until Gideon Toury reprinted it in his *Translation Across Cultures* (New Delhi: Bahri, 1987), 9–24. Holmes's study has since been reproduced in Venuti, ed., *The Translation Studies Reader*, 172–85.
66.   Holmes turns to Hempel's fascicle, *Fundamentals of Concept Formation in Empirical Sciences* (Chicago: University of Chicago Press, 1967), for his framework.
67.   Holmes, "The Name and Nature of Translation Studies" (Toury repr.), 15.
68.   Ibid.
69.   Gideon Toury, *Descriptive Translation Studies and Beyond* (Benjamins Translation Library 4; Amsterdam: John Benjamins, 1995), 7.

Holmes proposed splitting the discipline into *pure* and *applied* branches, with *theoretical* and *descriptive* studies as subsets of the pure branch. Descriptive translation studies (DTS) would then be subdivided according to orientation: *product-*, *process-*, and *function-oriented*. Product-oriented DTS describes existing translations; it is "text-focused translation description,"[70] which first gives rise to analyses of translations, which generally issue from comparison with other translations, and then moves on to surveys of larger corpuses of translations.[71] Function-oriented DTS "is not interested in the description of translations in themselves, but in the recipient socio-cultural situation: it is a study of contexts rather than texts."[72] The two foci of this function-oriented of DTS are choice—what texts did and did not get translated at different social, historical, and cultural junctures?—and the consequences of choice—what impact did these translations (or the lack of them) exert on a culture? The interest here is more with influence than method, with the social, historical, and cultural intersections within a text. Process-oriented DTS "concerns itself with the process or act of translation itself,"[73] with what goes on in the mind of the translator as he creates a new yet equivalent text.[74] What in the sensibility of the reteller (translator) engenders the retelling (translation) he offers? How does the retelling affect the status of the telling? The audience that receives the telling? These questions are central to our thinking about the literary afterlife of the Bible.

Polysystem Theory

The next major development in translation theory also provides concepts and vocabulary that are useful for thinking about the relationship between telling and retelling. André Lefevere's early work details seven strategies, or approaches, that translators take to the original. These are:

70. Holmes, "The Name and Nature of Translation Studies" (Toury repr.), 15.

71. "For instance, those made within a specific period, language and/or text discourse type. In practice the corpus has usually been restricted in all three ways: seventeenth-century literary translations into French, or medieval Bible translations," notes James S. Holmes in "The Name and the Nature of Translation Studies," in *The Translation Studies Reader*, 184. "But such descriptive surveys can also be larger in scope, diachronic as well as (approximately) synchronic and one of the eventual goals of product-oriented DTS might possibly be a general history of translation" (Holmes, "The Name and Nature of Translation Studies" [Toury repr.], 16).

72. Ibid., 16.

73. Ibid.

74. I. A. Richards avers that the mental activity of translators "may very probably be the most complex type of event yet produced in the evolution of the cosmos" (ibid.).

1. *Phonemic translation*, in which the translator strives to reproduce not only the sense of the foreign, but the sound as well. This is the premise at work in Everett Fox's translation of the Torah, in which the English is intended to echo the Hebrew.
2. *Literal translation*, in which the translator attempts a word-for-word translation.
3. *Metrical translation*, in which the emphasis falls on the faithful rendering of the target's meter rather than its meaning.
4. *Poetry into prose*, in which the sense is favored and such poetics traits as meter and rhyme are done away with.
5. *Rhymed translation*, in which the translator "enters into a double bondage" of meter and rhyme.
6. *Blank verse translation*, in which the translator is freed from the structure of the original and the focus of the translation falls on a greater accuracy and literalness of rendition.
7. *Interpretation*, which includes what Lefevere calls *versions*, in which the substance of the original is retained but the form is changed, and *imitations*, in which the translator produces a work of his own, one with "only title and point of departure, if those, in common with the source text."[75]

At the end of his list, Lefevere brings us back to those writings that depart from what is commonly understood to be translation, leading us to the end of the spectrum at which "translation proper" becomes "version" and "imitation." The inclusion of interpretation among modes of translation presages Lefevere's later work in polysystem theory which attempts to situate the translator(s) in a broader literary framework.

In his 1982 article, "Mother Courage's Cucumbers," Lefevere seeks to show "how a certain approach to translation studies can make a significant contribution to literary theory as a whole and how translations or, to use a more general term, refractions, play a very important part in the evolution of literatures."[76] He contends,

> A writer's work gains exposure and achieves influence mainly through 'misunderstandings and misconceptions,' or, to use a more neutral term, refractions. Writers and their work are always understood and conceived against a certain background or, if you will, are refracted through a certain spectrum, just as their work itself can refract previous works through a certain spectrum.[77]

75. André Lefevere, *Translating Poetry: Seven Strategies and a Blueprint* (Amsterdam: Van Gorcum, 1975).
76. André Lefevere, "Mother Courage's Cucumbers: Text, System and Refraction in a Theory of Literature," *Modern Language Studies* 12, no. 4 (1982), 3.
77. Ibid., 3.

The notion of refraction is closely linked to my idea of filter: it is the diffusion of a text through a particular lens. Lefevere speaks of three components that may contribute to refraction: patronage, poetics, and ideology. Patronage, the literary system's regulatory body, is manifest in the "person, persons, institutions (Maecenas, the Chinese and Indian emperors, the Sultan, various prelates, noblemen, provincial governors, mandarins, the Church, the Court, the Fascist or Communist Party) who or which extend(s) patronage"[78] to the literary system. Poetics, the literary system's code of behavior, "consists of both an inventory component (genre, certain symbols, characters, prototypical situations) and a 'functional' component, an idea of how literature has to, or may be allowed to, function in society."[79] Ideology indicates the way "language reflects culture."[80] These "constraints" operating on the system of language cause refraction; in our parlance, they are all categories of filter with the capacity to color the retelling. Lefevere insists on drawing attention to them, because these "other constraints are often much more influential in the shaping of the translation than are the semantic or linguistic ones."[81] They influence "the ways in which literature offers its knowledge";[82] they shape (or as Lefevere has it, refract) the very telling. They are, as it happens, the filter.

Deconstruction
(Or, Translation and the Vocabulary of Deformation)

To this point, all the thinkers we have considered have had, on the whole, a positive attitude toward the fact and act of translation. Antoine Berman's 1985 essay "Translation and the Trials of the Foreign" marks a departure from this view. Berman announces as the theme of his essay "translation as the trial of the foreign (*comme l'épreuve de l'étranger*)."[83] He takes the idea of translation and trial from Heidegger,[84] and extends to

78. Ibid., 6.
79. Ibid.
80. It is thus "often most troublesome to translators. Since different languages reflect different cultures, translations will nearly always contain attempts to 'naturalize' the different culture, to make it conform more to what the reader of the translation is used to" (ibid.).
81. Ibid., 7.
82. Ibid., 19.
83. Antoine Berman, "Translation and the Trials of the Foreign," in Venuti, ed., *The Translation Studies Reader*, 284.
84. Who uses it to define one pole of poetic experience in Hölderlin; with this poet, the trial is "essentially enacted by translation, by his version of Sophocles, which is in fact the last 'work' Hölderlin published before descending into madness" (ibid.).

it a double meaning. On the one hand, the phrase "establishes a relation-ship between the Self-Same (*propre*) and the Foreign by aiming to open up the foreign work to us in its utter foreignness";[85] on the other, "translation is a trial *for the foreign as well*, since the foreign work is uprooted from its own *language-ground* (*sol-de-langue*)."[86] In transla-tion, both the receptor and the transmitter, the target and the source, are tested. The translator's responsibility in the carrying across of a text into another language is to accentuate the strangeness of the foreign, while making the foreign intelligible. Accomplishing both disrupts the target and the source alike.

Translation of literary texts, as against the more rote or literal trans-lation of technical or scientific ones, undertakes more than merely semantic transfer. It is "concerned with *works*, that is to say texts so bound to their language that the translating act inevitably becomes a manipulation of signifiers, where two languages enter into various forms of collision and somehow *couple*."[87] The prevailing trend in the history of translation has detracted from the mutual aspect of the coupling, as translators have favored renderings that "naturalize" the foreign. Thus, argues Berman, translation has become not the trial of the foreign but its negation. The source's "most individual essence [becomes] radically repressed"[88] as a consequence of its acclimation to the target.

Berman seeks to retrieve translation as an *ethical* act, with the "prop-erly ethical aim"[89] of receiving the foreign as foreign. As a way of doing so, he proposes "an analysis that shows how (and why) that aim has, from time immemorial (although not always), been skewed, perverted, and assimilated to something other than itself, such as the play of hypertextual transformations."[90] In Berman's view, the translation has too quickly and easily moved outside the realm of translation pure and simple into that of hypertext; transformations take place where transla-tions should occur. As a corrective, he outlines twelve "deforming forces," all apparent throughout the Western translating tradition,[91] which "intervene" in the domain of literary prose.

85. Ibid.
86. Ibid.
87. Ibid., 285.
88. Ibid.
89. Ibid.
90. Ibid., 286.
91.   Berman contends that the deforming tendencies he outlines "are not ahis-torical. They are rather historical in an original sense. They refer back to the figure of translation based on Greek thought in the West or more precisely, Platonism. The 'figure of translation' is understood here as the form in which translation is deployed

That Berman has already dismissed these forces—or tendencies, as he also calls them—as hypertextual transformations suggests that, even more than some of the other vocabularies of translation we have encountered thus far, they have tremendous potential for appropriation for our uses. He isolates and names ways in which translations alter (or at least deviate from) the very texts they purport to recount, which is precisely the project at hand. Berman's deforming forces are as follows:

Rationalization. There are three basic traits of rationalization: it "recomposes sentences and the sequence of sentences, rearranging them according to a certain idea of discursive *order*";[92] it renders texts abstract,[93] thus "annihilat[ing]...prose's drive toward concreteness";[94] it "reverses the relations which prevail in the original between formal and informal, ordered and disorderly, abstract and concrete... It causes the work to undergo a change of *sign*, of *status*—and seemingly without changing form and meaning."[95] In fact, it is the act of reversal that best typifies rationalization, which in sum "deforms the original by *reversing* its basic tendency."[96]

Clarification. Berman identifies clarification as "a corollary of rationalization which particularly concerns the level of 'clarity' perceptible in words and their meanings";[97] it can take one of two very different forms. It might be an explanation of something that is concealed or repressed in the original, a making apparent of that which is not readily so. It may also be a removal of nuance or subtlety, thereby making explicit that which "does not wish to be clear in the original."[98] The first form is a movement from obscurity to clarity; the second, from polysemy to monosemy.

and appears to itself, before any explicit theory. From its very beginnings, western translation has been an embellishing restitution of meaning, based on the typically Platonic separation between spirit and letter, sense and word, content and form, the sensible and the non-sensible. When it is affirmed today that translation (including non-literary translation) must produce a 'clear' and 'elegant' text (even if the original does not possess these qualities), the affirmation assumes the Platonic figure of translating, even if unconsciously" (ibid., 296).

92.   Ibid., 288.
93.   It does so "not only by reordering the sentence structure, but—for example—by translating verbs into substantives, by choosing the more general of two substantives, etc." (ibid., 289).
94.   Ibid.
95.   Ibid.
96.   Ibid.
97.   Ibid.
98.   Ibid.

Expansion. The nature of translation is that it inevitably becomes larger than the original—it is inherently "inflationist," as Steiner says. This is due in part to the fact that rationalization and clarification both require expansion, but the expansion is "empty": it adds no semantic value to the original.

Ennoblement. What Berman calls "the culminating point of 'classic' translation," ennoblement is, in poetry, "poeticization" and in prose "rhetoricization."[99] It consists in "producing 'elegant' sentences while using the source text, so to speak, as *raw material*";[100] by definition it therefore compromises the original, by imposing upon it an idealized style. Berman notes that there is a negative counterpart to ennoblement: *popularization*, in which a text deemed too haughty or elevated, is rendered as pseudo-slang or in a style approximating spoken language.

Qualitative Impoverishment. The name of the category itself again betrays Berman's disdain for transformative translation. He uses the term to refer to "the replacement of terms, expressions, and figures in the original with terms, expressions, and figures that lack their sonorous richness or, correspondingly, their signifying or 'iconic'[101] richness."[102] When the replacement happens not merely with individual words, but across an entire text "to the whole of its iconic surface, it decisively effaces a good portion of its signifying process and mode of expression—what makes a work *speak* to us."[103] Thus in Berman's view, replacement is synonymous with depreciation.

Quantitative Impoverishment. All prose works present a "proliferation of signifiers and signifying chains"[104] that, when translated, become fixed signs with finite signifiers. Thus with every translation there is a lexical loss, a narrowing of possibility.

The Destruction of Rhythms. While this aspect of deformation is self-evidently true of translated poetry, Berman argues that "the novel is not less rhythmic than poetry. It even comprises a multiplicity of rhythms. Since the entire bulk of the novel is thus in movement, it is fortunately difficult for translation to destroy this rhythmic movement."[105] This is why, according to Berman, we are more willing to read a badly translated

---

99. Ibid.
100. Ibid.
101. A term is "iconic" when, "in relation to its referent, it 'creates an image,' enabling a perception of resemblance" (ibid., 291).
102. Ibid.
103. Ibid.
104. Ibid.
105. Ibid., 292.

novel than poorly translated poetry. Nonetheless, the destruction of rhythm can notably deform even a novel.

The Destruction of Underlying Networks of Signification. Beneath every literary work there is an "underlying text" wherein certain signifiers connect with others to link up disparate parts of the text itself. This subtext "carries the network of word-obsessions"—*Leitworter*—that contribute both to the rhythm and to the signifying process of a text. While these words as signifiers have "no particular value,"[106] the chain of them, their linking of the text to itself, lends semantic unity to the whole. Unless the same words are reproduced faithfully (which is to say consistently) throughout a translation, this "dimension of augmentation"[107] is in danger of being lost.

The Destruction of Linguistic Patternings. Beyond the level of signifiers and metaphors, "the semantic nature of the text…extends to the type of sentences, the sentence constructions employed."[108] Rationalization and clarification, in their expanding the text, destroy these linguistic patternings by introducing outside phrasing and form. The result is "a curious consequence: when the translated text is more 'homogeneous' than the original (possessing more 'style' in the ordinary sense), it is equally more *incoherent* and, in a certain way, more heterogeneous, more *inconsistent.*"[109] The trap of this kind of translation, then, is its appearing simultaneously homogeneous and inconsistent.

The Destruction of Vernacular Networks or Their Exoticization. Again the text is deformed or diminished when the richness imparted to it by the use of a vernacular is replaced in translation—even by another vernacular. Berman contends that "the effacement of vernaculars is…a very serious injury to the textuality of prose works,"[110] and argues that *exoticization,* the route translators take to retain the vernacular, is inadequate. Exoticization tends to take one of two forms: either italicization to isolate the foreign term, or a replacement of the foreign vernacular with a local one. This latter is particularly odious, in Berman's view, as "unfortunately, a vernacular clings tightly to its soil and completely resists any direct translating into another vernacular."[111] The effect of both means of exoticization, therefore, is a ridiculing of the original.

106. Ibid., 293.
107. Ibid.
108. Ibid.
109. Ibid.
110. Ibid., 294.
111. Ibid.

The Destruction of Expressions and Idioms. This category can go largely without explanation: idioms, as other translators have noted, need to be attended to in an other-than-literal fashion. The most obvious solution is to replace the idiom with a comparable idiom in the target.[112] Replacing an idiom with its equivalent, however, is an ethnocentrism (something to be avoided in Berman's schema), and when repeated on a large scale (as in a novel) results in an absurdity. Berman cautions that "to play with 'equivalence' is to attack the discourse of the foreign work."[113]

The Effacement of the Superimposition of Languages. The superimposition of languages "involves the relation between dialect and a common language, a *koine*, or the coexistence, in the heart of a text, of two or more *koine*."[114] When a text is translated, the relation of tension and integration between the two source languages is threatened; the homogeneity of the target language risks effacing the striations of the source. The heteroglossia or heterophony of the original is in danger of becoming a univocity.

All the tendencies Berman has outlined make for translation that may be "more 'clear,' more 'elegant,' more 'pure' than the original. But they are the destruction of the letter in favor of meaning"[115]and are therefore false to the extent that they privilege meaning over form. Berman is therefore profoundly suspicious of translation itself. He wonders whether translation should not focus more on the literal—which is to say that which is attached to the letter or to the work. His mistrust of the enterprise aside, he does provide us with a list of twelve evocative terms, all with the potential to be translated (or carried across) to a taxonomy of retelling.[116] More than any other vocabulary of translation, Berman's

---

112.   For example, "Il pleut à seaux" would become "It's raining cats and dogs."
113.   Berman, "Translation and the Trials of the Foreign," 295.
114.   Ibid.
115.   Ibid., 297.
116.   A note of caution here. While Berman's catalogue of transpositional moves provides us with a vocabulary ripe for appropriation, we should perhaps be cautious about a wholesale adoption of it. The list is a *via negativa*, a litany of ways the text is rendered less true when touched by other hands. While the negative slant may work in thinking about translation, which—as I have noted—we tend to expect to be faithful, it will need to be reconstituted somewhat more positively for our thinking here. Our consideration is not *How has this retelling deformed the telling?* but *What has this retelling done with the telling?* Thus, to dub a retelling a "qualitative impoverishment" would move us from the objective realm of nomenclature to the subjective realm of aesthetics. We should thus perhaps adopt the terms somewhat divorced from their (largely derogatory) definitions.

offers us a language for speaking of approach, for articulating how the retelling gains access to the telling. His twelve terms constitute a variety of relations a retelling may have to a telling. It may recompose order, render text abstract, or reverse relations within a text. It may clarify, make explicit that which is veiled in the original, remove nuance. It may expand upon the original. It may ennoble or popularize the language of the telling. It may replace terms, expressions, or figures with more recognizable ones. It may build signifiers and signifying chains. It may alter rhythm, making the poem prose or the prose poem. It may toy with the network of underlying text. It may render the telling homogeneous. It may substitute vernaculars. It may exoticize or familiarize. It may manipulate relations between languages within the text.

The Approach of the Translator

I have ended our discussion of theory with a lexicon of words that highlight the potentially devaluative and even destructive effects of translation. Returning to Steiner, who resisted the very idea of a theory translation, we find a narrative, rather than a theory, which describes what happens in translation. In Steiner's view, "the translator invades, extracts, and brings home."[117] This language of sacking and pillaging overstates Steiner's point: he asserts that the hermeneutic motion in translation is ultimately constructive.

Basing his description on the accounts and records of translators themselves, Steiner asserts that there is a four-beat movement in the act of translation: initiative trust; aggression; incorporation; reciprocity (or restitution). This four-part narrative describes what I have been calling approach: how the translator (or the author of the retelling) gains access to the original telling.

"Initiative trust" is what compels the translator to take on the task of translation in the first place. It is a belief in the significance, "in the 'seriousness' of the facing, or strictly speaking, adverse text."[118] It is a belief, based more on instinct than on evidence, that not only is there something worthwhile in the other, but that that something can be captured and conveyed through translation. This trust will be tested through the course of the translation, as the source and target gain and lose coherence under the translator's scrutiny.

---

117.   Steiner, *After Babel*, 314.
118.   Ibid., 312.

After trust comes "aggression": "the second move of the translator is incursive and extractive."[119] It is an attack, in the Heideggerian sense that understanding, recognition, and interpretation comprise an attack mode. "This manoeuvre of comprehension is explicitly invasive and exhaustive,"[120] for in the understanding involved in translation, where one must dissect a text in order to convey it into another idiom.

The third movement, "incorporation," shifts the focus from source to target. It is the importing of the source's meaning and form into the target, the naturalizing of them as they are moved across. The translated becomes a part of the world of the translator; the foreign influences the domestic. Steiner offers two metaphors for this stage: sacramental intake and infection. We are equally likely to be made strong as to be made lame by what we import.

The three stages alone are "dangerously incomplete"; they lack "the piston-stroke, as it were, that completes the cycle."[121] The incompleteness is in fact an imbalance: the act of translation throws the translator off kilter. As translators, we

> 'lean toward' the confronting text (every translation has experienced this palpable bending towards and launching at his target). We encircle and invade cognitively. We come home laden, thus again off-balance, having caused disequilibrium throughout the system by taking away from 'the other' and by adding…to our own.[122]

The motion of translation is cyclical or circular: we lean toward in trust, circle and invade in aggression, and wind up dizzy and off-tilt in the incorporation. We have taken but we have not given. Thus the fourth movement of "reciprocity" or "restitution" restores balance. This last motion happens after the "appropriative 'rapture' of the translator";[123] it is the act of imbuing something of the target in the source. "The work translated is enhanced":[124] its richness is reflected in the light of a new light language; its stature increased by its entering a new culture. The reciprocity is the coupling of the "outflow of energy from the source" with the "inflow into the receptor"[125] such that both are altered.

Steiner's four-movement hermeneutic is an abstraction of the act or approach of translation. It offers a poetic appraisal of what takes place in

119.   Ibid., 313.
120.   Ibid., 314.
121.   Ibid., 316.
122.   Ibid.
123.   Ibid.
124.   Ibid.
125.   Ibid., 317.

translation, but does not treat the concrete aspects of how translation might proceed. While the practical treatments of approach will ultimately provide us with a vocabulary on which to build, we cannot proceed without considering more broadly the philosophical concerns of translation.

Eugene Nida, who launched considerable debate and discussion about the act of translating, notes that there is a tendency to think of translation as having two poles—paraphrastic and literal. Nida, however, is quick to point out the grades of translation:

> There are, for example, such ultraliteral translations as interlinears, while others involve highly concordant relationships, e.g. the same source-language word is always translated by one—and only one—receptor-language word. Still others may be quite devoid of artificial restrictions in form, but nevertheless may be over traditional and even archaizing. Some translations aim at very close formal and semantic correspondence, but are generously supplied with notes and commentary. Many are not so much concerned with giving information as with creating in the reader something of the same mood as was conveyed by the original.[126]

An even more specific range of possible approaches had been outlined a few years earlier by two Canadians, Jean-Paul Vinay and Jean Darbelnet. In 1958, they published *Comparative Stylistics of French and English: A Methodology for Translation*, a textbook providing a theoretical basis for a variety of then-current translation methods.

Vinay and Darbelnet begin with an echo of the assertion Nida contests: that there are, in fact, only two basic modes of translation—literal and paraphrastic. In their account, these are labeled "literal" and "oblique." Literal translation is the transposition, element by element, of the source language message into the target language. This method is possible when the source and target are based either on "parallel categories, in which case we can speak of structural parallelism, or of parallel concepts, which are the result of metalinguistic parallelisms."[127] There may be places where gaps in the target language (lacks of equivalence) necessitate the translator's use of "corresponding elements, so that the overall impression is the same for the two messages";[128] the overall method, however, is an element-by-element carrying across. When the source and target languages exhibit structural or metalinguistic differences, certain stylistic effects cannot be transposed. In such cases, "more complex methods have to be used which at first may look unusual but which

126.   Nida, *Toward a Science of Translating*, 156.
127.   Jean-Paul Vinay and Jean Darbelnet, "A Methodology for Translation," in Venuti, ed., *The Translation Studies Reader*, 84.
128.   Ibid.

nevertheless permit translators a strict control over the reliability of their work";[129] this is oblique translation.

In one chapter, however, "A Methodology for Translation," the two assert what Nida also contends: that translation is polyvalent not polarized. Between literal and oblique is a spectrum of possibility. Despite its many shades, it is not, however, infinite. While there may appear to be countless possible ways to translate, there are in fact only seven basic modes, each more complex than the one before. The first three are designed to assist the translator in bridging the lacunae sometimes encountered when doing literal translation; the remaining four may be required in oblique translation:

Procedure 1: Borrowing. The simplest of all translation methods, borrowing is used "to overcome a lacuna, usually a metalinguistic one (e.g. a new technical process, an unknown concept)."[130] Vinay and Darbelnet note that translators sometimes use it for stylistic effect, retaining a word in the source language so as to give the reader of the target language a sense of the foreign. Thus, a translator might retain foreign currency, foods, personal or place names, even when there is an equivalent in the target, as a way of establishing setting. We see borrowing frequently in English translations of the Psalms that retain *Selah* at their close. It is a word with no precise English equivalent,[131] and in fact its exact Hebrew meaning is unknown. The effect of retaining the foreign word is a heightened sense of both the grandeur and the holiness of the psalm, and the Hebrew-cum-English word links the English reader into a venerable chain of worship that traces directly back to the ancient text.

Procedure 2: Calque. A calque is the borrowing of an expression from another language, and the subsequent literal translation of the elements within the expression. There are two types of calque. A *lexical calque,* "respects the syntactic structure of the [target language], whilst introducing a new mode of expression." An example would be rendering the English "Compliments of the Season!" in French as "*Compliments de la saison!*" rather than offering a known French holiday greeting like "*Meilleurs voeux.*" A *structural calque* "introduces a new construction into the language."[132] Vinay and Darbelnet offer as an example the English genre 'science-fiction' having become the French "science-fiction."

129. Ibid.
130. Ibid., 85.
131. *Webster's English Dictionary* defines it as "a Hebrew word of unknown meaning at the end of verses in the Psalms: perhaps a musical direction, but traditionally interpreted as a blessing meaning 'forever.'"
132. Vinay and Darbelnet, "A Methodology for Translation," 85.

Yiddish works at length with calques; it is thus that it brings the "*loshen koydesh*" (holy language) into the vernacular.

Procedure 3: Literal Translation. Literal translation is the "direct transfer of a source language text into a *grammatically* and idiomatically appropriate target language text in which the translator's task is limited to observing the adherence to the linguistic servitudes of the target language."[133] This procedure works best with languages in the same family, particularly when the languages share the same culture. The literal translation is "reversible and complete in itself";[134] its proceeding word by word through a text allows it to be readily undone.

According to Vinay and Darbelnet's instructions, the above three procedures—which do not involve any "special stylistic procedures"[135]— should comprise the first attempts made by the translator. If, however, the text when translated literally "gives another meaning; has no meaning; is structurally impossible; does not have a corresponding expression within the metalinguistic experience of the target language, or has a corresponding expression, but not within the same register,"[136] the translation is unacceptable. When the literal procedures do not yield an acceptable translation, the translator must resort to oblique translation, which has its own set of guidelines. Its four procedures are:

Procedure 4: Transposition. Transposition can be both an intra- and an interlingual translation device. It "involves replacing one word class with another without changing the meaning of the message."[137] There are two types of transposition: obligatory and optional. The obligatory transposition must take place in order for the translation to make sense. The optional transposition may be translated literally, but may also be transposed to give a fuller or more nuanced meaning. Vinay and Darbelnet offer as an example "*As soon as he gets up*" which may in French become either a calque—"*Dès son lever*"—or a transposition—"*Dès qu'il se lève.*"[138]

Procedure 5: Modulation. When a literal translation yields an utterance that is unidiomatic or awkward in the target language, the translator must use modulation. Here again we find two subsets: fixed and free modulation. Fixed modulation is linked to the language structure itself.

---

133. Ibid., 86.
134. Ibid.
135. Ibid., 87. These three procedures can be done by a computer; they turn on cases of the unambiguous transfer from source to target language.
136. Ibid.
137. Ibid., 88.
138. Ibid.

The negative English expression "It is not difficult to show..." must be translated as the positive French idiom "*Il est facile de démontrer...*" The translator who has facility in both target and source languages will simply know these phrases to be equivalent, despite the differences in their grammatical structures; he can seek confirmation of his choice of expression in a dictionary or grammar. In instances of free modulation, by contrast, the translator cannot seek recourse in set cases or rules; as these instances are unique, he must decide at each encounter how to proceed. When free modulation is "carried out as it should be, the resulting translation should correspond perfectly to the situation indicated by the source language";[139] it should "[make] the reader exclaim, 'Yes, that's exactly what you would say.'"[140] The difference, then, between fixed and free modulation is one of degree: "free modulation...tends towards a unique solution, a solution which rests upon an habitual train of thought and which is necessary rather than optional."[141] When a free modulation is used often enough to be found in a dictionary, it becomes fixed, and a translation that does not employ the now-standard import would be deemed inadequate.

Procedure 6: Equivalence. In transmitting certain expressions and idioms the act of translation cannot be literal, but demands that the translator find the equivalent formulation in the target language. The rooster in the French children's book should not say "Cock-a-doodle-do" but rather "*Cocorico.*" A clumsy Englishman would never be described as being "*Comme un chien aux quilles*" ("like a dog at a bowling game"); any reasonable translator would take the literal phrase and render it "Like a bull in a china shop."[142] Such expressions cannot be translated with a calque—they must be conveyed by equivalent idioms or expressions.

Procedure 7: Adaptation. Vinay and Darbelnet describe this last procedure as "the extreme limit of translation."[143] It is used in cases where the situation referred to in the source language is unknown in the target (e.g. rendering the Italian "*bocci*" as "lawn bowling"). When a translator refuses to make a necessary adaptation, the reader will detect the impact not only on the syntactic structure, but also on the development of ideas.[144]

---

139.   Ibid., 89.
140.   Ibid.
141.   Ibid.
142.   Ibid., 90.
143.   Ibid.
144.   Ibid., 91.

Through this seven part analysis, we are introduced to a vocabulary that allows one to speak. The translation is not to be described as merely oblique or literal, the process of translation itself is detailed more precisely. Borrowing, calque, literal translation, transposition, modulation, equivalence, and adaptation, all tell us how a translator can enter into the text to be translated, all signal what he might do as he tries to convey literature in a new idiom. It is a vocabulary for thinking about how the translator gains access to the work to be translated. Thus, at points, the concerns of what I have been calling approach overlap with those of stance. Stance is what the translator conceives of himself as doing; this is a distinct concern from the mechanics of what he does in translating (that is, his approach, the way he gains access to the source (as by interlinear translation). What role does the translated text play for translator? For the translation? Assuming, as we are, an analogy between translation and retelling, we can also ask: What is the role of telling in light of the retelling? How does the retelling stand in relation to the telling?

Chapter 8

UNTO ALL LANGUAGES THAT DWELL IN THE EARTH

Steiner has shown us the hermeneutic motion—what happens in a translation, how the translator accesses the source—and Nida, Vinay, and Darbelnet have pointed to a range of possible approaches. The next question is how the translation reflects the source. This is the question of stance: How does the rewritten text (the translation or the retelling) stand in relation to the text it treats?

In exploring the idea of the translator's stance, and in co-opting the language of translation studies to speak about the stances of retellings, this chapter will use as its biblical prooftext the David story.

The Stance of the Translator

The range of understandings of the relationship between translated and translation is broad, and we will explore some of the variations within it. It is perhaps helpful to begin with Foucault, who, in a widely cited review of Pierre Klossowski's translation of *The Aeneid*, casts into high relief the poles of translation. He asserts that there are two kinds of translation, and they share neither function nor nature. In the one type, "something (meaning, aesthetic value) must remain identical, and it is given passage into another language; these translations are good when they go 'from like to the same.'"[1] The other kind consists of those translations "that hurl one language against another…taking the original text for a projectile and treating the translating language like a target. Their task is not to lead a meaning back to itself or anywhere else; but to use the translated language to derail the translating language."[2] "From like to the same" and the hurled projectile represent not just the two extremes of translation, but "the two kinds" of translation. Foucault's is the radical

---

1. Michel Foucault, "Les mots qui saignent" (trans. Lawrence Venuti), *L'Express* 29 (August 1969): 30.
2. Ibid.

view; as we will see, other thinkers have posited more nuanced, more complex understandings of the possible stances involved in translation.

From within what he describes as the narrow framework of translation, Hugo Friedrich asks broad questions about the moving of a text from one language to another:

> Is translation something that concerns the cultural interaction of an entire nation with another? Is translation just the reaction of one writer to another? Does translation resurrect and revitalize a forgotten work, or does it just keep a work alive to satisfy tradition? Does the translation create levels of meaning that were not necessarily visible in the original text so that the translated text reaches a higher level of aesthetic existence? What is the relationship between translation and interpretation: when do the two meet and when does translation follow its own laws?[3]

These are questions that could equally be asked of the retelling. Does it involve the dialogue of cultures, or merely of authors? Is it a resurrection or a mummification of the telling? Can it surpass the original? When does it take place on its own terms, and when does it adhere to the text from which it derives? In an attempt to answer some of the questions he raises of translation, Friedrich, a scholar of Romance languages, offers a historical overview of the art, highlighting in particular two modes (or stances): conquest and embrace. The concept of translation as conquest had already been well-articulated by Nietzsche in *The Gay Science*. Just as Heinemann and Stern argue that the midrash reflects the concerns of its writers more than anything in the text itself, so Nietzsche argues that translation is conditioned by the period in which a translator lived. The translator's approach is determined by her own culture's view of history. Thus, conversely, if one closely examines a translation one can determine the historical sensibilities of the period in which it was written. So Nietzsche asserts that "one can estimate the degree of an age's historical sense from the way it makes *translations* and seeks to absorb past ages and books."[4]

The Romans, in Nietzsche's estimation, translated the Greeks "violently and naively," laying waste to "everything good and lofty in the older Greek antiquity." Their translations were marked by a lack of concern for the original creation and a tremendous estimation of the

---

3. Hugo Friedrich, "On the Art of Translation" (trans. Rainer Schulte and John Biguenet), in *Theories of Translation* (ed. Rainer Schulte and John Biguenet; Chicago: University of Chicago Press, 1992), 11–12.

4. Friedrich Nietzsche, "83. Translations," in *The Gay Science* (ed. Bernard Williams; trans. Josefine Nauckhoff and Adrian Del Caro; Cambridge: Cambridge University Press, 2001), 83.

createrly capabilities of the translator. They translated by "leaving out the historical…adding allusions to the present and, above all, crossing out the name of the poet and replacing it with one's own—not with any sense of theft but with the very best conscience of the *imperium Romanum.*" The Romans conceived of themselves as breathing new life into dead bodies—of translating things into the "Roman present." They stripped away the Greek particulars and replaced them with "what was contemporary and Roman"—"what was past and alien was embarrassing to them."[5] Theirs was a conception of translation as conquest, undergirded by a sense of—if not what Nietzsche calls theft—what many of our contemporaries would label imperialism. These poet-translators conducted themselves in the literary front as their empire behaved on the political one.

Friedrich fleshes out this idea of translation as imperialism. Initially, he notes, when the ancient Romans began translating from the Greek, they so gave themselves over to the original that awkward Graecisms would enter the Latin. In time, however, the Roman tendency became to subsume the original in the target language. For the Romans, translation came to mean "the appropriation of the original; [it] meant transformation in order to mold the foreign into the linguistic structures of one's own culture."[6] Thus the target language dictated how the translation took place. This attitude is reflected in Cicero's precept not to translate *verbum pro verbo*, and in his comments about his translation of Demosthenes. Cicero claims not to have translated "as an interpreter, but as an orator, keeping the same ideas and the forms, or as one might say, the 'figures' of thought, but in language that conforms to our usage (*verbis ad nostram consuetudinem aptis*)."[7] In not translating word for word, Cicero understood himself to be preserving the "general style (*genus*) and force (*vis*) of the language" of the original, but one might argue that he was as concerned with the target.

This philosophy pervaded Latin translations, serving also as the underpinning for St. Jerome's translation of the Septuagint, where the target again dictated the flow of the translation. In *De Optimo Genere*

---

5. All quotations in the paragraph, ibid., 84.
6. Friedrich, "On the Art of Translation," 12.
7. "Converti enim ex Atticis duorum eloquentissimorum nobilissimas orationes inter seque contrarias, Aeschinis et Demosthenis; nec converti ut interpres, sed ut orator, sententiis isdem et earum formis tamquam figuris, verbis ad nostram consuetudinem aptis. In quibus non verbum pro verbo necesse habui reddere, sed genus omne verborum vimque servavi. Non enim ea me adnumerare lectori putavi oportere, sed tamquam appendere" (Cicero, *De Optimo Genere Oratorium* 5.14).

Interpretandi, his treatise on translation, St. Jerome makes overt the notion of translation as conquest, noting that "the translator considers thought content a prisoner which he transplants into his own language with the prerogative of a conqueror."[8] In this cultural imperialism, the original must be wrestled into submission.

By Friedrich's account, Roman translation was as much marked by contest as it was by conquest. The goal of the translation was to surpass the original. This perspective goes hand in hand with the imperialism of conquest: by improving the original, the translated work became a truly Roman creation. Historically, the movement from translation to enrichment to surpassing was followed by yet another approach, this one "based on the premise that the purpose of translation is to go beyond the appropriation of content to a releasing of those linguistic and aesthetic energies that heretofore had existed only as pure possibility in one's own language and had never been materialized before."[9] In this tack, the original is still brought over to the target—the target does not give way to the original—in order to reveal "the latent stylistic possibilities in one's own language that are different from the original."[10] According to Friedrich, this use of the original as a springboard for the development of the target language itself is seen most clearly in Malherbe's rendering of Seneca's letters in French. Malherbe brought across Seneca's short, laconic sentences, linking them together with conversational connections and interactions, arranging them in order of significance, repeating their content in different form. His appropriation of the content of the original, combined with his creation of a new style unknown to both the source and target languages, marks the beginning of Classical French writing.

This seventeenth-century literary variation on the idea of translation as conquest or carrying over served to open up a new style of writing, but it eventually gave way to another vision of translation, one in which the target language ceded to the original rather than the other way around. The period's increasing tolerance of cultural difference reduced "the artistic, intellectual or any other rivalry between languages and [gave] equal standing to all languages."[11] The result of shifts in perceptions of language, as well as in understandings of the limits of the enterprise of translation, made for a new norm in translation: a movement away from the target to the source.

8. Friedrich, "On the Art of Translation," 12–13.
9. Ibid., 13.
10. Ibid.
11. Ibid., 14.

Two things come out of this movement toward the source. The first is an inclination to uphold the original, casting it in as good a light as possible. Here we see Dryden's bias toward glorifying the original writer, toward "[making] his author appear as charming as he possibly can"—so long, that is, as he is faithful to the author's character. Here Dryden likens translation to life-drawing, "where every one will acknowledge that there is a double sort of likeness, a good one and a bad." A bad likeness captures the true outlines, proportions, coloring of the model; a good one preserves these but makes them "graceful, by the posture, the shadowings, and chiefly, by the spirit which animates the whole."[12] This instinct towards making the original graceful for its own sake,[13] and not for the sake of outdoing it, marks a sharp departure from the surpassing movement of the Roman translations.

The second new motion also counters the philosophy of the later Roman translations, but falls in line with those earlier ones that erred toward a Graecizing of the Latin. Proponents of this view sought to uphold the foreignness of the source, even to the point of "foreignizing" the target such that it echoes the source. Or, as Schleiermacher asks, "Should [the translator] try to bring two people together who are so totally separated from each other—as his fellow man, who is completely ignorant of the author's language, and the author himself are—into such an immediate relationship as that of author and reader?" And even if he does want "to open up to his readers only the same relationship and the same pleasure that he enjoys, marked by traces of hard work and imbued with a sense of the foreign, how can he achieve all this with the means at his disposal?" Schleiermacher answers his own questions: "If [the translator's] readers are supposed to understand, then they must comprehend the spirit of the language that was native to the writer, and they must be able to see his peculiar way of thinking and feeling."[14]

Translation here is an embrace of the foreign rather than a conquest of it, a drawing of the reader near to the original rather than the original to the reader: "the translator's goal must be to provide his reader with the same image and the same pleasure as reading the work in the original

12.   John Dryden, "Preface to Sylvae," in *Of Dramatick Poesy and Other Essays*, Vol. 1 (ed. George Watson; London: Dent, 1968), 252–53.

13.   The instinct does not always play out well. In this, we see the theme of betrayal by augment. Steiner describes the sonnets of Louise Labe as originals to which (after Rilke's *Umdichtung*) we no longer return because the translation is of a higher magnitude.

14.   Friedrich Schleiermacher, "From *On the Different Methods of Translating*" (trans. Waltraud Bartscht), in Schulte and Biguenet, eds., *Theories of Translation*, 39.

language offers to the man educated in this way."[15] The effect of reading a translation must be comparable to the effect of reading the original in its source language: the reader must be aware of the foreignness of the text, despite the familiarity of the language in which it is now written.

There is a range of opinions about the degree to which the target should be foreignized. In the introduction to his 1816 translation of *Agamemnon*, Wilhelm von Humboldt asserts that "a translation should indeed have a foreign flavor to it, but only to a certain degree"[16]—there is a clear line that must not, in his view, be crossed. "As long as one does not feel the foreignness (*Fremdheit*) yet does feel the foreign (*Fremde*), a translation has reached its highest goal; but where foreignness appears as such, and more than likely even obscures the foreign, the translator betrays his inadequacy.[17]

Von Humboldt's rule stands in sharp distinction to those laid out by Martin Buber and Franz Rosenzweig, who, in their translation of the Hebrew Bible into German, responded against the fluidity of Luther's translation, in which the Reformer sought "to produce clear language, comprehensible to everyone, with an undistorted sense and meaning."[18] Rosenzweig describes Luther's translation as a "trumpet-call in the ear of those who had fallen asleep happy in their possession of the 'received and certified text'":[19] initially it awakened Germans to a scripture that had been remote. It became, however, a national document, a Protestant one at that, which more reflected contemporary Germany than it did the Bible. Thus Buber and Rosenzweig set about producing their own translation, Hebraicizing the German, peppering it with archaisms and replicating the *Leitworte* that recur in the Hebrew. Their aim was to make the overly familiar Bible as foreign as possible. Years later, Everett Fox used their theories of translation to bring the Hebrew Bible into English, publishing the very foreignized *The Five Books of Moses*.

The ideas of conquest, embrace, and foreignization raised in this discussion of the translator's stance are all of potential use to the present consideration of retellings. We might rightly understand Joseph Heller's *God Knows*[20] to be a conquest, in which the perspective of the biblical

15. Ibid., 44.

16. Wilhelm von Humboldt, "From his 'Introduction to *Agamemnon*'" (trans. Sharon Sloane), in Schulte and Biguenet, eds., *Theories of Translation*, 58.

17. Ibid.

18. Franz Rosenzweig, "Scripture and the Word: On the New Bible Translation," in Martin Buber and Franz Rosenzweig *Scripture and Translation* (trans. Lawrence Rosenwald; Bloomington: Indiana University Press, 1994), 40.

19. Ibid., 57.

20. Joseph Heller, *God Knows* (New York: Scribner, 1997).

history is undermined, and a new authority is offered in its stead. Heller's book is a chronicle of David's life, recounted by the king in his old age. Acutely self-aware, and aware of the tradition that has sprung up around him,[21] Heller's David recasts his own biblical story. Early on, David sets the stage for his telling, positioning himself within the canon, but irreverently so. He writes:

> Of the making of books there is no end and the longer I reflect on this tale of mine, the stronger grows my conviction that killing Goliath was just about the biggest mistake I ever made. Fucking Bathsheba, then fucking her again, then again and again and again, and holding her in my arms until I almost could not hold her any longer, and could not bear separating from her—that could have been my second biggest mistake.[22]

This David, much in keeping with the "authorized" one of the Bible, is driven by his body; his remembrance has largely to do with his carnal pleasures (especially with regard to Bathsheba).

Beyond his sexual escapades, however, the story attends in part to David's relationship with God, which is what we, as readers of the Bible, expect:

> I've got a love story and a sex story, with the same woman no less, and both are great, and I've got this ongoing, open-ended Mexican stand-off with God, even though He might now be dead. Whether God is dead or not hardly matters, for we would use Him no differently anyway. He owes me an apology, but God won't budge so I won't budge. I have my faults, God knows, and I may even be among the first to admit them, but to this very day I know in my bones that I'm a much better person than He is. Although I never actually *walked* with God, I did talk with Him a lot and got along with Him in perfect rapport until I offended Him the first time; then He offended me, and later we offended each other. Even then He promises to protect me. And He has? But protect me from what? Old age? The deaths of my children and the rape of my daughter?[23]

David's telling here is animated but world-weary, and his garrulous cynicism replaces the piety of the biblical account. This David and his God have struggled, but neither has prevailed. The conquest here is of perspective: the authoritative version is rendered much less authoritatively when presented by an author with his own subjective version. In

---

21.   Both propensities are seen in his comment that "Joseph is a collateral ancestor with whom I can easily identify and sympathize, even at his infantile worst" (ibid., 35).

22.   Ibid., 16.

23.   Ibid., 8.

telling the story from the perspective of the jaded old king, Heller is not only adding a subjective element, but fundamentally unhinging the biblical truth.

The unhinging is accomplished because Heller's David knows himself to be the maker of the biblical truth of the Bible (particularly, of the Authorized Version). David knows how great his contribution to literary tradition is, in part because of his (clearly anachronistic) familiarity with the King James translation. This textual self-referencing appears throughout the book, usually wryly. David speaks as the self-recognized psalmist:[24]

> It was from this end-of-day activity, incidentally, that I drew my widely quoted "separating the sheep from the goats, and the men from the boys," which stands out so prominently in one of my lesser-known psalms, I think, or perhaps in one of those proverbs of mine for which authorship is often credited to Solomon or someone else. I know beyond doubt that my "separating the sheep from the goats" is used in more than one of the works by that overrated hack William Shakespeare of England, whose chief genius lay in looting the best thoughts and lines from the works of Kit Marlowe, Thomas Kyd, Plutarch, Raphael Holinshed and me. The idea for *King Lear*, of course, he got from me and Absalom. Are you going to tell me no? Who else but me was every inch a king? Do you think the unscrupulous plagiarist could have written *Macbeth* and never heard of Saul?[25]

As is evident in the references to Absalom, this David's story is aware of the details of the actual biblical story; it is the personalized version of that account, told in the distinct voice of a frustrated and sarcastic David, a David not seen in the Bible. This David makes frequent reference to the record of his story (history) in 1 and 2 Samuel, while dismissing the version in Chronicles as the most white-washed, watered-down version conceivable, one which divests him entirely of his character and his life of scandal. Thus the conquest of the Bible by *God Knows* is achieved in part because the biblical truth stands right alongside this new David's, and because it is corrected at every turn by the very king who lived through these chronicles.

---

24. "Bathsheba, mind you, is slyly credited with the more famous psalms, which David notes did not rhyme and lacked meter—he characterizes her as having a tin ear. She brings him a poem, and he replies, "And here's another big error. Either 'valley of death' or 'shadow of death,' not both. Bathsheba, give it up. You don't have the head for it. You think writing psalms is a snap? Go back to your macramé" (ibid., 272).

25. Ibid., 65.

If Heller's novel conquers the biblical text, other retellings engage in embrace and foreignization. Recastings of the figure of Abishag, the concubine tendered to warm David in his old age, can illustrate these movements. In Heller's version, Abishag's function is reproach. She is the symbol of Bathsheba's reproach of David,[26] of God and David's mutual reproach, of David's reproach of his own legacy. The aged king takes cold comfort in Abishag: when she comes to his room toward the end of the book, he remarks plaintively, "I want my God back, and they send me a girl."[27] The givens of the Bible are altogether done away with: the hero warrior is only human; the omnipresent God is mostly absent. Heller's story replaces the biblical one; it offers the truth behind the lore.

By contrast, Rainer Maria Rilke's poem "Abishag" is an embrace of the biblical account. It does not seek to do away with its forerunner, but to enhance it through only the gentlest of expansions. Rilke offers the relationship between David and Abishag from the third person point of view, the very perspective of the Bible itself. And yet, from this distance, he engenders the reader's empathy toward the aged king and his young concubine both.

Abishag[28]
I.
She lay. And her childlike arms were bound
by servants around the withering king,
on whom she lay throughout the sweet long hours,
a little frightened of his many years.

And now and then she turned her face
in his beard, whenever an owl cried;
and all that was night came and flocked
around her with fear and longing.

The stars trembled just as she did,
a scent went searching through the sleeping room,
the curtain stirred and made a sign,
and her gaze went softly after it—.

But she kept clinging to the dark old man
and, not reached by what the nights call forth,
lay on his potent slumber's deepening chill
with virgin lightness, like a buoyant soul.

---

26.   The beloved wife approaches the husband solely to petition for the kingdom on Solomon's behalf.

27.   Heller, *God Knows*, 353.

28.   Translated from the German by Edward Snow.

II.

The king sat thinking through the empty day
of deeds accomplished, of unfelt pleasures,
and of his favorite dog, on whom he doted.
But in the evening Abishag arched
over him. His tangled life lay
abandoned like an ill-famed coast
beneath the constellation of her silent breasts.

And now and then, as one adept in women,
he recognized through his eyebrows
the unmoved, kissless mouth;
and saw: her feeling's green divining rod
did not point downward to his depths.
A chill went through him. He hearkened like a hound
and sought himself in his last blood.

The poem is an embrace, a gentle expansion of the biblical text: it expands rather than contradicts, drawing the reader in by drawing out the details only hinted at in scripture. The poem is wholly specific—it is the story of David and Abishag—and yet it touches on the universal themes of love, loss, trepidation at the approach of death. But these themes, implicit in the biblical account, when made explicit do not compromise or overwhelm the primary tale.

Rilke accomplishes his gentle embrace of the biblical characters by drawing his reader close to them, making the reader intimate with them and with their own lack of intimacy. Similarly, Shirley Kaufman zooms in on the biblical text, invokes its minute details. In her poem, "Abishag," she describes in uncomfortable detail the tense relationship between the frail old king and the young woman, "ordered / for the old man / to dangle around his neck." They are opposite in every respect: her flesh is bright, his hands, if pinched, might turn to powder. He shivers against her warm body, "her breasts / against him like an accusation." The pair take no pleasure in each other, nor comfort either: "he can do nothing else / but wear her, pluck at her body / like a lost bird / pecking in winter." He is the lost bird, the lost traveler, who has "[spread] her out / like a road-map," but who still cannot find his way. "He's cold from the fear / of death, the sorrow / of failure," even her bright flesh cannot warm him. She can make no use of him either: "she feels his thin claws, his wings / spread over her like arms, not bones / but feathers ready to fall." When his feeble body jerks, she tells him cruelly, "Take it easy."

The effect is foreignization, rather than embrace. The familiar figures of David and Abishag, recognizable at a distance, become distorted on closer examination. The details—his frail arms, his feeble legs, her submissiveness—make the couple foreign to us, make us aware of how unfamiliar they actually are. The biblical text let us think we knew the king and the woman brought to warm him, but Kaufman's poem, with its images of decay, assure us we do not. The picture she paints reverberates against the biblical portrait, such that both become more remote to us.

Translating the Language of Translation

In the absence of a set vocabulary to account for what happens to a work through the course of translation, translators have offered a range of their own words to describe what we have been calling the approach and stance toward a text. Already we have encountered two words that we can incorporate into a discussion of stance: Nietzsche and Friedrich's "conquest" and its corollary, "embrace"; Buber and Rosenzweig's idea of "foreignization." These are but two words in a relatively long list of possible designations, many of which we will explore below.

We have heard a little about the so-called disease of translation from Dryden. He also gives an account of the various ways the disease might manifest itself. As part of his preface to his rendering of *Ovid's Epistles* in English, Dryden ventures his own three-part description of the trans-lation of poetry. In his view, "all translation…may be reduced into these three heads": metaphrase, paraphrase, and imitation. Metaphrase is the "turning an author word by word, and line by line, from one language into another."[29] He cites as an example Ben Jonson's translation of Horace's *Art of Poetry*. Paraphrase he describes as "translation with latitude, where the author is kept in view by the translator, so as never to be lost, but his words are not so strictly followed as his sense; and that too is admitted to be amplified, but not altered." The example he gives here is Waller's translation of Virgil's Fourth *Aeneid*. In imitation, "the translator (if now he has not lost that name) assumes the liberty, not only to vary from the words and sense, but to forsake them both as he sees occasion; and taking only some general hints from the original, to run division on the groundwork, as he pleases."[30] Imitation is, in Dryden's view, the best term to describe Crowley's rendering of two Odes of Pindar, and one of Horace, into English.

Dryden champions the paraphrase, the compromise between the metaphrase, which suffers from the pedantry of being overly faithful, and the imitation, which is the "most advantageous way for a translator to show himself, but the greatest wrong which can be done to the memory

---

29. John Dryden, *Ovid's Epistles* (London: J. & R. Jonson, 1748), 11.
30. Ibid.

and reputation of the dead."[31] It is through paraphrase that "the spirit of an author may be transfused and yet not lost";[32] the ideal, for Dryden, is a translation that reflects what the original would have been like had it been composed in the target language. The best translation stands perfectly between metaphrase and imitation, with source and target allowed equal influence on the resultant rendering.

A century and a half later, Goethe put forth another tripartite understanding of modes of translation, although his turns on three phases of translation through which every literature—individual texts and entire literary heritages alike—must pass. These three "epochs" represent three stances the target can take to the source. The first of these "acquaints us with the foreign country on our own terms":[33] it brings the source to the target. Prose is the best medium for this type of translation, as it can express "foreign splendors in the midst of our own national domestic sensibility."[34] Goethe points to Luther's Bible as reflecting the ability of the foreign to uplift in a new way, while maintaining the guise of the familiar.[35]

In the second type of translation, the translator "endeavors to transport himself into the foreign situation but actually only appropriates the foreign idea and represents it as his own";[36] it is an endeavor that Goethe deems "parodistic." Men of wit (like the French, apparently) are drawn to the parodistic: "in the same way that the French adapt foreign words to their pronunciation, they adapt feelings, thoughts, even objects; for every foreign fruit there must be a substitute grown in their own soil."[37] The movement in this case is a transformation of the original into the translator's own linguistic and cultural idiom, where the translator only treats those aspects of the source text that resonate with the sensibility of his age. Consequently, his is a diminished effort, as it represents neither the genius of the original nor its strangeness.

Goethe deems the third class of translation the highest of the three. In this mode, "the goal of the translation is to achieve perfect identity with

---

31. Ibid., 14.

32. Ibid., 15.

33. Johann Wolfgang von Goethe, "Translations" (trans. Sharon Sloane), in Schulte and Biguenet, eds., *Theories of Translation*, 60.

34. Ibid.

35. An example for which Steiner takes him to task, asking "Can he really have meant to say that Luther's immensely conscious, often magisterially violent reading is an instance of humble style, imperceptibly insinuating a foreign spirit and body of knowledge into German?" (Steiner, *After Babel*, 272).

36. Goethe, "Translations," 60.

37. Ibid., 61.

the original, so that the one does not exist instead of the other but in the other's place."[38] Once the German public ear had become accustomed to the negation of its nation's tones, German literature benefited, with its own authors exhibiting a heightened versatility and its "Germanized foreigners" becoming central to the nation's linguistic and literary development.

Steiner describes this philosophy of translation, which understands translation to be "an exemplary case of metamorphosis,"[39] as being rooted in Goethe's central philosophic beliefs. Translation's process is marked by "an organic unfolding towards the harmonic integrity of the sphere or cloud circle which Goethe celebrates throughout the realms both of spirit and of nature. In perfect translation as in the genetics of evolution there is a paradox of fusion and new form without the abolition of component parts."[40] Translation is a form of evolution that preserves the best of the original and adapts it for survival in a new setting.

As Steiner notes, in his conviction that "life of the original is inseparable from the risks of translation," Goethe presages Benjamin. Both uphold the afterlife as assuring the life of the original. A text "dies if it is not subject to transformation."[41] Again we see the translation not only as life-giving—the transplant or transfusion needed to ensure a text's continued existence—but as organic: it necessarily grows out of the text. It is part of its natural genetic evolution.

Like Dryden and Goethe, Roman Jakobson has a triadic understanding of translation. In his view, though, every word-sign, whether foreign or familiar, triggers translation. He outlines the cross-relation between translation and interpretation: "both [for] linguists and [for] ordinary word-users, the meaning of any linguistic sign is its translation into some further, alternative sign, especially a sign 'in which it is more fully developed.'"[42] Meaning and translation are inseparable; for a sign to signify, it must be translated. Jakobson maps out three classes of translation of verbal signs: intralingual translation, interlingual translation, and intersemiotic translation.[43] Intralingual translation is the rewording of a word-sign through other signs in the same language; it thus comprises all

38. Ibid.
39. Steiner, *After Babel*, 273.
40. Ibid.
41. Ibid.
42. Jakobson here borrows the wording of C. S. Peirce. Ibid., 274.
43. Roman Jakobson, "On Linguistic Aspects of Translation" (1959), in *Selected Writings: Word and Language*, Vol. 2 (The Hague: Mouton, 1971), 261, cited by Steiner, *After Babel*, 274.

definition and all explanation. Interlingual translation is what we would think of as translation proper: the understanding of a word-sign through signs in another language. Intersemiotic translation or transmutation, however, is the translation of a word-sign through non-verbal sign systems; it is the recreation of the word in pictures, gestures, numbers, and music.[44] We could certainly speak of Michelangelo's statue of David as transmutation: the word-sign, David, is recreated in marble. It is less clear whether one could use the term to speak of Kyle Baker's graphic novel *King David* or Gregory Peck and Susan Hayward's 1951 epic film *David and Bathsheba*, for instance.

Perhaps these latter examples fall more squarely under "creative transposition." This is another of Jakobson's terms, born out of the notion that, poetry is by definition untranslatable.[45] Thus "only 'creative transposition' is possible: from one poetic form into another in the same language, from one tongue into another, or between quite different media and expressive codes."[46] While English poetry cannot, in Jakobson's view, be translated into French poetry, it can be recreated as other poetry in English or, picking up on our discussion of King David, be transposed to a graphic novel or a screenplay. One wonders whether Jakobson is thus describing precisely the type of revisionist activity that lies at the center of our discussion.

In discussing translation, Gregory Rabassa posits that what we call translation might more accurately be dubbed transformation. In Rabassa's view, translation "is a form of adaptation, making the new metaphor fit the original metaphor";[47] there are no metaphoric equals, merely equivalences. Not only does the French dog say "Oua oua" and the English "Bow wow," but in some Muslim populations the dog is considered a vile creature, while it is doted on in many parts of Europe. To translate a barking dog might be to transform him, have him connote the appropriate status as well as speak the appropriate dog dialect.

In two novels by Thomas Hardy, we find retellings of the David story. *Far From the Madding Crowd* treats a Victorian Bathsheba, a woman torn between lovers. In *The Mayor of Casterbridge*, Hardy plays with the biblical relationship between Saul and David. Here we see examples of what we might describe as transformation: Hardy fashions the details of

44. Ibid., 261.
45. This is because of paronomasia, the relationship between the phonemic and the semantic unit (as in a pun) (Steiner, *After Babel*, 275).
46. Steiner, *After Babel*, 275.
47. Rabassa, "No Two Snowflakes are Alike," 2.

his own text so that the new metaphor and the old fit one another. The connections between the novel and the Bible are made through explicit allusion and thematic parallel both. Michael Henchard, the protagonist, is described as feeling "like Saul at his reception by Samuel"; a mayor, he is the older ruler (the Saul) who is threatened by Donald Farfrae, a younger man who courts his daughter. As Saul was with David, Henchard is attracted to Farfrae's musical ability. The beloved king, however, is not valorized but humanized. Hardy accentuates the leader's frailty: his David is modeled on the king depicted in the books of Samuel, not the one in Chronicles. Like his biblical forerunner, Henchard experiences a decline that leads him to a lonely death, although Hardy's David is so transformed as to die alone, dejected, in the countryside, not even covered by a lovely young maiden. The theme of alienation is underscored, as the transformation pushes at the limits of the biblical text. Throughout the novel, Hardy resituates the biblical tropes so that they speak to his contemporary audience.

Steiner, in a debate about the "morality of appropriation via translation," uses the word *transfiguration*, in which "the intrinsic weight and radiance of the translation eclipses that of the source."[48] We can assume that the author of Chronicles intended to transfigure the books of Samuel, or at least the shape of David in those books. Chronicles' David is not sullied by his affair with Bathsheba; he is the upstanding leader. Through omission, addition, and alteration of the books of Samuel and Kings, the author of Chronicles transfigures not just David but Israel itself.

Along with the idea of transfiguration, Steiner introduces the even more loaded *transubstantiation*. The context for his usage is a discussion of Jorge Luis Borges' wonderful short story, "Pierre Menard, Author of the *Quixote*," which Steiner calls "the most acute, most concentrated commentary anyone has offered on the business of translation."[49] "Pierre Menard" is the story of an author who writes a book that is literally identical to Cervantes' *Don Quixote*:

> Cervantes' text and Menard's are verbally identical, but the second is almost infinitely richer. (More ambiguous, his detractors will say, but ambiguity is richness.)
> It is a revelation to compare Menard's *Don Quixote* with Cervantes'. The latter, for example, wrote (part one, chapter nine):

48. Steiner, *After Babel*, xvi.
49. Ibid., 73. That Steiner insists that the story is a translation points to the close relationship between the theoretical discourses I juxtapose here; as we will see, Gerard Genette treats "Pierre Menard" in his discussion of intertextuality.

...truth, whose mother is history, rival of time, depository of deeds, witness of the past, exemplar and adviser to the present, and the future's counselor.

Written in the seventeenth century, written by the "lay genius" Cervantes, this enumeration is a mere rhetorical praise of history. Menard, on the other hand, writes:

> ...truth, whose mother is history, rival of time, depository of deeds, witness of the past, exemplar and adviser to the present, and the future's counselor.
>
> History, the *mother* of truth: the idea is astounding. Menard, a contemporary of William James, does not define history as an inquiry into reality, but as its origin. Historical truth, for him, is not what has happened; it is what we judge to have happened. The final phrases—*exemplar and adviser to the present, and the future's counselor*—are brazenly pragmatic.
>
> The contrast in style is also vivid. The archaic style of Menard—quite foreign after all—suffers from a certain affectation. Not so that of his forerunner, who handles with ease the current Spanish of his time.[50]

Despite the distinctions Borges's fictive translator makes, the sole feature that distinguishes Menard's book from Cervantes's—the feature that lends it its "richness"— is the two centuries of history that come between the first writing and the second. This lapse of time necessarily gives Menard's *Don Quixote* a meaning completely distinct from Cervantes's. And it is this lapse that has Steiner refer to Menard's activity as "total translation, or as one might more rigorously say, transubstantiation."[51] It is "a translation of a perfect transcription,"[52] a near impossible task.

Where might we find an example of transubstantiation in literature having to do with David? The theological resonance in the term itself makes one wonder whether it might be applied to passages in the New Testament that are taken verbatim from the old, and then interpreted Christologically. One thinks, for instance, of God's covenant with David—specifically, his promise "I will be a father to him, and he shall be a son to me" (2 Sam. 7:14)—which the author of Hebrews incorporates into his assertion that Jesus is superior to the angels (Heb 1:5). Paul refers to the verse in 1 Corinthians, but does not transcribe it verbatim (1 Cor 6:18). Whether these examples might simply be classified as

50. Jose Louis Borges, "Pierre Menard, Author of *Don Quixote*" (trans. James E. Irby), in *Labyrinths: Selected Stories and Other Writings* (New York: New Directions, 1964), 42–43. Rabassa reports that Borges "had a fine sense of how words are used and of their Swiftian limitations when he told his translator not to write what he said but what he wanted to say" (Rabassa, "No Two Snowflakes are Alike," 2).

51. Steiner, *After Babel*, 74.

52. Ibid., 76.

typology, rather than transubstantiation remains open for debate. J. Hillis Miller would call them misprisions: a text has been extracted from its original context and resituated elsewhere. In its new setting, it has come to mean something quite different than it first had. This is total translation indeed.

After transubstantiation, Steiner puts forth *translucencies* to describe situations in which the translator treats a work in a language or culture very similar to her own. In such instances, the translator is drawn in to "concentric circles of linguistic-cultural self-consciousness, presumptive information and recognition."[53] She is bound by the "legacy of mutual contact"[54] between the source and target. The overlap of etymologies and associations makes the text to be translated denser and the relations of what is "near" the translator more ambiguous.

In this context, we might think of Dryden's *Absalom and Achitophel*, his satire inspired by the royal crisis that ultimately brought England to the revolution of 1688. Two successors contested Charles II's throne: his brother James and his illegitimate son James Scott, Duke of Monmouth. The situation suggested the rebellion of Absalom to Dryden, and was immediately recognizable to his readers. The "legacy of mutual contact" between source and target inspired the poem and determined its successful reception; operating within the "concentric circles of linguistic-cultural self-consciousness, presumptive information and recognition" Dryden was able to equate David and Charles II, Absalom and Monmouth, Achitophel and Shaftesbury translucently, such that the audience could see the shadows of the contemporary players beyond Dryden's biblical shapes.

Steiner gives us *transfiguration* and *transubstantiation*, John Hollander gave us *transumption*, and Jakobson intersemiotic translation, which can be described as *transmutation*. Add to these Jakobson and Genette's distinct understandings of *transposition*, as well as the terms *transplant* and *transfusion* (all of which we will consider presently), and a vocabulary of relevant "trans-" words begins to emerge.

Transmutation and creative transposition, the two trans- terms put forth by Jakobson, are both to be found in *The Scarlet Letter*. As we have seen, Jakobson's transmutation is a translation between distinct media or expressive modes. It can be the recreation of the word in pictures, as is the case with the Gobelin tapestry on the walls of Reverend Dimmesdale's room. Depicting "the Scriptural story of David and Bathsheba, and

53. Ibid., 380.
54. Ibid.

Nathan the prophet, in colors still unfaded,"[55] it is not only transmutation but mirror: the tapestry points the reader back to the world of the room in which it hangs, that the reader may see the correspondences between the two tales' adulterers.

Creative transposition is the movement from one creative form into another in the same language. Here we think of the scarlet letter Hester Prynne is obliged to wear: it is a "creative transposition" of the prophet Nathan's declaration "Thou art the man!" The context is shifted, Nathan's sentence becomes Hester's letter, but both the accusation and the A stand for the same thing: a condemnation of adulterous behavior.

Genette's transposition is distinct from Jakobson's. In his discussion of parody, Genette derives an etymology of the word: "*ode,* that is the chant; *para,* along, beside. *Parodeis,* whence *parodia,* would therefore mean singing beside: that is, singing off key, or singing in another voice—in counterpoint; or again, singing in another key—deforming, therefore, or *transposing* a melody."[56] The transposition of an epic could "therefore consist of a stylistic modification that would, for example, transfer it from its noble register to a more familiar, even vulgar one."[57]

As an example, one which requires little by way of analysis, we have Josephine Miles's poem "David." In this retelling, Goliath is "strong" and "determined," "clear in the assumption of status." He is "determined by the limits of his experience"—a quality shared by surgeons, sergeants, deans, and other men who possess a certain type of power. By contrast, Miles's David "made few assumptions / Had little experience" and thus was open to more and new things. Faced with this green opponent, Goliath was hindered by his assumptions; David, "with his few hypotheses" feared not "the power of status which is but two-footed." So the young man "shot, and shouted!" Miles takes the players from their biblical setting and invests in them familiar characteristics. They become not legends but men we have known—surgeons, sergeants, those who test pebbles, test giants. The transposition here does not render vulgar, but familiar: Miles psychologizes our figures, and thus brings them down from their "noble register."

Next are transplant and transfusion, closely related medical terms. To transplant is to extract an essential organ and reposition it in another body, such that it gives life to something else; to transfuse is to pour

55. Nathaniel Hawthorne, *The Scarlet Letter* (New York: Penguin, 2002), 111.
56. Gerard Genette, *Paratexts: Thresholds of Interpretation* (trans. Jane E. Lewin; Cambridge: Cambridge University Press, 1997), 10.
57. Ibid., 11.

blood from a healthy being into an ailing body.[58] In the case of the transplant, although the original body is no longer vital, the transplanted organ revitalizes the recipient. With the transfusion, the original body and the receiving body thrive following the procedure. The transplant leaves the original body behind; the transfusion creates two interdependent bodies.

We might describe as a transplant Faulkner's use of the David story in *Absalom! Absalom!* Faulkner transplants the plot of the novel: his is the story of Thomas Sutpen who, like David, loses two sons in the prime of their lives, and of an incestuous triangle that echoes that of Tamar, Absalom and Amnon. While, as Alter notes, "David, Absalom and the rape of Tamar are never explicitly alluded to in Faulkner's novel...the title directs us to an elaborate set of correspondences of plot and theme between the ancient tragedy and the modern stories."[59] Faulkner's story stands on its own, but is enriched by its biblical heart.

By contrast, the epic poems that amplify biblical narratives are much more within the domain of transfusion. George Peele's *The Love of King David and Fair Bethsabe* (1599) and Charles Heavysedge's *Saul* (1868) flesh out the biblical accounts, providing lengthy narrative and exhaustive detail. Although they offer so much by way of biblical account that the reader need not turn back to the original, they have no autonomous existence outside their relation to the Bible. The Bible provides their lifeblood, and yet the Bible remains a vital being itself.

Translation as Cure

At the outset of this chapter, we considered whether Miller's misprision, mistranslation, and translation are subsets of retelling, or whether retelling is itself a subset of translation. As this chapter has made clear, more than it is a form of intertextuality or midrash, retelling is a mode of translation. It is a carrying across of texts from one language (broadly defined) to another. It may be interlingual, bringing a linguistically incomprehensible text to a new audience. But it may also be an intralingual enterprise, made necessary or desirable by the language of the source and the language of the target having become mutually indecipherable because of remoteness of time, place, or culture.

---

58.   The *OED* offers as a first definition, "Cause to pass from one person or thing to another; cause to have gradual and complete influence." The connection between transfusion and influence is germane to the present discussion.

59.   Alter, *Canon and Creativity*, 10.

Both types of translation, as Benjamin notes, occur at the point that the text has found its place in history. Translation then becomes a way of continuing the text's life, of imbuing it with an afterlife. In this respect, then, the translation and the retelling have precisely the same outcome: they create an afterlife. The language of translation theory, with its concern for what we are calling stance, speaks about how the afterlife responds to the life—or, about what the retelling "thinks" of the telling. Benjamin's description of the afterlife-giving properties of translation suggests that the life is somehow worth continuing, which is not a certainty with regard to the afterlife-giving of a retelling.

Friedrich, in speaking of Roman practices of translation, allows us to see that the translation can be a quashing or an appropriation of the original. Even more damning, Berman argues that every translation is destructive, not restorative at all; the very act of translating destroys the foreignness (and thus the worth) of the original. Likewise, although it takes the telling as its starting point, the retelling may not hold its forerunner in a place of honor. It may in fact seek to supplant the original, to strip it of its worth (or stature) even as it springs forth from it. Here lies the difference between Foucault's translations that move "from like to the same" and those that "hurl one language against another." We see, then, that the language of translation theory is especially helpful in our context. It allows us to think in terms of stance, to speak of retelling as conquest, embrace, foreignization. Better still, the accumulated theorists give us a host of useful terms: among them, transposition, transmutation, transfiguration, transfusion, transplant, transmutation, and transumption.

As if this were not enough to recommend it, translation theory provides with a means of talking about approach. The act of translation has, as Nida notes, two far-flung poles: the literal and the paraphrastic. But those who have theorized translation have attended to the many points between the two. Vinay and Darbelnet's four procedures of oblique translation are perhaps too specific to be of use to us, but they do provide four words—transposition, modulation, equivalence, adaptation—that we could conceivably wrest from their contexts and redefine. Dryden's metaphrase, paraphrase, and imitation are also useful for speaking generally about retelling. Lefevere offers imitation and version. And Berman, in his polemic, provides us with a litany of descriptors.

What ultimately makes translation theory the most compelling vocabulary from which to cull, however, is its ability to think in terms of filter as well. As we saw, Descriptive Translation Studies occupies itself with what texts did and did not get retold; it attempts to situate the translation (or, for our purposes, the retelling) within the larger literary culture, to assess what drove and determined a particular revisiting of a text. Poly-system theory, with its attention to the patronage, poetics, and ideology that inform, constrain, and mold the literary system, is also illuminating for thinking about filter.

To understand, and thereby to speak about, a retelling, one must be able to articulate three essential characteristics about it. How does it gain access to the telling? What does it do to the telling once it has accessed it? And why does it access it in this way? These are the questions behind approach, stance, and filter. Only in translation theory do we find developed vocabularies that enable us to think about the three factors that lie at the heart of any retelling.

Chapter 9

THESE ARE THE WORDS

Over the course of this book, we have encountered a variety of terms from a range of fields that treat or touch on questions of retelling. Considering the languages of literary criticism and theory, of midrashic studies, and of translation theory has provided us with a wide variety of possibilities, many of which will have been appealing to readers. The aim now is to glean from these languages a vocabulary that is specific enough to be illuminating but limited enough to be manageable.

If it seems curious to turn to other fields for our language, we must consider the mimetic process here. In coming to speak about the literary afterlife of the Bible, we appropriate the language of other fields and disciplines. We retell. This is how we keep language alive, ourselves alive. We recycle language to speak about retelling, about how later works reuse earlier ones. As I noted in the second chapter, J. Hillis Miller reads the story of Ruth as a parable of the transformation of theory. When theory travels, it is translated or deformed. In a new country, a theory (like Ruth) "is put to new uses that cannot be foreseen":[1] these uses are "an alienation of the theory, its translation into a new idiom, and its appropriation for new, indigenous purposes."[2] Those in Judah who encounter the Israelite story of Ruth make it their own so as to ensure their own cultural vitality. They

> assimilate the alien, making the different into the same, but at the same time changing that same, in order to ensure that vitality, just as works of traveling theory are transformed in the new country or in a new discipline. In the new place a theory is made use of in ways the theory never intended or allowed for, though it also transforms the culture or discipline it enters.[3]

1. Miller, "Border Crossings," 219.
2. Ibid.
3. Ibid.

Theories, like tellings, by their very nature allow themselves to be recast.[4] Both are transformed in the retelling:

> The somewhat disturbing openness of theory to translation, its promiscuity, so to speak, reveals something essential about the original theory. Far from being a definitive expression of some way of language or another kind of sign works, a theoretical formulation is always provisional and idiomatic, never wholly clear and never wholly satisfactory. The evidence for that is the way the formulation is amenable to having quite different effects in different contexts.[5]

What happens in a retelling is a transformation of code: words, which meant one thing in their original setting, take on new value in another. In the literary retelling, the recycling of ancient plots may serve to illuminate a later author's contemporary situation. Figures recast may serve as analogues or foils in ways they had not before. In the theoretical retelling, the language of translation may be made to speak of literary retelling. All retellings imbue new value, as "any cultural event that is incorporated into a specific poetic context is reordered within that particular text (whether it is long or short) in accordance with the needs of that text."[6] The languages of literary theory, midrash, and translation become the language of retelling once they find themselves within the context of a discussion of retellings. These languages are reordered in accordance with new needs, and take on their own afterlives.

To understand, and thereby to speak about, a retelling, one must be able to articulate three essential characteristics about it. How does it gain access to the telling? (Does it borrow a phrase, a character, a plot, an image?) What does it do to the telling once it has accessed it? (Does it deepen understanding of the original? Displace it?) And why does it access it in this way? (Is it reading the earlier text through a particular theological or ideological lens? With a particular aesthetic?) These are the questions behind approach, stance, and filter. Together, literary theory, midrashic studies, and translation theory offer multiple insights into these three aspects of retelling.

---

4. This may have everything to do with the very nature of both story and theory. Miller asserts that "theory's openness to translation is a result of the fact that theory, in spite of performances, is a performative, not a cognitive, use of language" (ibid., 223). Stories, too, are performative, and thus mutable: they alter with each presentation.

5. Ibid.

6. Conte, *The Rhetoric of Imagination: Genre and Poetic Memory in Virgil and Other Latin Poets* (trans. Charles Segal. Ithaca: Cornell University Press, 1986), 48.

What is the What?

The early literary critics spoke of imitation and invention. Ben Jonson gave us purposeful remaking; Piero Boitani rescripting; Barbara Godorecci re-writing. Translation theorists speak in terms of source and target. Throughout this discussion, I have used the term "retelling." It is a simple enough word, requires no explanation, and suggests the existence of a telling. Let us keep the term.

The Language of Approach

How does the retelling gain entry into the telling? What parts of the earlier texts does it use? These are, to some extent, the questions of midrashic study, which examines what Judah Goldin called the scriptural provocations to midrash (or, in James Kugel's terms, the surface irregularity in the Bible that gives rise to interpretation). Thus various terms in midrash are helpful for thinking about approach. Likewise translation theory, with its extensive discussion of approach. (One thinks in particular of Vinay and Darbelnet's catalogue of borrowing; calque; literal translation; transposition; modulation; equivalence; and adaptation. Also useful are Berman's rationalization; clarification; expansion; ennoblement; qualitative and quantitative impoverishment; and his various modes of destruction and effacement.) In the realm of literary theory, Gerard Genette was particularly productive; some of his terms, combined with others we encountered, make a cluster of related "trans-" words. To focus on the terms that follow is not to dismiss the many others we have encountered: these are proffered because together they comprise a finite, inter-related vocabulary.

Transfocalization—shifting the point of view of the story. Anita Diamant's *The Red Tent*, which tells Genesis from the perspective of the women, is a transfocalization. Also useful here is the idea of *defocalization*, which removes the point of view of the original.

Transfusion—importing the lifeblood of the original. One could read *The Scarlet Letter* as a transfusion of the David and Bathsheba story.

Transgression—using the original as a springboard for another work, taking some dimension of the original and using it as a departure point.

Transiency—the brief introduction of an element from the original; an unsustained allusion.

Transition—the setting of a story in a new era or period. The spate of 1990s films that set Shakespeare's plays in contemporary American high schools is a transition (and a translocation).

Translation—the carrying across of the original to a new cultural setting. This may involve transition and translocation as well.

Translocation—the setting of a story in a new place. Faulkner's moving the David story to America in *Absalom! Absalom!* is a translocation. (Genette would call this a heterodiegetic transposition.)

Translucency—a significant transposition of the original, which nonetheless maintains the shape or form of the original: one can see the telling through the retelling. Here, perhaps, we might think of Thomas Hardy's *Mayor of Casterbridge*.

Transmodalization—the changing of the form of the original. David Pinsky's rendering the narrative of David's life as a play is a transmodalization. The retelling still operates within the literary mode, but alters the literary form.

Transmutation—the alteration of the medium of the retelling. Films like *The Ten Commandments* or *Prince of Egypt*, which adapt biblical literature to a new medium, are transmutations.

Transplantation—the extraction of a particular element of the original story. Consider Kafka's use of Job's unexplained test in *The Trial.*

Transposition—following Genette, a serious transformation of the original.

Transumption—a quoting of the original.

Transvaluation—a reframing that shifts the evaluative connotation from negative to positive or from positive to negative.

Transvocalization—the telling of the story in another voice. Here we might think of Franco Ferrucci's *The Life of God (as Told by Himself)*.

The Language of Stance

Stance is concerned with the attitude of the later text to the earlier. Here the language of translation theory is particularly useful, with its explicit concern for the relationship between source and target.

Conquest—a retelling that renders the original invalid or unnecessary. There are mischievous conquests, like Jeanette Winterson's *Boating for Beginners*, which renders the biblical flood story absurd, and well-intentioned conquests, like we see in children's bibles, which often obviate the desire to read the original.

Embrace—the upholding of the sensibility of the original. David Maine's *The Preservationist* is an embrace of the biblical flood story.

Foreignization—destabilizing the original by rendering it less familiar or unfamiliar. Queen Jane's bible, a translation which uses vulgar English and contemporary slang and which flags sexual acts with marginalial icons, is a foreignization.

Inversion—a retelling that lays bare complexities or difficulties in the telling, thus turning us back to the original, causing us to read rather than resist or replace the telling.

Misprision—a misapprehension of the original text, so that it is put to the service of something anathema, or is made to speak in a way contrary to itself. Bloom calls the use of Ruth by Christians a misprision.

Reversion—a retelling that underscores or upholds the sensibilities or ideas of the earlier text.

Subversion—an undermining of the original. An example would be Timothy Findley's *Not Wanted on the Voyage*, in which the narrator presents a passage from Gen 7 and follows it "Everyone knows it wasn't like that."

The Language of Filter

To consider filter is to consider the lens through which the retelling examines the telling. Not all retellings have filters, but the words that best describe filter are already part of the shared lexicon. These are often –isms: a later text scrutinizes an earlier through the lens of atheism, capitalism, feminism, or Marxism for instance. Likewise, it may look at it through the lens of Christianity or modernity. We do not need to introduce a vocabulary for describing filter, but we need to ensure that the questions of filter are asked when considering a retelling: what is the later text's sensibility and how does that contribute to the transformation of the earlier.

These lists above are hardly comprehensive—they do not approach the precision of Genette's descriptive vocabulary, but they are more manageable. They provide a beginning, a common vocabulary that allows us to think about approach, stance, and filter, and yet leaves room for other words to enter the lexicon organically. They tap into, but do not exhaust, the vocabularies of literary theory, midrashic study, and translation theory. And this is what we, author and reader, have been working together to develop: a limited series of words that recall a prolonged consideration of the very many ways telling and retelling interrelate.

Sustaining Fictions

As I close, a few thoughts about the proliferation of retelling. What do we make of all this returning to ancient texts, of carrying them forward to another cultural setting? In general, what does the act of retelling do for the telling? Does the retelling replace the telling? Revive it? Rekindle it? Reaffirm it? Relegate it to the past? Beyond the very specific questions of one text's stance toward its forerunner are broader questions about the place of later writing in relation to earlier. These we have alit upon in passing, but it is worthwhile to articulate them more cohesively (and perhaps coherently) now.

Christopher Ricks speaks of allusion in terms of literary inheritance, noting that "the inheritor needs to be not only generous but responsible, given that an inheritance is held in trust."[7] Allusion (broadly defined) connects the past to the present, but places it in different hands. It is by its very nature, however, fragmented: it is a portion of the past, and a portion which comes to be the present when wrested from the past. In *The Archaeology of Knowledge*, Foucault grapples with the idea of continuity, wondering whether there can be a cohesiveness among the fragments. He asserts that each act of discourse (or, in his parlance, "historical irruption") has a "specific existence,"[8] and exists only in the moment of its utterance. Thus, "we do not seek below what is manifest in the half silent murmur of another discourse; we must show why it could not be other than it was, in what respect it is exclusive of any other, how it assumes, in the midst of others and in relation to them, a place that no other could occupy."[9] Barbara Godorecci, who turns to Dilthey to frame her thinking about Machiavelli's own rewriting and others' rewriting of Machiavelli, comments that

> the term re-writing, as it is here presented graphologically, is itself suggestive of temporal and creative processes. In its hyphenated form, it doubles for neither *writing* nor *rewriting*, yet curiously embraces the two: separating, while at the same time binding. Emphasized are both the creative newness proper to 'writing' and the 'historical' profundity that is implicit in the use of the prefix *re-*.[10]

To re-tell is simultaneously to break with and retain tradition.

This is particularly apt when it comes to rethinking about the retelling of the Bible. The religion and literature scholars of the 1950s and 1960s would certainly have claimed that there is something particular about biblical retelling. Nathan Scott and Amos Wilder saw modern poets and novelists as "the outriders of the faith. They continue its exploration, its advance, and its witness at a distance from the main body. If they are

---

7. Christopher Ricks, "Keats's Sources, Keats's Allusions," in *The Cambridge Companion to Keats* (ed. Susan J. Wolfson; New York: Cambridge University Press, 2001), 152.

8. Michel Foucault, *The Archaeology of Knowledge* (trans. A. M. Sheridan Smith; New York: Pantheon, 1982), 28.

9. Ibid.

10. Barbara Godorecci, *After Machiavelli: "Re-Writing" and the "Hermeneutic Attitude"* (Purdue Studies in Romance Literatures 3; Purdue, IN: Purdue University Press, 1993), 9.

heretics we may yet recall the paradoxical thesis that the blood of the heretics is often the seed of the church. We should indeed recognize the contribution of those who are well outside the church."[11] Literary retelling is the renewal of scripture, if not from within tradition then from only slightly without. The point, for Scott and Wilder, seems to be that even the secular is fundamentally sacred.

By inscribing a sacredness in the secular, Scott and Wilder fail to account for the phenomenon of "strange secular afterlives of biblical texts,"[12] however. Just because a later text uses the Bible does not absolutely mean that it upholds the Bible. As Sherwood has noted, "the secular is not always *kind* to the biblical, and sometimes seeks to expose it, and the God behind it, as an old, moribund, and dribbling parent. It aims to make the text stammer and stutter; to use the present as a spanner in the mechanisms of its logic."[13] Sherwood suggests that "an intrinsic part of this traumatic unhinging of the text is simply to make it as puzzled and alienated by us as we are by it, to register within the Bible the sense of disjunction between the naïve past and the knowing present."[14] The act of retelling may be an act of putting the Bible on equal footing with its reader, and with the reader of the retext. It may be a leveling of the statures of both scripture and literature.

It may also be an attempt to wrest tradition from those who have claimed exclusive right to it. As Sherwood notes, among modern writers who return to scripture,

> the prevailing sense seems to be that the Bible needs somehow to be reclaimed, either from its own history—from the long chain of tradition which has bound it to a world that is not the artist's—or from the hands of those who have misclaimed it—from the fundamentalists or the evangelicals or even merely the religiously lost.[15]

This reclamation or rehabilitation of the Bible, particularly by nonreligious writers, Sherwood casts as a "rescue mission, an effort to draw a book adrift into the safety of the rational waters, or better to the secular shore."[16] The mission is driven by a concern to return to the Bible "control over the dissemination of its own image"—a control scripture is

11. Amos Wilder, *Modern Poetry and the Christian Tradition* (New York: Scribner, 1952), 243–44.
12. Sherwood, *A Biblical Text and Its Afterlives*, 201.
13. Ibid. 205.
14. Ibid.
15. Ibid., 206.
16. Ibid.

understood to have lost when it became part of the "'semiotic repertoire' of culture."[17] Overly familiar, it is treated with contempt. Counter-intuitively, secular writers seek to restore to the Bible, if not its status as sacred, then at least its status as exceptional.

The idea of rescue is intriguing, as is making the Bible available to us on our terms. The appropriation and recasting is a fundamentally human activity, and, Sherwood's point notwithstanding, one that many would argue is fundamentally religious. Boitani sees re-scripting as a means of moving *toward* God. In re-scripting scripture, in revisiting the stories about the recognition of God by Abraham, by Jacob, writers enable us to recognize God as well. To read about another's act of recognition will not suffice; we must re-enact the recognition through re-scripting. We apprehend God in the act of appropriating his word. This is not an exclusively (post-)biblical phenomenon: the interpretation and re-inter-pretation of scripture is a common characteristic of all textually oriented religious traditions. This impetus to return again and again to the same texts, looking to them to speak to us in continually new ways, has, in Michael Fishbane's view, become a deeply ingrained dimension of "our modern literary inheritance."[18] It gives rise to a cultural (and religious) imagination that "responds to and is deeply dependent upon received traditions; an imagination whose creativity is never entirely a new crea-tion, but one founded upon older and authoritative words and images."[19] We might go so far as to suggest that with any literary retelling, not merely one with a biblical basis, we enact a religious rite. Retelling is re-creation; imitation, *imitatio dei*.

And so. Tellings beget retellings. Tellings themselves are retellings. Literary creation is preconditioned by previous literary creation. Creation itself, if we listen to Fishbane, if we look at Genesis, is literary:[20] it is the speaking into being of the world. From the moment God first said, creation has been re-saying. And creation is not alone in its respeaking. The rabbis imagined God himself studying and interpreting his own Torah. Fishbane reflects on the image: "it is nothing if not tradition's own realization that there is no authoritative teaching which is not also the source of its own renewal, that revealed traditions are a dead letter

17. Ibid.
18. Michael Fishbane, *The Garments of Torah: Essays in Biblical Hermeneutics* (Bloomington: Indiana University Press, 1989), 3.
19. Ibid.
20. This is, of course, a naïve articulation, which wrongly situates Genesis as a primordial text. It is in fact only an account of a primordial act. Genesis, as many biblical scholars will eagerly argue, is itself a response to literature.

unless revitalized in the mouth of those who study them."[21] Without retelling, traditions die. Unless we retell, we die too. In *Headhunter*, Timothy Findley's recasting of the Western canon, protagonist Marlow tells us that it is "this way we write each other's lives—by means of fictions. Sustaining fictions. Uplifting fictions. Lies. This way we lead one another toward survival. This way we point to the darkness—saying: *come with me into the light.*"[22] Fiction sustains us; we sustain fictions. By now incapable of experiencing and describing "natural" conditions, we write and rewrite, tell and retell. This is our sustenance.

21. Ibid., 3.
22. Timothy Findley, *Headhunter* (Toronto: HarperCollins Canada, 1999), 512.

BIBLIOGRAPHY

I. *Retellings*

A. *Retellings and the Biblical Canon*
i. *The Bible as Retelling*

Aichele, George, and G. A. Philips. *Intertextuality and the Bible*. Atlanta: Scholars Press, 1995.

Alter, Robert. *The Art of Biblical Narrative*. New York: Basic, 1981.

Carson, D. A., and H. G. M. Williamson. *It is Written: Scripture Citing Scripture*. New York: Cambridge University Press, 1988.

Eslinger, Lyle M. "Hosea 12:5a and Genesis 32:29: A Study in Inner Biblical Exegesis." *Journal for the Study of the Old Testament* 18 (1980): 91–99.

_____. "Inner-biblical Exegesis and Inner-biblical Allusion: The Question of Category." *Vetus Testamentum* 42 (1992): 47–58.

Fewell, Dana Nolan, ed. *Reading Between Texts: Intertextuality and the Hebrew Bible*. Louisville: Westminster/John Knox, 1992.

Fishbane, Michael. *The Garments of Torah: Essays in Biblical Hermeneutics*. Bloomington: Indiana University Press, 1989.

_____. "Inner Biblical Exegesis: Types and Strategies of Interpretation in Ancient Israel." Pages 19–37 in *Midrash and Literature*. Edited by Sanford Budick and Geoffrey Hartman. New Haven: Yale University Press, 1986.

_____. "Revelation and Tradition: Aspects of Inner-Biblical Exegesis." *Journal of Biblical Literature* 99 (1980): 343–61.

Greenstein, Edward L. "An Inner-biblical Midrash of the Nadab and Abihu Episode" [Hebrew]. Pages 71–78 in *Proceedings of the Eleventh World Congress of Jewish Studies*. Jerusalem: World Union of Jewish Studies, 1994.

Kaiser, Walter C. "Inner Biblical Exegesis as a Model for Bridging the 'Then' and 'Now' Gap: Hosea 12:1–6." *Journal of the Evangelical Theological Society* 28 (1985): 33–46.

Rosenblatt, J. P., and J. C. Sitterson. *Not in Heaven: Coherence and Complexity in Biblical Narrative*. Bloomington: Indiana University Press, 1991.

Rosenstock, Bruce. "Inner-Biblical Exegesis in the Book of the Covenant: The Case of the Sabbath Commandment." *Conservative Judaism* 44 (1992): 37–49.

Sommer, Benjamin D. *A Prophet Reads Scripture: Allusion in Isaiah 40–66*. Stanford, Calif.: Stanford University Press, 1998.

Sternberg, Meir. *The Poetics of Biblical Narrative: Ideological Literature and the Drama of Reading*. Bloomington: Indiana University Press, 1987.

Weingreen, Jacob. *From Bible to Mishna: The Continuity of Tradition*. Manchester: Manchester University Press, 1976.

ii. *On the Bible and Retelling*

Abramson, Glenda. "Amichai's God." *Prooftexts* 4 (1984): 111–26.

_____. "The Reinterpretation of the Akedah in Modern Hebrew Poetry." *Journal of Jewish Studies* 41 (1990): 101–14.

Alter, Robert. *Canon and Creativity: Modern Writing and the Authority of Scripture.* New Haven: Yale University Press, 2000.

_____. *The World of Biblical Literature.* New York: Basic, 1992.

Atwan, Robert, and Laurence Wieder. *Chapters into Verse: Poetry in English Inspired by the Bible.* 2 vols. Oxford: Oxford University Press, 1993.

Avni, Abraham. *The Bible and Romanticism: The Old Testament in German and French Poetry.* Paris: Mouton, 1969.

Baker, Carlos. "The Place of the Bible in American Fiction." *Theology Today* (April 1960): 71.

Bartel, Roland, ed. *Biblical Images in Literature.* Nashville: Abingdon, 1975.

_____. "Teaching Wilfred Owen's War Poems and the Bible." Page 199 in *Biblical Images in Literature.* Edited by Roland Bartel. Nashville: Abingdon, 1975.

Berkeley, David S. "Typology." In *A Dictionary of Biblical Tradition in English Literature.* Edited by David Lyle Jeffrey. Grand Rapids, MI: Eerdmans, 1992.

Besserman, Lawrence. *Chaucer and the Bible.* New York: Garland, 1988.

Blackburn, Ruth. *Biblical Drama Under the Tudors.* The Hague: Mouton, 1971.

Boitani, Piero. *The Bible and Its Rewritings.* Oxford: Oxford University Press, 1999.

Brown, Douglas C. *The Enduring Legacy: Biblical Dimensions in Modern Literature.* New York: Charles Scribner & Sons, 1975.

Budick, Sanford. "Milton and the Scene of Interpretation: From Typology toward Midrash." Pages 195–212 in *Midrash and Literature.* Edited by Sanford Budick and Geoffrey Hartman. New Haven: Yale University Press, 1986.

Butterworth, Charles C. *The Literary Lineage of the King James Bible.* Philadelphia: University of Pennsylvania Press, 1941.

Charity, A. C. *Events and Their Afterlife: The Dialectics of Christian Typology in the Bible and Dante.* Cambridge: Cambridge University Press, 1966.

Clines, David. *The Bible in the Modern World.* Sheffield: Sheffield Academic Press, 1997.

Cohn, Norman. *Noah's Flood: The Genesis Story in Western Thought.* New Haven: Yale University Press, 1996.

Cowley, Abraham. *Poems.* Cambridge: Cambridge University Press, 1905.

Crook, Margaret B. *The Bible and Its Literary Allusions.* New York: Abingdon, 1937.

Curzon, David, ed. *Modern Poems on the Bible: An Anthology.* Philadelphia: Jewish Publication Society, 1994.

Cushing, Lesleigh. "The Missing Missus." Pages 103–33 in *Sacred Text, Secular Times: The Hebrew Bible in the Modern World.* Edited by J. L. Greenspoon and B. F. Lebeau. Omaha: Creighton University Press, 2000.

Donnelly, Susan. "Eve Names the Animals." Page 62 in *Modern Poems on the Bible.* Edited by David Curzon. Philadelphia: Jewish Publication Society, 1994.

Elliott, Emory. "Milton's Biblical Style in *Paradise Regained*." *Milton Studies* 6 (1974): 227–42.

Findley, Timothy. *Headhunter.* Toronto: HarperCollins Canada, 1999.

Fowler, David. *The Bible in Early English Literature.* Seattle: Washington University Press, 1976.

_____. *The Bible in Middle English Literature.* Seattle: Washington University Press, 1984.

Freud, Sigmund. *Moses and Monotheism.* New York: Vintage, 1955.

Fulghum, Walter B. *A Dictionary of Biblical Allusion in English Literature.* New York: Holt, Rinehart & Winston, 1965.

Glück, Louise. "The Gift." In *First Four Books of Poems—Louise Glück.* San Francisco: HarperCollins, 1996.

Goldman, Solomon. "Echoes and Allusions." Pages 127–355 in *The Book of Books: An Introduction.* New York: Harper, 1948.

Goodman, Allegra. "Sarah." Pages 208–33 in *The Family Markowitz.* New York: Washington Square Press, 1997.

Gunn, Giles. *The Bible and American Arts and Letters.* Philadelphia: Fortress, 1983.

Hardy, Thomas. *Far From the Madding Crowd.* London: Pan Books, 1967.

Hawkins, Peter S. *Dante's Testaments: Essays in Scriptural Imagination.* Stanford: Stanford University Press, 2000.

Hawthorne, Nathaniel. *The Scarlet Letter.* New York: Penguin, 2002.

Hecht, Anthony. "Naming the Animals." In *Chapters into Verse,* vol. 1. Edited by Robert Atwan and Laurance Weider. New York: Oxford University Press, 1997.

Heller, Joseph. *God Knows.* New York: Scribner, 1997.

Holstein, J. "Melville's Inversion of Jonah in *Moby Dick.*" *The Iliff Review* 35 (1978): 13–19.

Hook, Brian S., and R. R. Reno. "Abraham and the Problems of Modern Heroism." Pages 135–62 in *Sacred Text, Secular Times: The Hebrew Bible in the Modern World.* Edited by J. L. Greenspoon and B. F. Lebeau. Omaha: Creighton University Press, 2000.

Hornback, Bert G. *Noah's Arkitecture: A Study of Dickens's Mythology.* Athens: Ohio University Press, 1972.

Jacobson, David C. *Does David Still Play Before You? Israeli Poetry and the Bible.* Detroit: Wayne State University Press, 1997.

Jasper, David, and Steven Prickett. *The Bible and Literature.* Cambridge, Mass.: Blackwell, 1998.

Jeffrey, David Lyle. *A Dictionary of the Bible in English Literature.* Grand Rapids: Eerdmans, 1992.

Kartun-Blum, Ruth. *Profane Scriptures.* Cincinnati: Hebrew Union College Press, 1999.

Katz, David S. *God's Last Words: Reading the English Bible from the Reformation to Fundamentalism.* New Haven: Yale University Press, 2004.

Kermode, Frank. *The Genesis of Secrecy.* Cambridge, Mass.: Harvard University Press, 1979.

Kreitzer, Larry Joseph. *The Old Testament in Fiction and Film.* Sheffield: Sheffield Academic Press, 1994.

Kuschel, Karl-Josef. *Abraham: Sign of Hope for Jews, Christians and Muslims.* New York: Continuum, 1995.

Larson, Janet L. *Dickens and the Broken Scripture.* Athens: University of Georgia Press, 1985.

Leivick, H. "Sacrifice." Page 238 in *The Penguin Book of Modern Yiddish Verse,* by Irving Howe, Ruth R. Wisse, and Khone Shmeruk. Translated by Robert Friend. New York: Viking, 1987.

Levenson, Jon D. *The Death and Resurrection of the Beloved Son.* New Haven: Yale University Press, 1993.

Liptzin, Sol. *Biblical Themes in World Literature.* Hoboken: Ktav, 1985.

McConnell, Frank D. *The Bible and the Narrative Tradition.* New York: Oxford University Press, 1986.

McNeil, Brian. "Typology." Page 713 in *A Dictionary of Bible Interpretation.* Edited by R. J. Coggins and J. L. Houlden. London: SCM, 1990.

Meltzer, Françoise. *Salome and the Dance of Writing: Portraits of Mimesis in Literature.* Chicago: University of Chicago Press, 1987.

Milosz, Czeslaw. "Linnaeus." In *Provinces: Poems 1987–1991.* Manchester: Carcanet, 1993.

Mosley, Virginia Douglas. *Joyce and the Bible.* DeKalb: Northwestern University Press, 1967.

Nathan, Esther. *Haderekh lemeitey Midbar.* Tel Aviv: Hakibbutz Hameuhad, 1993.

Naveh, Gila Safran. *Biblical Parables and Their Modern Recreation: From "Apples of Gold in Silver Settings" to "Imperial Messages."* New York: SUNY Press, 1999.

Norris, Pamela. *Eve: A Biography.* New York: New York University Press, 1999.

Norton, David. *A History of the English Bible as Literature.* Cambridge: Cambridge University Press, 2000.

Ostriker, Alicia. *Feminist Revision and the Bible.* Cambridge, Mass.: Blackwell, 1993.

_____. "A Word Made Flesh: The Bible and Revisionist Women's Poetry." *Religion and Literature* 23, no. 3 (1991): 9–26.

Pelikan, Jaroslav. *Jesus Through the Centuries: His Place in the History of Culture.* New Haven: Yale University Press, 1985.

Petit, Susan. "Co-Creations with God: How Michel Tournier Rewrites the Story of Eden." Pages 193–207 in *Reform and Counterreform: Dialectics of the World in Western Christianity since Luther.* Edited by John C. Hawley. Berlin: Mouton de Gruyter, 1994.

Phillips, John A. *Eve: The History of an Idea.* San Francisco: Harper & Row, 1984.

Pippin, Tina. *Apocalyptic Bodies: The Biblical End of the World in Text and Image.* New York: Routledge, 1999.

Pippin, Tina, and George Aichele. *The Monstrous and the Unspeakable: The Bible and Fantastic Literature.* Sheffield: Sheffield Academic Press, 1997.

Prickett, Stephen. *Origins of Narrative: The Romantic Appropriation of the Bible.* Cambridge: Cambridge University Press, 1996.

Prothero, Stephen. *Jesus in America.* New York: Farrar, Strauss & Giroux, 2003.

Purdy, Dwight H. *Joseph Conrad's Bible.* Norman: University of Oklahoma Press, 1984.

Roston, Murray. *Prophet and Poet: The Bible and the Growth of Romanticism.* London: Faber & Faber, 1965.

Schaar, Claes. *The Full Voic'd Quire Below: Vertical Context Systems in* Paradise Lost. Lund: CWK Gleerup, 1982.

Schneidau, Herbert. *Sacred Discontent: The Bible and Western Tradition.* Berkeley: University of California Press, 1976.

Schwartz, Regina, ed. *The Book and the Text: The Bible and Literary Theory.* Cambridge, Mass.: Blackwell, 1990.

Sherwood, Yvonne. *A Biblical Text and Its Afterlives: The Survival of Jonah in Western Culture.* Cambridge: Cambridge University Press, 2000.

Sims, James H. *The Bible in Milton's Epics.* Gainesville: University of Florida Press, 1962.

_____. *Biblical Allusions in Shakespeare's Comedies.* Forsyth, Ga.: Tift College, 1960.

_____. *Dramatic Uses of Biblical Allusions in Marlowe and Shakespeare*. Gainesville: University of Florida Press, 1966.

Sims, James H., and Leland Ryken, eds. *Milton and Scriptural Tradition: The Bible into Poetry*. Columbia, Miss.: University of Missouri Press, 1984.

Solle, Dorothee, Joe H. Kirchberger, and Herbert Haag. *Great Women of the Bible in Art and Literature*. Macon, Ga.: Mercer University Press, 1994.

Soltes, Ori Z. "The Bible and Art at the End of the Millennium: Words, Ideas and Images." Pages 163–96 in *Sacred Text, Secular Times: The Hebrew Bible in the Modern World*. Edited by J. L. Greenspoon and B. F. Lebeau. Omaha: Creighton University Press, 2000.

Stevens, James S. *The English Bible*. New York: Abingdon, 1921.

Stewart, Randall. *American Literature and Christian Doctrine*. Baton Rouge: Louisiana State University Press, 1958.

Stone, Michael E., and Theodore E. Bergren. *Biblical Figures Outside the Bible*. Harrisburg: Trinity Press International, 1998.

Wilder, Amos. *Modern Poetry and the Christian Tradition* New York: Scribner, 1952.

Wright, Melanie J. *Moses in America: The Cultural Uses of Biblical Narrative*. Oxford: Oxford University Press, 2003.

Wright, Nathalia. *Melville's Use of the Bible*. Durham, N.C.: Duke University Press, 1949.

Yehoshua, A. B. "Three Days and a Child." In *The Continuing Silence of a Poet: The Collected Short Stories of A. B. Yehoshua*. Syracuse, N.Y.: Syracuse University Press, 1998.

B. *Retellings and Other Canons*

i. *On Retellings of Myths and Classics*

Abramson, Glenda. "Hellenism Revisited: The Uses of Greek Myth in Modern Hebrew Literature." *Prooftexts* 10 (1990): 237–55.

Conte, Gian Biagio. *The Rhetoric of Imagination: Genre and Poetic Memory in Virgil and Other Latin Poets*. Translated by Charles Segal. Ithaca: Cornell University Press, 1986.

Farrell, Joseph. *Virgil's Georgics and the Traditions of Ancient Epic: The Art of Allusion in Literary History*. New York: Oxford University Press, 1991.

Fuchs, Jacob. *Pope's Imitations of Horace*. Lewisburg: Bucknell University Press, 1989.

Garner, Richard. *From Homer to Tragedy: The Art of Allusion in Greek Poetry*. London; New York: Routledge, 1990.

Greene, Thomas M. *The Light in Troy: Imitation and Discovery in Renaissance Poetry*. New Haven: Yale University Press, 1982.

Hamilton, Donna B. *Virgil and the Tempest: The Politics of Imitation*. Columbus: Ohio State University Press, 1990.

Hinds, Stephen. *Allusion and Intertext: Dynamics of Appropriation in Roman Poetry*. New York: Cambridge University Press, 1998.

Hollander, John. *The Figure of Echo: A Mode of Allusion in Milton and After*. Berkeley: University of California Press, 1981.

Mitchell, W. J. T. *The Last Dinosaur Book*. Chicago: University of Chicago Press, 1998.

Panofsky, Dora, and Erwin Panofsky. *Pandora's Box: The Changing Aspects of a Mythical Symbol*. 1956. Repr., Princeton: Mythos, 1991.

Payne, Alina, Anne Kuttner, and Rebekah Smick. *Antiquity and Its Interpreters*. New York: Cambridge University Press, 2000.

Segal, Charles. "Foreword" to Gian Biagio Conte, *The Rhetoric of Imitation: Genre and Poetic Memory in Virgil and Other Latin Poets*. Ithaca: Cornell University Press, 1986.

Smith, Alden. *Poetic Allusion and Poetic Embrace in Ovid and Virgil*. Ann Arbor: University of Michigan Press, 1997.

Thomas, Richard F. *Reading Virgil and His Texts: Studies in Intertextuality*. Ann Arbor: University of Michigan Press, 1999.

ii. *On Retellings of/in the Western Literary Canon*

Atherton, James S. *The Books at the Wake: A Study of Literary Allusions in James Joyce's* Finnegans Wake. Mamaroneck, N.Y.: Appel, 1974.

Baranowski, Anne-Marie. "De l'amour et de l'argent. Écriture féminine et réécriture contestatrice: les deux épouses de Mr. Rochester." *La Revue LISA* 2, no. 5 (2004): 97–106.

Cancogni, Annapaola. *The Mirage in the Mirror: Nabokov's Ada and Its French Pretexts*. New York: Garland, 1985.

Dane, Joseph A. *Who is Buried in Chaucer's Tomb? Studies in the Reception of Chaucer's Book*. East Lansing: Michigan State University Press, 1995.

Dasenbrock, Reed Way. *Imitating the Italians: Wyatt, Spenser, Synge, Pound, Joyce*. Baltimore: Johns Hopkins University Press, 1991.

Eco, Umberto. "Casablanca: Cult Movies and Intertextual Collage." Pages 197–211 in *Travels in Hyperreality*. Translated by William Weaver. San Diego: Harcourt Brace Jovanovich, 1986.

Gerli, Michael E. *Refiguring Authority: Reading, Writing, and Rewriting in Cervantes*. Louisville: University Press of Kentucky Press, 1995.

Godorecci, Barbara. *After Machiavelli: "Re-Writing" and the "Hermeneutic Attitude."* Purdue Studies in Romance Literatures 3; Purdue, IN: Purdue University Press, 1993.

Gresser, Michel, and Noel Polk. *Intertextuality in Faulkner*. Jackson: University Press of Mississippi, 1995.

Gross, John J. *Shylock: Four Hundred Years in the Life of a Legend*. London: Vintage, 1994.

Gutleben, Christian. *Nostalgic Postmodernism: The Victorian Tradition and the Contemporary British Novel*. Postmodern Studies 31. Amsterdam: Editions Rodopi, 2002.

McKenna, Andrew. "Biblioclasm: Joycing Jesus and Borges." *Diacritics* 8 (1978): 15–29.

Moses, Carole. *Melville's Use of Spenser*. New York: Peter Lang, 1989.

Ostriker, Alicia. "The Thieves of Language: Women Poets and Revisionist Mythmaking." Pages 314–38 in *The New Feminist Criticism*. Edited by Elaine Showalter. New York: Pantheon, 1985.

Pillière, Linda. "Michael Cunningham's *The Hours*: Echoes of Virginia Woolf." *La Revue LISA* 2, no. 5 (2004): 133–43.

Rich, Adrienne. "When We Dead Awaken: Writing as Re-vision." *College English* 34 (1972): 18–30.

Roblin, Isabelle. "De la parodie à la réécriture: Margaret Mitchell's *Gone with the Wind* (1936) vs Alice Randall's *The Wind Done Gone* (2001). *La Revue LISA* 2, no. 5 (2004): 120–31.

Schwartz-Gastine, Isabelle. "Shakespeare revisité, entre fidélité et parodie: de La Nuit des Rois à Shake de Dan Jemmett. *La Revue LISA* 2, no. 5 (2004): 75–85.

Scott, Robert. "'But hey, this is Africa, man': Water Music and the Postmodernization of the Eighteenth Century Novel." *La Revue LISA* 2, no. 5 (2004): 87–95.

The Shakspere Allusion-Book: A Collection of Allusions to Shakspere from 1591 to 1700. Originally compiled by C. M. Ingleby, L. Toulmin Smith, and F. J. Furnivall, with the assistance of the New Shakspere Society (1909). Re-issued with a Preface by Sir Edmund Chambers. Freeport, N.Y.: Books for Libraries Press, 1970.

Weiner, Andrew D. "Sidney/Spenser/Shakespeare." Pages 245–70 in *Influence and Intertextuality in Literary History*. Edited by Jay Clayton and Eric Rothstein. Madison: University of Wisconsin Press, 1991.

Williams, Todd. "Eliot's Alteration of Renaissance Drama through Frazer in *The Waste Land*." *La Revue LISA* 2, no. 5 (2004): 61–73.

II. *Literary Criticism and Theory*

A. *Allusion, Imitation, Invention, Influence, Mimesis*

Auerbach, Erich. *Mimesis: The Representation of Reality in Western Literature.* Princeton: Princeton University Press, 1953.

_____. "Odysseus' Scar." Page 12 in *Mimesis*. Princeton: Princeton University Press, 1953.

Bate, W. Jackson. *The Burden of the Past and the English Poet.* Cambridge, Mass.: Harvard University Press, 1970.

Baxandall, Michael. *Patterns of Intention: On the Historical Explanation of Pictures.* New Haven: Yale University Press, 1985.

Bloom, Harold. *The Anxiety of Influence: A Theory of Poetry.* Oxford: Oxford University Press, 1973.

_____. *A Map of Misreading.* Oxford: Oxford University Press, 1975.

Bruns, Gerald. *Inventions: Writing, Textuality and Understanding in Literary History.* New Haven: Yale University Press, 1982.

Coste, Didier. "Rewriting, Literariness, Literary History." *La Revue LISA* 2, no. 5 (2004): 9–24.

Desmet, Christy, and Robert Sawyer, eds. *Shakespeare and Appropriation.* New York: Routledge, 1999.

Dodge, R. E. Neil. "A Sermon on Source-Hunting." *Modern Philology* 9 (1911): 211–23.

Dryden, John. "Preface to Sylvae." Pages 252–52 in Volume 1 of *Of Dramatick Poesy and Other Essays*. Edited by George Watson. London: Dent, 1968.

Eliot, T. S. "Tradition and the Individual Talent." In *Selected Prose of T. S. Eliot*. New York: Harcourt Brace, 1975.

Hassan, Ihab H. "The Problem of Influence in Literary History: Notes Toward Definition." *Journal of Aesthetics and Art Criticism* 14 (1955): 165–89.

Heninger, S. K. *Sidney and Spenser: The Poet as Maker.* University Park: Pennsylvania State University Press, 1989.

Hermeren, Goran. "Allusions and Intentions." Pages 203–20 in *Intention and Interpretation*. Edited by Gary Iseminger. Philadelphia: Temple University Press, 1992.

_____. *Influence in Art and Literature.* Princeton: Princeton University Press, 1975.

Hoesterey, Ingeborg. *Pastiche: Cultural Memory in Art, Film, Literature.* Bloomington: Indiana University Press, 2001.

Horace. "Art of Poetry." In *Critical Theory Since Plato. Edited by* Hazard Adams. New York: Harcourt Brace Jovanovich, 1971.

Lhermitte, Corinne. "Adaptation as Rewriting: Evolution of a Concept." *La Revue LISA* 2, no. 5 (2004): 27–44.

Mahoney, John L. *The Whole Internal Universe: Imitation and the New Defense of Poetry in British Criticism, 1660–1830*. New York: Fordham University Press, 1985.

McLaughlin, Kevin. *Writing in Parts: Imitation and Exchange in Nineteenth-Century Literature*. Stanford: Stanford University Press, 1995.

McLaughlin, Martin L. *Literary Imitation in the Italian Renaissance: The Theory and Practice of Literary Imitation in Italy from Dante to Bembo*. New York: Oxford University Press, 1995.

Minnis, Alastair J. *Medieval Theory of Authorship: Scholastic Literary Attitudes in the Late Middle Ages*. Philadelphia: University of Pennsylvania Press, 1988.

Newlyn, Lucy. *Coleridge, Wordsworth, and the Language of Allusion*. New York: Oxford University Press, 1986.

Ostriker, Alicia. *Stealing the Language*. Boston: Beacon Press, 1990.

Peterson, Richard. *Imitation and Praise in the Poems of Ben Jonson*. New Haven: Yale University Press, 1982.

Pope, Alexander. "An Essay on Criticism." Pages 274–82 in *Critical Theory Since Plato*. Edited by Hazard Adams. New York: Harcourt Brace Jovanovich College Publishers, 1992.

Pucci, Joseph Michael. *The Full-Knowing Reader: Allusion and the Power of the Reader in the Western Literary Tradition*. New Haven: Yale University Press, 1998.

Quint, David. *Origin and Originality in Renaissance Literature: Versions of the Source*. New Haven: Yale University Press, 1983.

Rebei, Marian. "A Different Kind of Circularity: From Writing and Reading to Rereading and Rewriting." *La Revue LISA* 2, no. 5 (2004): 45–58.

Ricks, Christopher. "Allusion: The Poet as Heir." Pages 209–40 in *Studies in the Eighteenth Century III: Papers Presented at the Third David Nichol Smith Memorial Seminar*. Edited by R. F. Brissenden and J. C. Eade. Toronto: University of Toronto Press, 1976.

_____. "Beckett's Allusions to Shakespeare." (Lecture) Boston University Translation Seminar, 31 January 1997.

_____. "Keats's Sources, Keats's Allusions." Pages 152–69 in *The Cambridge Companion to Keats*. Edited by Susan J. Wolfson. New York: Cambridge University Press, 2001.

Saprisou, Mihai, ed. *Mimesis in Contemporary Theory: An Interdisciplinary Approach*. Philadelphia: J. Benjamins, 1984.

Sidney, Sir Philip. *An Apology for Poetry*. In *Critical Theory Since Plato*. Edited by Hazard Adams. New York: Harcourt Brace Jovanovich, 1971.

_____. *In Defense of Poesy*. Edited by Lewis Soens. Lincoln: University of Nebraska Press, 1970.

Slochower, Harry. *Mythopoesis: Mythic Patterns in Literary Classics*. Detroit: Wayne State University Press, 1973.

Sörbom, Göran. *Mimesis and Art. Studies in the Origin and Early Development of an Aesthetic Vocabulary*. New York: Humanities, 1966.

Todorov, Tzvetan. *The Poetics of Prose*. Translated by R. Howard. Ithaca: Cornell University Press, 1977.

Urdang, Laurence, and Frederick G. Ruffner, Jr., ed. *Allusions: Cultural, Literary, Biblical, and Historical: A Thematic Dictionary*. Detroit, Mich.: Gale Research Co., 1982.

Waugh, Patricia. *Metafiction: The Theory and Practice of Self-Conscious Fiction*. London: Methuen, 1984.

Wellek, René. "The Concept of Evolution in Literary History." Pages 37–53 in *Concepts of Criticism*. New Haven: Yale University Press, 1963.

B. *Literary and Reception Theories*

Abrahams, M. H. *Doing Things With Texts: Essays in Criticism and Critical Theory*. New York: Norton, 1991.

Bakhtin, Mikhail. *Speech Genres and Other Late Essays*. Translated by V. W. McGee. Austin: University Texas Press, 1986.

Barthes, Roland. "From Work to Text." Pages 73–81 in *Textual Strategies: Perspectives in Post-Structuralist Criticism*. Edited by Josue V. Harari. Ithaca: Cornell University Press, 1979.

Berg, Henk de. "Reception Theory or Perception Theory?" Pages 23–30 in *The Systematic and Empirical Approach to Literature and Culture as Theory and Application*. Edited by Steven Totosy de Zepetnek and Irene Sywensky. Siegen University: Institute for Empirical Literature and Media Research, 1997.

Bérubé, Michael. *Public Access: Literary Theory and American Cultural Politics*. London: Verso, 1994.

Bloom, Harold. *Ruin the Sacred Truths: Poetry and Belief from the Bible to the Present*. Cambridge, Mass.: Harvard University Press, 1989.

Cavell, Stanley. "Aesthetic Problems of Modern Philosophy." Pages 24–36 in *Critical Theory Since 1965*. Edited by Hazard Adams and Leroy Searle. Tallahasee: Florida State University Press, 1990.

Cornis-Pope, Marcel. *Hermeneutic Desire and Critical Rewriting: Narrative Interpretation in the Wake of Poststructuralism*. New York: St. Martin's Press, 1992.

Cowart, David. *Literary Symbiosis: The Reconfigured Text in Twentieth-Century Writing*. Athens: University of Georgia Press, 1993.

Culler, Jonathan. *On Deconstruction: Theory and Criticism after Structuralism*. London: Routledge, 1993.

_____. *The Pursuit of Signs: Semiotics, Literature, Deconstruction*. London: Routledge, 1981.

_____. *Structuralist Poetics: Structuralism, Linguistics, and the Study of Literature*. London: Routledge, 1975.

Derrida, Jacques. *Of Grammatology*. Translated by Gayatri Chakravorty Spivak. Baltimore: Johns Hopkins University Press, 1976.

Eagleton, Terry. *Literary Theory: An Introduction*. Minneapolis: The University of Minnesota Press, 1995.

Fish, Stanley. *Is There a Text in This Class? The Authority of Interpretive Communities*. Cambridge, Mass.: Harvard University Press, 1980.

Foucault, Michel. "What is an Author?" Pages 196–210 in *Modern Criticism and Theory*, Edited by David Lodge; London: Longman, 1988.

Frye, Northrop. *Anatomy of Criticism*. Princeton: Princeton University Press, 1973.

_____. *The Great Code*. Toronto: Harcourt Brace Jovanovich, 1982.

_____. *The Secular Scripture: A Study of the Structure of Romance*. Cambridge, Mass.: Harvard University Press, 1976.

Gadamer, Hans-Georg. *Truth and Method*. New York: Continuum, 1993.

Hartman, Geoffrey. *Criticism in the Wilderness*. New Haven: Yale University Press, 1980.

_____. "The Culture of Criticism." Pages 17–56 in *Minor Prophecies: The Literary Essay in the Culture Wars*. Cambridge, Mass.: Harvard University Press, 1991.

Hawkes, Terence. *Structuralism and Semiotics*. London: New Accents, 1989.

Holland, Peter, and Hanna Scolnicov. *Reading Plays: Interpretation and Reception*. Cambridge: Cambridge University Press, 1991.

Holub, Robert C. *Crossing Borders: Reception Theory, Poststructuralism, Deconstruction*. Madison: University Wisconsin Press, 1992.

_____. "Reception Theory: School of Constance." Pages 319–46 in *The Cambridge History of Literary Criticism*. Vol. 8, *From Formalism to Poststructuralism*. Edited by Raman Selden. Cambridge: Cambridge University Press, 1995.

Hutcheon, L. *A Theory of Parody: The Teachings of Twentieth Century Art Forms*. London: Methuen, 1989.

Iser, Wolfgang. *The Implied Reader: Patterns of Communication in Prose Fiction from Bunyan to Beckett*. Baltimore: Johns Hopkins University Press, 1974.

_____. *The Act of Reading: A Theory of Aesthetic Response*. Baltimore: Johns Hopkins University Press, 1978.

Jauss, Hans Robert. "Levels of Identification of Hero and Audience." *New Literary History* 5 (1974): 283–317.

_____. "Literary History as a Challenge to Literary Theory." Pages 3–45 in *Toward an Aesthetic of Reception*. Translated by Timothy Bahti. Minneapolis: University Minnesota Press, 1982.

_____. "The Theory of Reception: A Retrospective of Its Unrecognized Prehistory." Pages 53–73 in *Literary Theory Today*. Edited by Peter Collier and Helga Geyer-Ryan. Cambridge: Polity, 1990.

_____. *Toward an Aesthetic of Reception*. Translated by Timothy Bahti. Minneapolis: University of Minnesota Press, 1982.

Machor, James L., and Philip Goldstein. *Reception Study: From Literary Theory to Cultural Studies*. New York: Routledge, 2001.

Mailloux, Steven. *Reception Histories: Rhetoric, Pragmatism, and American Cultural Politics*. Ithaca: Cornell University Press, 1998.

_____. *Rhetorical Power*. Ithaca: Cornell University Press, 1989.

Medvedev, P. N., and M. M. Bakhtin. *The Formal Method in Literary Scholarship*. Baltimore: Johns Hopkins University Press, 1978.

Moraru, Christian. *Rewriting: Postmodern Narrative and Cultural Critique in the Age of Cloning*. Albany: SUNY Press, 2001.

Ricoeur, Paul. *Interpretation Theory: Discourse and the Surplus of Meaning*. Fort Worth: Texas Christian University Press, 1976.

Riffaterre, Michael. "The Making of the Text." Pages 54–70 in *Identity and the Literary Text*. Edited by Mario J. Valds and Owen Miller. Toronto: University of Toronto Press, 1985.

_____. *Text Production*. Translated by Terèse Lyons. New York: Columbia University Press, 1983.

Saussure, Ferdinand de. *Cours de Linguistique Generale*. Paris: Payot, 1967.

C. *Intertextuality*

Allen, Graham. *Intertextuality*. New York: Routledge, 2000.

Bakhtin, Mikhail M. *The Dialogic Imagination*. Edited by Michael Holquist. Translated by Caryl Emerson and Michael Holquist. Chicago: University of Chicago Press, 1984.

Barthes, Roland. "The Death of the Author." Pages 142–48 in *Image-Music-Text*. Translated by Stephen Heath. New York: Hill & Wang, 1977.

_____. *The Pleasure of the Text*. Translated by Richard Miller. New York: Hill & Wang, 1973.

_____. *S/Z*. Translated by Richard Miller. New York: Hill & Wang, 1970.

Barthes, Roland, and Francis Bovon. *Structural Analysis and Biblical Exegesis: Interpretational Essays*. Translated by Alfred M. Johnson. Pittsburgh: Pickwick, 1974.

Clayton, Jay, and Eric Rothstein. "Figures in the Corpus: Theories of Influence and Intertextuality." Pages 3–36 in *Influence and Intertextuality in Literary History*. Edited by Jay Clayton and Eric Rothstein. Madison: University of Wisconsin Press, 1991.

Culler, Jonathan. "Presupposition and Intertextuality." Pages 100–18 in *The Pursuit of Signs: Semiotics, Literature, Deconstruction*. Ithaca: Cornell University Press, 1981.

Derrida, Jacques. *The Truth in Painting*. Translated by Geoff Bennington and Ian McLeod. Chicago: University Chicago, 1987.

Fleming, Richard, and Michael Payne. *Criticism, History, and Intertextuality*. Toronto: Associated University Press, 1988.

Foucault, Michel. "The Discourse on Language." Pages 215–37 in *The Archaeology of Knowledge and the Discourse of Language*. Translated by A. M. Sheridan Smith. New York: Harper & Row, 1972.

_____. "What Is an Author?" Revised version. Translated by Josué V. Harari. Pages 141–60 in *Textual Strategies: Perspectives in Post-Structuralist Criticism*. Edited by Josué V. Harari. Ithaca: Cornell University Press, 1979.

Frow, John. "Intertextuality." Pages 125–69 in *Marxism and Literary History*. Cambridge, Mass.: Harvard University Press, 1986.

Genette, Gerard. *Architext: An Introduction*. Translated by Jane E. Levin. Berkeley: University of California Press, 1992.

_____. *Introduction à l'architexte*. Paris: Seuil, 1979.

_____. *Palimpsests: Literature in the Second Degree*. Translated by Channa Nouman and Claude Doubinsky. Lincoln: University of Nebraska Press, 1997.

_____. *Palimpsestes: la littérature au second degré*. Paris: Seuil, 1982.

_____. *Paratexts: Thresholds of Interpretation*. Translated by Jane E. Lewin. Cambridge: Cambridge University Press, 1997.

Kristeva, Julia. *Desire in Language: A Semiotic Approach to Literature and Art*. Edited by Leon S. Roudiez. Translated by Thomas Gora, Alice Jardine, and Leon S. Roudiez. New York: Columbia University Press, 1980.

_____. *La révolution du langage poetique*. Paris: Seuil, 1974.

_____. *Sémeiotiké: Recherches pour une sémanalyse*. Paris: Seuil, 1969.

Miller, J. Hillis. *Fiction and Repetition*. Oxford: Oxford University Press, 1982.

Miller, Nancy. "Arachnologies: The Woman, The Text and The Critic." Pages 77–101 in *Subject to Change: Reading Feminist Writing*. New York: Columbia University Press, 1988.

O'Donnell, Patrick, and Robert Con Davis, eds. *Intertextuality and Contemporary American Fiction.* Baltimore: Johns Hopkins University Press, 1989.

Queneau, Raymond. *Exercises in Style.* Translated by Barbara Wright. New York: New Directions, 1981.

Rex, Janet. "Heterogeneous Contradiction: Toward a Kristevan Practice." *Poetics Today* 7, no. 4 (1986): 767.

Stewart, Susan. *Nonsense: Aspects of Intertextuality in Folklore and Literature.* Baltimore: Johns Hopkins University Press, 1980.

Todorov, Tzvetan. *Mikhail Bakhtin: The Dialogical Principle.* Translated by Wald Godzvich. Manchester: Manchester University Press, 1984.

III. *Midrash and the Language of (Jewish) Retelling*

A. *Midrashim*

Midrash Rabbah. Translated by H. Freedman and M. Simon. 10 vols. London: Soncino, 1939.

Charles, R. H. *The Apocrypha and Pseudepigrapha of the Old Testament in English.* 2 vols. Oxford: Clarendon, 1913.

Charlesworth, J. H., ed. *The Old Testament Pseudepigrapha.* 2 vols. New York: Doubleday, 1983.

Ginzberg, Louis, et al. *Legends of the Jews.* 7 vols. Repr., Baltimore: Johns Hopkins University Press, 1998.

Kugel, James. *The Bible as It Was.* Cambridge, Mass.: The Belknap Press of Harvard University Press, 1999.

Nickelsburg, George W. E. *Jewish Literature Between the Bible and the Mishnah.* Philadelphia: Fortress, 1981.

Steinsaltz, Adin. *The Talmud: The Steinsaltz Edition.* Volume 1, *A Reference Guide.* New York: Random House, 1989.

Stern, David. "Introduction." In *The Book of Legends—Sefer Ha Aggadah* Edited by Hayim Nahum Bialik and Yehoshua Hana Ravnitzky. Translated by William G. Braude. New York: Schocken, 1992.

Stone, Michael. *Jewish Writings of the Second Temple Period.* Philadelphia: Fortress, 1984.

Urbach, Ephraim E. *The Sages: Their Concepts and Beliefs.* Cambridge, Mass.: Harvard University Press, 1989.

B. *On Midrash*

Ben-Ami, I., and J. Dan, eds. *Studies in Aggadah and Jewish Folklore.* Jerusalem, 1983.

Bland, Kalman P.. "The Rabbinic Method and Literary Criticism." Pages 16–23 in *Literary Interpretation of Biblical Narrative.* Edited by Kenneth R. R. Gross Louis et al. Nashville: Abingdon, 1974.

Bowker, John. *The Targums and Rabbinic Literature.* Cambridge: Cambridge University Press, 1969.

Charlesworth, James H. *LXX: The Pseudepigrapha and Modern Research.* Septuagint and Cognate Studies 7. Ann Arbor: Scholars Press, 1981.

_____. "In the Crucible: The Pseudepigrapha as Biblical Interpretation." In *The Aramaic Bible: Targums in their Historical Context.* Edited by D. R. G. Beattie and M. J. McNamara. Sheffield: JSOT Press, 1994.

Collins, John J., and George W. E. Nickelsburg. *Ideal Figures in Ancient Judaism: Profiles and Paradigms.* Atlanta: Scholars Press, 1980.

Daube, David. "Rabbinic Methods of Interpretation and Hellenistic Rhetoric." *Hebrew Union College Annual* 22 (1949): 239–64.

Dimant, Devorah. "Use and Interpretation of Mikra in the Apocrypha and Pseudepigrapha." Pages 379–419 in *Mikra: Text, Translation, Reading and Interpretation of the Hebrew Bible in Ancient Judaism and Early Christianity.* Edited by Martin Jan Mulder. Philadelphia: Fortress Press, 1988.

Fishbane, Michael. *The Exegetical Imagination: On Jewish Thought and Theology.* Cambridge, Mass.: Harvard University Press, 1998.

Fraade, Steven D. *From Tradition to Commentary: Torah and Its Interpretation in the Midrash Sifre to Deuteronomy.* Albany: SUNY Press, 1991.

Frankel, Israel. *Peshat in Talmudic and Midrashic Literature.* Toronto: LaSalle, 1956.

Ginzberg, Louis. *Jewish Law and Lore.* Philadelphia: Jewish Publication Society, 1962.

Goldenberg, Robert. "History and Ideology in Talmudic Narrative." Pages 159–71 in Volume 4 of *Approaches to Ancient Judaism.* Edited by William Scott Green. 5 vols. Chico, Calif: Scolars Press, 1983.

Goldin, Judah. "The Freedom and Restraint of Aggadah." Pages 57–76 in *Midrash and Literature.* Edited by Sanford Budick and Geoffrey Hartman. New Haven: Yale University Press, 1986.

_____. "From Text to Interpretation and from Experience to Interpreted Text." Pages 271–82 in *Studies in Midrash and Related Literature.* Edited by Barry L. Eichler and Jeffrey Tigay. Philadelphia: Jewish Publication Society, 1988.

_____. "Reflections on Translation and Midrash." Pages 239–52 in *Studies in Midrash and Related Literature.* Edited by Barry Eichler and Jeffrey Tigay. Philadelphia: Jewish Publication Society, 1988.

_____. *The Song at the Sea: Being a Commentary on a Commentary in Two Parts.* New Haven: Yale University Press, 1971.

Gordis, Robert. "Midrash: Its Method and Meaning." *Midstream* (1959): 91–96.

Green, William Scott. "Writing with Scripture: The Rabbinic Uses of the Bible." Pages 7–23 in *Writing with Scripture: The Authority and Uses of the Hebrew Bible in the Torah of Formative Judaism.* By Jacob Neusner with William Scott Green. Repr., Minneapolis: Fortress Press, 1989.

Guttman, Theodore. *Hamashal Bitkufat Hatannaim.* Jerusalem, 1949.

Halivni, David Weiss. *Midrash, Mishnah, and Gemara: The Jewish Predilection for Justified Law.* Cambridge, Mass.: Harvard University Press, 1986.

_____. *Peshat and Derash: Plain and Applied Meaning in Rabbinic Exegesis.* New York: Oxford University Press, 1991.

Heinemann, Joseph. *Agadot ve-toldotehen: iyunim be-hishtalshelutan shel masorot.* Jerusalem: Bet Hotsaah Keter, 1974.

_____. "The Nature of the Aggadah." Pages 41–55 in *Midrash and Literature.* Edited by Sanford Budick and Geoffrey Hartman. New Haven: Yale University Press, 1986.

_____. "Profile of a Midrash." *Journal of the American Academy of Religion* 39 (1971): 141–50.

Heinemann, Joseph, and Dov Noy, eds. *Studies in Aggadah and Folk Literature.* Jerusalem: Magnes, 1978.

Heinemann, Yitzhak (Isaac). *Darkhei Ha'Aggadah.* Jerusalem: Magnes, Hebrew University, 1970.

Horgan, M. P. *Pesharim: Qumran Interpretations of Biblical Books*. Catholic Biblical Quarterly Monograph Series 8. Catholic Biblical Society of America, 1979.

Idel, Moshe. "Midrash vs. Other Jewish Hermeneutics." Pages 45–58 in *The Midrashic Imagination: Jewish Exegesis, Thought and History*. Edited by Michael Fishbane. Albany: SUNY Press, 1993.

Jacobs, Irving. *The Midrashic Process: Tradition and Interpretation in Rabbinic Judaism*. Cambridge: Cambridge University Press, 1995.

Jacobs, Louis. *Studies in Talmudic Logic and Methodology*. London: Vallentine, Mitchell & Co., 1961.

Kadushin, Max. *The Rabbinic Mind*. 3d ed. New York: Bloch, 1972.

Kugel, James. *In Potiphar's House*. Cambridge, Mass.: Harvard University Press, 1994.

_____. "Two Introductions to Midrash." Pages 77–103 in *Midrash and Literature*. Edited by Geoffrey Hartman and Sanford Budick. New Haven: Yale University Press, 1986.

Loewe, Raphael. "The 'Plain' Meaning of Scripture in Early Jewish Exegesis." *Papers of the Institute of Jewish Studies* 1 (1964): 140–85.

Neusner, Jacob. *The Halakhah and the Aggadah: Theological Perspectives*. Lanham, Md.: University Press of America, 2001.

_____. *Midrash as Literature: The Primacy of Documentary Discourse*. Lanham, Md.: University Press of America, 1987.

_____. *The Torah in the Talmud: A Taxonomy of Uses of Scripture in the Talmud*. Atlanta: Scholars Press, 1993.

_____. *What is Midrash? and A Midrash Reader*. Atlanta: Scholars Press, 1994.

_____. *Writing With Scripture: The Authority and Use of the Hebrew Bible in the Torah of Formative Judaism*. With William Scott Green. Atlanta: Scholars Press, 1993.

Nickelsburg, George, and Michael Stone. *Faith and Piety in Early Judaism*. Philadelphia: Fortress, 1983.

Quarles, Charles L. *Midrash Criticism: Introduction and Appraisal*. Lanham, Md.: University Press of America, 1998.

Rabinowitz, Abraham Hirsch. *The Jewish Mind in Its Halakhic Talmudic Expression*. Jerusalem: Hillel Press, 1978.

_____. *The Study of Talmud: Understanding the Halachic Mind*. Northvale, N.J.: Jason Aronson, 1996.

Roitman, Betty. "Sacred Language and Open Text." Pages 159–75 in *Midrash and Literature*. Edited by Geoffrey Hartman and Sanford Budick. New Haven: Yale University Press, 1986.

Rosenblatt, Samuel. *The Interpretation of the Bible in the Mishnah*. Baltimore: Johns Hopkins University Press, 1975.

Sarason, Richard S. "Toward a New Agendum for the Study of Rabbinic and Midrashic Literature." Pages 55–73 in *Studies in Aggadah, Targum, and Jewish Liturgy in Memory of Joseph Heinemann*. Edited by Jakob J. Petuchowski and Ezra Fleischer. Jerusalem: Magnes, 1981.

Schwarz, Howard. *Reimagining the Bible: The Storytelling of the Rabbis*. Oxford: Oxford University Press, 1999.

Slonimsky, Henry. "The Philosophy Implicit in Midrash." *Hebrew Union College Annual* (1968): 235–90.

Spiegel, Shalom. *The Last Trial: On the Legends and Lore of the Command to Abraham to Offer Isaac as a Sacrifice*. Translated by Judah Goldin. Woodstock, Vt.: Jewish Lights, 1993.

Stern, David. "Midrash and the Language of Exegesis." Pages 105–24 in *Midrash and Literature*. Edited by Geoffrey Hartman and Sanford Budick. New Haven: Yale University Press, 1986.

_____. *Parables in Midrash: Narrative and Exegesis in Rabbinic Literature*. Cambridge, Mass.: Harvard University Press, 1991.

Strack, Hermann L., and Günter Stemberger. *Introduction to the Talmud and Mishnah*. Translated by Markus Bockmuehl. Minneapolis: Augsburg Fortress, 1992.

Strack, Hermann L., and Gunter Stemburger. *Introduction to the Talmud and Midrash*. Translated by Markus Bockmuehl. Minneapolis: Fortress Press, 1996.

Weingreen, Jacob. *From Bible to Mishna: The Continuity of Tradition*. Manchester: Manchester University Press, 1976.

Wright, Addison. *The Literary Genre: Midrash*. Staten Island: Alba House, 1967.

Yerushalmi, Yosef Hayim. *Zakhor: Jewish History and Jewish Memory*. Seattle: University of Washington Press, 1996.

C. *Midrash and Literary Theory*

Atkins, G. Douglas. "Dehellenizing Literary Criticism," *College English* 41 (1980): 769–79.

Berlin, Adele. "Literary Exegesis of Biblical Narrative: Between Poetics and Hermeneutics." Pages 120–28 in *"Not in Heaven": Coherence and Complexity in Biblical Narrative*. Edited by Jason Press. Rosenblatt and Joseph C. Sitterson, Jr. Bloomington IN: Indiana University Press, 1991.

Bible and Culture Collective, The. "Lacan as Midrashist, Biblical Scholar and Theologian." Pages 196–211 in *The Postmodern Bible*. New Haven: Yale University Press, 1995.

Boyarin, Daniel. *Carnal Israel: Reading Sex in Talmudic Culture*. Berkeley: University of California Press, 1993.

_____. *Intertextuality and the Reading of Midrash*. Bloomington: Indiana University Press, 1990.

Bruns, Gerald. *Hermeneutics Ancient and Modern*. New Haven: Yale University Press, 1992.

_____. "Midrash and Allegory: The Beginnings of Scriptural Interpretation." Pages 625–46 in *The Literary Guide to the Bible*. Edited by Robert Alter and Frank Kermode. Cambridge, Mass.: Harvard University Press, 1987.

Callaway, Mary. *Sing, O Barren One: A Study in Comparative Midrash*. Atlanta: Scholars Press, 1986.

Faur, Jose. *Golden Doves With Silver Dots: Semiotics and Textuality in Rabbinic Tradition*. Bloomington: Indiana University Press, 1986.

Handelman, Susan. *The Slayers of Moses: The Emergence of Rabbinic Interpretation in Modern Literary Theory*. Albany: SUNY Press, 1982.

Hartman, Geoffrey. "The Struggle for the Text." Pages 3–18 in *Midrash and Literature*. Edited by Geoffrey Hartman and Sanford Budick. New Haven: Yale University Press, 1986.

Jaffee, Martin. "The Hermeneutical Model of Midrashic Studies: What It Reveals and What It Conceals." *Prooftexts* 11 (1991): 67–76.

Silberman, Lou H. "Toward a Rhetoric of Midrash: A Preliminary Account." Pages 15–26 in *The Biblical Mosaic: Changing Perspectives*. Edited by Robert Polzin and Eugene Rothman. Philadelphia: Fortress, 1982.

Stein, Kenneth. "Exegesis, Maimonides and Literary Criticism." *Modern Language Notes* 88 (1973): 1134–54.

Stern, David. *Midrash and Theory: Ancient Jewish Exegesis and Contemporary Literary Studies*. Evanston, Ill.: Northwestern University Press, 1997.

_____. "Literary Criticism or Literary Homilies? Susan Handelman and the Contemporary Study of Midrash." *Prooftexts* 5 (1985): 102–3.

_____. "Midrash and Indeterminacy." *Critical Inquiry* 15, no. 3 (1988): 132–61.

Werman, Golda. *Milton and Midrash*. Washington, D.C.: Catholic University of America Press, 1996.

D. *Modern Midrash*

Alter, Robert. *Hebrew and Modernity*. Bloomington: Indiana University Press, 1994.

_____. *Necessary Angels: Tradition and Modernity in Kafka, Benjamin and Scholem*. Cambridge, Mass.: Harvard University Press, 1991.

Bloom, Harold. *The Strong Light of the Canonical: Kafka, Freud, and Scholem as Revisionists of Jewish Culture and Thought*. New York: City College, 1987.

Curzon, David. "A Hidden Genre: Twentieth-Century Midrashic Poetry." *Tikkun* 9 (1994): 70–71, 95.

_____. "Tradition Unbound: Poetry from Midrash." *Tikkun* 6 (1991): 30–31, 95.

Holtz, Barry. "Midrash and Modernity: Can Midrash Serve a Contemporary Religious Discourse?" Pages 377–391 in *The Uses of Tradition: Jewish Continuity in the Modern Era*. Edited by Jack Wertheimer. New York: Jewish Theological Seminary of America, 1992.

Jacobson, David C. *Modern Midrash: The Retelling of Traditional Jewish Narratives by Twentieth Century Hebrew Writers*. Albany: SUNY Press, 1987.

Mintz, Alan. *Hurban: Responses to Catastrophe in Jewish Literature*. New York: Columbia University Press, 1984.

Schwartz, Howard. "The Aggadic Tradition." *Judaism* 32 (1983): 84–101.

IV. *Translation*

A. *Translation Studies*

Aichele, George. "Translation, Narrative and Theology." *Explorations* 9 (1991): 61–80.

Bassnett Susan. *Translation Studies*. London: Routledge, 1991.

_____. "When is a Translation Not a Translation?" Pages 25–40 in *Constructing Cultures*. Edited by Susan Bassnett and André Lefevere. Philadelphia: Multilingual Matters, 1998.

Bassnett, Susan, and André Lefevere, eds. *Translation, History and Culture*. London: Pinter, 1990.

_____. "Translation Practice(s) and the Circulation of Cultural Capital: Some Aeneids in English." Pages 41–56 in *Constructing Cultures*. Edited by Susan Bassnett and André Lefevere. Philadelphia: Multilingual Matters, 1998.

Benjamin, A. *Translation and the Nature of Philosophy*. London: Routledge, 1989.

Benjamin, Walter. "The Task of the Translator." Pages 15–22 in *The Translation Studies Reader*. Edited by Lawrence Venuti. New York: Routledge, 2000.

Berman, Antoine. "Translation and the Trials of the Foreign." Pages 284–97 in *The Translation Studies Reader*. Edited by Lawrence Venuti. New York: Routledge, 2000.

Biguenet, John, and Rainer Schulte, eds. *The Craft of Translation*. Chicago: University of Chicago Press, 1989.

Brower, Reuben, ed. *On Translation*. Cambridge, Mass.: Harvard University Press, 1959.

Budick, Sanford. "Crises of Alterity: Cultural Untranslatability and the Experience of Secondary Otherness." Pages 1–12 in *The Translatability of Cultures: Figurations of the Space Between*. Edited by Sanford Budick and Wolfgang Iser. Stanford: Stanford University Press, 1996.

Chamberlain, Lori. "Gender and the Metaphorics of Translation." Pages 57–73 in *Difference in Translation*. Edited by Joseph F. Graham. Ithaca: Cornell University Press, 1985.

Derrida, Jacques. "Des Tours de Babel." Pages 165–207 in *Difference in Translation*. Edited by Joseph F. Graham. Ithaca: Cornell University Press, 1985.

Dryden, John. "On Translation." Pages 17–31 in *Theories of Translation: An Anthology of Essays from Dryden to Derrida*. Edited by Rainer Schulte and John Biguenet. Chicago: University of Chicago Press, 1992.

Even-Zohar, Itamar. "The Position of Translated Literature within the Literary Polysystem." Pages 192–97 in *The Translation Studies Reader*. Edited by Lawrence Venuti. New York: Routledge, 2000.

Folkart, Barbara. "Modes of Writing: Translation as Replication or Invention." *Romance Languages Annual* 5 (1993): xv–xxii.

Foucault, Michel. "Les mots qui saignent." Translated by Lawrence Venuti. *L'Express* (29 aout 1969): 30.

Frame, Donald. "Pleasures and Problems of Translation." Pages 70–92 in *The Craft of Translation*. Edited by John Biguenet and Rainer Schulte. Chicago: University of Chicago Press, 1989.

Friedrich, Hugo. "On the Art of Translation." Translated by Rainer Schulte and John Biguenet. Pages 11–12 in *Theories of Translation*. Edited by Rainer Schulte and John Biguenet. Chicago: University of Chicago Press, 1992.

Gentzler, E. *Contemporary Translation Theories*. 2d rev. ed. Clevedon: Multilingual Matters, 2001.

Goethe, Johann Wolfgang von. "Translations." Translated by Sharon Sloane. Pages 60–63 in *Theories of Translation: An Anthology of Essays from Dryden to Derrida*. Edited by Rainer Schulte and John Biguenet. Chicago: University of Chicago Press, 1992.

Hempel, Carl G. *Fundamentals of Concept Formation in Empirical Sciences*. Chicago: University of Chicago Press, 1967.

Holmes, James S. "The Name and the Nature of Translation Studies." Pages 180–93 in *The Translation Studies Reader*. Edited by Lawrence Venuti. New York: Routledge, 2000.

Humboldt, Wilhelm von. "From his 'Introduction to *Agamemnon*.'" Translated by Sharon Sloane. Pages 55–59 in *Theories of Translation*. Edited by Rainer Schulte and John Biguenet. Chicago: University of Chicago Press, 1992.

Jakobson, Roman. "On Linguistic Aspects of Translation." Pages 232–39 in *On Translation*. Edited by Reuben Brower. Cambridge, Mass.: Harvard University Press, 1959.

Keeley, Edmund. "Collaboration, Revision, and Other Less Forgivable Sins in Translation." Pages 54–69 in *The Craft of Translation*. Edited by John Biguenet and Rainer Schulte. Chicago: University of Chicago Press, 1989.

Kelly, Douglas. "*Translatio* Studii: Translation, Adaptation, and Allegory in Medieval French Literature." *Philological Quarterly* 57 (1978): 287–310.

Kelly, Louis G. *The True Interpreter: A History of Translation Theory and Practice in the West*. Oxford: Blackwell, 1979.

Lefevere, André. *Translating Poetry: Seven Strategies and a Blueprint*. Amsterdam: Van Gorcum, 1975.

_____. *Translation, Rewriting, and the Manipulation of Literary Fame*. New York: Routledge,1992.

_____. "Translation Studies: The Goal of the Discipline." Pages 172–85 in *Literature and Translation: New Perspectives in Literary Studies with a Basic Bibliography of Books on Translation Studies*. Edited by James S. Holmes et al. Leuven: Acco, 1978.

Nietzsche, Friedrich. "83. Translations." Pages 82–83 in *The Gay Science*. Edited by Bernard Williams. Translated by Josefine Nauckhoff and Adrian Del Caro. Cambridge: Cambridge University Press, 2001.

Pound, Ezra. *Literary Essays of Ezra Pound*. Edited T. S. Eliot. London: Faber & Faber, 1954.

Quine, W. V. O. "Meaning and Translation." Pages 148–72 in *On Translation*. Edited by Reuben Brower. Cambridge, Mass.: Harvard University Press, 1959.

_____. *Word and Object*. New York: Oxford University Press, 1960.

Rabassa, Gregory. "No Two Snowflakes are Alike." Pages 1–12 in *The Craft of Translation*. Edited by John Biguenet and Rainer Schulte. Chicago: University of Chicago Press, 1989.

Robinson, D., ed. *Western Translation Theory from Herodotus to Nietzsche*. Manchester: St. Jerome, 1997.

Schleiermacher, Friedrich. "From *On the Different Methods of Translating*." Translated by Waltraud Bartscht. Pages 36–54 in *Theories of Translation*. Edited by Rainer Schulte and John Biguenet. Chicago: University of Chicago Press, 1992.

Steiner, George. *After Babel: Aspects of Language and Translation*. Oxford: Oxford University Press, 1992.

Sullivan, J. P. "The Poet as Translator—Ezra Pound and Sextus Propertius." *The Kenyon Review* 23, no. 3 (Summer 1961): 37.

Toury, Gideon. *Descriptive Translation Studies and Beyond* Benjamins Translation Library 4. Amsterdam: John Benjamins Publishing Co., 1995.

_____. *Translation Across Cultures*. New Delhi: Bahri Publications, 1987.

Van Gorp, Hendrick. "Translation and Literary Genre: The European Picaresque Novel in the 17th and 18th Centuries." Pages 136–48 in *The Manipulation of Literature: Studies in Literary Translation*. Edited by Theo Hermans. New York: St. Martin, 1985.

Vermeer, Hans J. "Skopos and Commission in Translational Action." Translated by Andrew Chesterman. Pages 221–32 in *The Translation Studies Reader*. Edited by Lawrence Venuti. New York: Routledge, 2000.

Vinay, Jean-Paul, and Jean Darbelnet. "A Methodology for Translation." Translated by Juan C. Sager and M.-J. Hamel. Pages 84–93 in *The Translation Studies Reader*. Edited by Lawrence Venuti. New York: Routledge, 2000.

B. *Scripture and Translation*

Assman, Jan. "Translating Gods: Religion as a Factor of Cultural (Un)Translatability." Pages 25–36 in *The Translatability of Cultures: Figurations of the Space Between*. Edited by Sanford Budick and Wolfgang Iser. Stanford: Stanford University Press, 1996.

Bailey, L. R., ed. *The Word of God: A Guide to English Versions of the Bible*. Atlanta: John Knox, 1982.

Beekman, J., and J. Callow. *Translating the Word of God*. Grand Rapids: Zondervan, 1974.

Besserman, Lawrence. "Augustine, Chaucer and the Translation of Biblical Poetics." Pages 68–84 in *The Translatability of Cultures: Figurations of the Space Between*. Edited by Sanford Budick and Wolfgang Iser. Stanford: Stanford University Press, 1996.

Buber, Martin and Franz Rosenzweig. *Scripture and Translation*. Translated by L. Rosenwald with E. Fox. Bloomington: Indiana University Press, 1994.

Falk, Marcia. *Song of Songs: A New Translation and Interpretation*. San Francisco: Harper, 1990.

Fox, Everett. *The Five Books of Moses: A New Translation With Introductions, Commentary, and Notes*. New York: Schocken, 1995.

Goodspeed, Edgar J. *Problems of New Testament Translation*. Chicago: University of Chicago Press, 1945.

Greenstein, Edward L. *Essays on Biblical Method and Translation*. Atlanta: Scholars Press, 1989.

_____. "Theories of Modern Bible Translation." *Prooftexts* 8 (1983): 9–39.

Hammond, Gerald. "English Translation of the Bible." Pages 647–666 in *The Literary Guide to the Bible*. Edited by Robert Alter and Frank Kermode. Cambridge, Mass.: Harvard University Press, 1987.

Miller, J. Hillis. "Border Crossings, Translating Theory." Pages 207–23 in *The Translatability of Cultures: Figurations of the Space Between*. Edited by Sanford Budick and Wolfgang Iser. Stanford: Stanford University Press, 1996.

Nida, Eugene. "Principles of Correspondence." Pages 126–40 in *The Translation Studies Reader*. Edited by Lawrence Venuti. New York: Routledge, 2000.

_____. *Toward a Science of Translating, With Special Reference to Principles and Procedures Involved in Bible Translation*. Leiden: Brill, 1964.

Reicher, Klaus. "'It Is Time': The Buber-Rosenzweig Translation in Context." Pages 169–85 in *The Translatability of Cultures: Figurations of the Space Between*. Edited by Sanford Budick and Wolfgang Iser. Stanford: Stanford University Press, 1996.

Rosenzweig, Franz. "Scripture and Word: On the New Bible Translation." Pages 40–46 in *Scripture and Translation* by Martin Buber and Franz Rosenzweig. Translated by Lawrence Rosenwald. Bloomington: Indiana University Press, 1994.

Schwarz, Werner. *Principles and Problems of Biblical Translation*. Cambridge: Cambridge University Press, 1955.

Waard, J. de, and Eugene Nida. *From One Language to Another: Functional Equivalence in Bible Translating*. Nashville: Nelson, 1986.

INDEXES

INDEX OF REFERENCES

INDEX OF AUTHORS